STUMBLING TO THE PRIESTHOOD

Stumbling to the Priesthood

Vernon J. Schaefer

North Star Press of St. Cloud, Inc.

Design: Corinne Dwyer
Cover Art: Jessica Johnson

Published by:
North Star Press of St. Cloud, Inc.
P.O. Box 451
St. Cloud, Minnesota 56302

Dedication

To the Priests, Brothers, and Sisters who encountered me in the various institutions of learning as I stumbled to the priesthood, I joyfully dedicate this tome.

VJS

Author's Note

This is a journal of my early life and my rocky road to the Catholic priesthood. It is written in the third person with liberal literary license, allowing for imagination in the telling of the story and the addition of a generous dose of humor. All of this will serve, I hope, to better capture the reader's interest and hold it.

STUMBLING TO THE PRIESTHOOD

1

President Warren G. Harding was snarling at all the crooks in his administration. Henry Ford was making a big success with his Model T, and the nation was about to go on a big spree until 1929.

On a blizzardy December day, the 30th, 1919, Joseph John Pesch tried to clean out his barn. He heard something that sounded like the screech of the haymow door when first opened in the summer, only like it was ten miles away and muffled by the wind.

Joseph Pesch poked his unshaven face toward the house on the hill above the barn, and saw a woman standing outside the kitchen door waving her arm.

"Could be Maggie is having her baby," Joseph muttered and started walking up the hill to the house.

Standing in his smelly overshoes inside the kitchen door, he heard the thin cry of an infant. His sister-in-law, Veronica Knott, who had delivered the child, appeared.

"You have a son, Joe. Now get those dirty, stinkin' overshoes off before you go in to see Maggie."

In his stocking feet Joe strode to the bedroom and peered at the baby encased in the blanket Maggie held beside her in the bed.

Joe was a man of few words, and now he didn't know what to say. He smiled to indicate his pleasure that his son sucked oxygen into his nostrils after his arrival into this cruel old world. His wife, Maggie, ignored him and focused all her attention on the infant, whose breathing noticeably became wheezing.

"The baby's sick," announced Veronica who came into the bedroom. "In fact, he looks like he's gonna croak. Better get a priest to baptize him."

Joe cranked the wall telephone to get "central" who in turn rang the rectory of St. Cyril and Methodius in Lake Hebron eleven miles away.

Father Matthew Joachim, worthy pastor of said church answered, "Halloo."

"Fadder Joachim?" Joseph yelled into the instrument on the wall. He didn't understand how a voice could be carried by wire eleven miles down the road unless he yelled into the phone.

"Yah, I'm Father Joachim."

1

"Fadder, we got a baby out here dat don't look too good. Maybe we ought to get it baptized today."

"Vell, the vetter is bad, but I try to come out. If I can't make it, you baptize the baby yourself, Joe. Yah?"

"Ach, I don't know widder I know how to do dat, but maybe this woman here could."

He turned away from the phone and shouted at Veronica.

"Hey, Veronica, if the priest can't make it, can you baptize the kid?" She nodded vigorously.

"Fadder, yah, she said she could, but I would radder have you do it. You come, yah?"

The good Bavarian priest did buck the snowdrifts with his big Chrysler sedan, and the engine threw enough manifold heat into the interior of the car to keep him from blowing on his hands and shivering.

And that's how Paul Joseph Pesch was relieved of the guilt of original sin and inducted into the lobby of the kingdom with rights to move in if he behaved himself, provided he overcame his present crisis. But if he went, he would have it made as far as the Kingdom was concerned.

Father Joachim was served coffee and kuchen. As he was putting on his overcoat and hat to leave, he hesitated at the door and remarked, "Seems to me dat if the Lord wanted me to come out in this blizzard to baptize dat little feller, the least he could do now is make him a priest some day."

"Amen," said Joseph the elder.

The nineteen twenties came in, a decade when the nation became unsure whether it was really the promised land, and the people somehow knew in their hearts that the "war to end all wars" was not going to eliminate warfare in the future after all.

In the meantime, the nation started craving excitement; freewheeling became the mood of the day. Respectable citizens started doing the Charleston. Women bobbed their hair. Prohibition had been voted in, but, in defiance, young men carried pocket flasks, and people crowded into speakeasies.

President Calvin Coolidge inspired nobody and said few words, except folks took for granted that he probably was against sin.

But the wild spirit of the age did not filter very far into rural America. On farms like the one Joe Pesch rented north of Lake Hebron, farmers tilled the soil by the sweat of their brows unaware that in the cities people were "going to the dogs," as they would have put it.

Meanwhile, little Paul Pesch survived what ailed him and began to romp around, exploring the world about him while regularly wetting his diapers in the process.

Maggie Pesch, on her part, pined to be nearer town where she could help make quilts in the winter with the other ladies as they discussed how best to treat their children's croup and keep their husbands' hands off illegal moonshine. But especially she wanted to live near town so that her children would attend the parochial school in Lake Hebron.

Accordingly, the Pesches began looking for a farm closer to town and bought one at the worst time of all—during the short-lived agricultural boom following World War I. Joe bought a farm and paid a hundred dollars an acre more than it was worth. When the recession set in following the boom, he lost the beautiful estate including all his savings—ten thousand dollars, a very tidy sum in those days.

This unfortunate turn of events served to impoverish the family in which Paul grew up. Consequently, little Paul was delivered from the embellishments of the world, flesh, and the devil, which often derailed the rich on their journey to the Kingdom.

"Joe," Maggie whined one day, feeling low, "I wish we never seen this farm."

Nevertheless, the Schuff farm they bought and on which they still lived was indeed a handsome-looking place, near enough to town, that the children could easily walk to Sacred Heart School. The house was an imposing two-story mansion with a large porch all along the front—stylish architecture in those days. The barn was a neat-looking, hip-roofed building in good repair as were the hoghouse and chickenhouse. A large grove of trees provided an adequate windbreak. Less than a mile north of the farm lay Duck Lake. A lake attached to any estate was always considered an asset.

Maggie continued to wail, "It just seems like we've thrown ten thousand dollars into that lake. Where will we go next, Joe? We might have to live in a shack like Chicken King does."

Chicken King lived in a unique estate across the road from the Pesch farm. He had about half an acre of land on which he had planted an orchard of apples and plums. In the middle of the orchard he had hung a two-room shack, pieced together with bits of lumber and tin. He dignified his Camelot, as he called his dwelling, by planting two evergreens in front to frame the door.

Near the door he had dug a well, which he called Jacob's Well. And like at that famous well in Samaria one had to draw water by means of a pail and a rope.

Chicken King, scarcely five feet tall, weighed hardly one hundred pounds. About sixty years old, he had lost all his hair except for a wispy crown and a thin beard which came down a few inches below his chin.

Occasionally he went around the Lake Hebron municipal golf course, which surrounded his place, and looked for lost golf balls. Then King would appear among a twosome or foursome of golfers holding up a small bag of golf balls for which he usually received a dime apiece. He said, "It seems to me foolish for man to spend a few hours of what time he has been allotted on earth to poke a little white ball across the breast of Mother Nature, and then lose it. But when I find it I am enriched a bit to buy coffee and sugar."

King often came across the road to the "Pesch Palace," as he called it, and sat in Maggie's kitchen enunciating his philosophy of life in a sing-song nasal twang. Little Paul became accustomed to climbing up on King's lap and pulling at his beard, but King hardly seemed to notice the torture.

"You indeed feel very low, I suppose," he said one day as he commented on the upcoming foreclosure of the Pesch farm. "But it is only money you've lost. You have your health, your life, and your children, one of whom is bound and determined, it seems, to deprive me of a few more strands of my beard."

"Paul, stop pulling at his whiskers, d'ya hear?" Maggie commanded. But little Paul continued to pull at what strands he could wind about his small fist.

"As I was saying," King continued, "Man has a bad habit of worshipping gold instead of his Creator. You're making too much fuss about losing your ten thousand dollars."

"You should talk!" stormed Maggie. "If you had a house full of kids to raise, you might be singing a different tune. And while you're talking about worshipping God, I never see you ever go to church."

"Ah, but 'judge not lest ye be judged,' my good woman," sang out King, "I find the Lord dwelling in the inner recesses of my soul."

"Well, I don't particularly care whether you think He dwells. All I know is that we're dern hard up right now."

At this point Joe Pesch came into the kitchen and said, "King, do you suppose you could give me a hand tomorrow and drive that binder 'harvesting the fruit of the land,' as you call it, while I shock up the bundles? I'm getting too far behind in the shocking."

"Such manual labor hardly befits a person of my ancestry," said King. "I am, after all, descended from the House of Hapsburg. But, yes, I shall give you a hand out there in the golden stubble tomorrow."

And thus, in the absence of the master of Camelot, a distressing scene took place the next afternoon on King's estate.

Alvina Pesch, always called "Toots," trailed by her two-year-old brother, Paul, sauntered across the road to King's palace. She was wont to visit King quite frequently of late, looking for eggs that the hens liked to hide in the orchard. When she found some, King rewarded her with a few jelly beans he bought with part of the proceeds of selling golf balls.

Toots approached the well and decided to let down the old wooden pail as she had watched King do many times. She grasped the crank and unwound the rope from its dowel, allowing the pail to descend.

At this point the angel of darkness put an idea into her head, and she lifted Paul and placed him in the pail. Then she started cranking the pail with Paul in it up above the stone parapet, and reversed the cranking, which lowered the pail and its passenger into the depths of the well. Paul did not object to getting a free ride, but when he entered the cool darkness of the well he registered his disapproval of the strange surroundings by whimpering. At first it was a weak whimper which escalated into a wail, and when the echo of that reached his ears, he became very alarmed and sang a mighty dirge.

Toots peered down into the recesses of the well and observed the pail containing her screeching sibling bobbing around in the water below. She was undecided as what to do next.

Meanwhile, Maggie, bustling about the Pesch kitchen baking bread, experienced one of those maternal hunches that all was not well with her offspring somewhere outside. She ya-hoo-ed to them from the front porch but, getting no response, walked across the road to King's and soon became aware of Paul's mournful dirge emanating from the depths of Jacob's Well. She rushed to the well and saw Toots calmly standing at the parapet, looking down with the lack of concern as manifested by Judah gazing down at his brother, Joseph, languishing in the well at Dothan.

With trembling hands, Mother Pesch hastily extracted her first-born son from the depths of the well and then collapsed to the ground in a dead faint. After regaining consciousness, she collected her two off-spring, hurried back to the manor where she: 1. Spanked Toots. 2. Poured herself a glass of strong homemade wine her sister, Nora, had brewed. 3. Looked into the mirror to see if her hair had turned white.

When King reported to the kitchen for supper that evening, she told him about the incident and also informed him that, hereafter, Camelot was off-limits to her children.

King murmured, "Ah, many important things have happened at Jacob's well in Holy Writ. There was the Samaritan woman whom Jesus converted there, for instance. I perceive that little Paul, like Joseph in the book of Genesis, has been selected by the Lord for special service."

"I don't see why you don't just cover that well and pump water like everyone else," snapped Maggie.

3

When September 1925 rolled around, Joe and Maggie Pesch, looked at their eldest son, then six years old, and determined that some academic training would be in order for the lad.

Chicken King had made some reference to the subject along about August first as he sat on his kitchen stool while Maggie canned tomatoes from her extensive garden.

"It is most fitting," he said, "that a descendant of the House of Hapsburg begin the discipline of the liberal arts at an appropriate age, such as seven, in order that he might carry on the culture fostered so faithfully by his ancestors, Emperor Francis Joseph and Empress Maria Theresa."

"Why don't you come right out and say that Paul should start school?" Maggie inquired. "It's a good thing Joe isn't in the house listening to your lingo again or he'd tell you to stick your beard into a bowl of sheep dip. Paul, where are you?"

Paul rarely enthroned himself on King's lap anymore since the short old gent with the sparse beard and nearly bald head no longer fascinated him. He preferred mischief outside, which at the moment involved catching a baby pig. The squealing piglets roused the sow into putting on a demonstration of wrath, and Paul felt more secure if he dropped the noisy creature. He went to pick a few potato bugs in the garden to roll down sister Toot's neck, which usually caused her to put on a performance clearly outstripping that of the enraged sow. Then Paul hid in the corncrib until Maggie's wrath cooled off a bit.

In the village of Lake Hebron stood an ancient frame building where the children of the Sacred Heart parish were deposited beginning at the age of seven to learn the three Rs and the contents of the Baltimore catechism. Four female members of the Franciscan Congregation of Our Lady of Lourdes, for the love of God and daily board and room, labored faithfully to educate the children of the parish committed to their care. These women were called "sisters" and were highly thought of as being quite holy by the peasants of the parish whose children they taught.

"Now Paul," Maggie said as she braked the old boxy Chevy to a stop in front of the Sacred Heart parochial school, "you go with me to the first grade room, and Sister Ruth will take care of you the rest of the day till I pick you up again at three thirty."

"Naa, I ain't going to no school," Paul stated quite firmly, but his mother had a lock-tight grip on his left arm and dragged him, kicking and screaming, into the academic world.

Paul solemnly regarded Sister Ruth swathed in her brown woolen habit and black veil. He concluded that she must be a witch of great power, and decided not to cross her at the moment lest he be cooked in a big kettle for the evening meal in that haunted house. Paul had been great at looking through papers and magazines even though he couldn't read, and he had seen pictures of these witches that everyone called "sisters." He decided to do their bidding until such time as he could escape.

The school, originally built as a public school not long after the Civil War, sported high windows, high ceilings, worn wooden floors, and a cupola above the front steps in which rested a badly cast bell. In the rear of the school a newer two-story addition had been tacked on, an addition housing the four handmaids of the Lord who wielded the rulers and sticks in the classroom, plus a "cook" sister in the kitchen.

"My goodness, vat haff ve here?" chanted Sister Winifred, the cook Sister, one morning in her kitchen. Standing on a chair by the cupboard and about to explore for some cookies was Paul.

"I am tired of sitting in my desk and I want something to eat," Paul calmly stated.

"Ach, du lieber, diss is not goot. Come, vee go back to see Sister Ruth, ya wohl." And Sister Winifred escorted a recalcitrant Paul back to his classroom.

"Paul, come up here and receive your punishment," sternly commanded Sister Ruth. Paul bravely marched up and obediently extended his hands for the sharp blows of the ruler and then decided that sneaking away from his desk did not pay.

Meanwhile, the pastor of Sacred Heart church and school, Father Matthias Joachim, straightened up from his task of picking ground cherries in his garden and once more looked sorrowfully at his ancient school building.

"Truly, it's got to go," he sighed very deeply. He had built a beautiful towering Romanesque church some ten years previously. The school, by comparison, was a grevious eyesore at least to his critical orbs. "I must indeed find a way to build a new school."

Schultz, his brown German shepherd dog that followed him around inside and outside the house, sat on a tomato plant and looked solemnly up at his master, sharing his apparent grief.

"Schultz, get off that tomato plant! I told you to stay out of my garden, didn't I?"

Schultz moved over and sat on his haunches between rows of tomato plants.

"Schultz, how can we get that old school burned down to collect the insurance and build a new one? The old shack is an affront to the eye of a cultured gentleman and certainly not a tribute to the honor and glory of God. But those stupid farmers of mine can't appreciate harmony of architecture and wouldn't cough up enough money to build a new one unless they absolutely had to. Schultz, it is indeed a distressing situation."

Schultz showed he agreed by licking his jowls before he resumed cooling off his body by extending his tongue and panting. It was hot that September in the garden.

"Far be it for me, of course, to commit arson, Schultz, but lightning could strike the old shack. I must pray every day that it happens."

He began weekly fire drills in the hope his prayers would be answered.

One day Chicken King legged it to town from his "Belvedere Palace," as he now called his shack where he and his chickens resided, and King was a most observant man. Hardly a detail escaped his vision. As he walked past Widow Sorenson's house, he glanced up at the Sacred Heart School and immediately noticed a small tongue of flame flickering from a wooden shingle on the roof. He bolted to the door of the nearby rectory and informed Father Joachim of his discovery. The priest thanked King for the good news and, instead of leaping for the telephone to call the fire department, stood for a moment while his soul churned in great turmoil.

"If I don't call the fire department," he thought, "I'll be in great difficulty. Besides someone else will discover the flame." He looked out of the window again to check the progress of the fire, which increased very slowly.

"Shucks, Schultz," he muttered at his dog curled up on the settee in the office, "they'll get the fire out anyway whether I call or not. This is not my lucky day." And he cranked the wall phone to get "central," the telephone operator who sat in front of a switchboard in an upstairs room over the bank.

"Pauline, get that fire department over to put out the fire on my school roof. Yah, sure it's on fire! I wouldn't be calling if Sister Winifred's roast was burning."

Pauline turned on the siren located on top of the city hall, and a half dozen dogs, including Schultz, started howling.

"Shut up, Schultz, and get off that settee! How many times must I tell you to sleep on the rug!"

Father called over to Sister Valentia, the Sister Superior, to initiate the well-rehearsed fire drill to get the kids out of the building.

Once Sister had the building empty of her charges, she gave the order for them to march over to the church where they would all recite rosary that the firemen would get out the blaze. What the children wanted, of course, was to remain and watch the firemen at work, and they wore distress on their faces as they scuffed along. Especially distressed was Paul who vowed that he would quit the Church some day for sure.

4

P aul Pesch became nine, and his parents with four other children, paid little more attention to him than to the others. But he did make an impression on them one cold January night as 1929 dawned.

As the New Year came and went, King was full of predictions. "I'm afraid the economy is going to crack," he remarked one evening perched on the bar stool the Pesches acquired one day from Uncle Thorval who operated a bar in Springfield until Prohibition closed it down and he went into bootlegging.

"What do you mean, the economy is going to crack?" asked Joe eyeing the plate of his favorite food, potato pancakes, which Maggie put on the table. "Come on and sit down at the table, King," he added perhaps reluctantly.

King happily moved his sparse frame into his slot at the south end of the table next to the high chair where two-year-old Maggie was perched. She gurgled happily as she threw a portion of food from her plate on King's bald head. But the old prophet patiently bore this punishment as he had patiently endured the pulling of his beard when Paul was two.

"As you know," King began after forking a pancake onto his plate, "things are booming out there, Joe, even though nobody seems to do much buying around here. People are now buying things on the installment plan. Sixty percent of the cars are bought on the installment plan, seventy percent of the furniture, eighty percent of vacuum cleaners, radios, and refrigerators, et cetera."

"If people don't have the money to buy something they should wait till they do," interjected Joe. "This going into debt is not a healthy sign."

"Well, I recall we went way into debt when we bought that Shumacher place," observed Maggie. She received a dark look from her husband.

"Anyway," continued King, "the nation is on a buying spree. Not only are they buying merchandise, they are playing the stock market. One and a half million ordinary folk are speculating and buying stocks on margin. Said Roger Babson, and economist in the Wall Street Journal, 'Sooner or later a crash is coming, and it may be terrific.' Yessir, we're going to have a gigantic stock market crash soon."

10

"I suppose Johnny Mulrooney, the banker in town gets that New York paper," said Joe, "and you pick up old copies from the garbage box behind the bank."

Joe was worried. He had invested a thousand dollars Maggie had inherited into General Electric stock without telling her. He decided he'd better sell the stock before the crash old King predicted came. At the moment the stock had doubled in value—a good time to take his profits and run.

"Ma, why can't we have a radio?" whined Toots, ten. "Everybody else's got one, and the other kids in school always talk about listening to Paul Whiteman and his orchestra and Duke Ellington."

Joe thought to himself, "That's the first thing I'm going to buy after selling that stock. A new radio."

"KDKA, Pittsburg, has been on the air now almost ten years," observed King. "Since then 618 radio stations in the nation have come on the air."

"Golly, King, you sure got a good memory," said Maggie, then turned to her youngest daughter. "Maggie LaVera! You do that again, and I'll spank you good." Maggie grabbed a dishrag and wiped the mess off King's head where little Maggie had deposited a piece of potato pancake dripping with syrup.

The next day Joe went down to the First State Bank of Lake Hebron and told Johnny Mulrooney to liquidate his General Electric stock.

"Hell's Bells, Joe!" Johnny snorted. "Whaddya want to sell now, for? That stock has been going up like a coon with a dog on his tail?"

"Ask me that in a few more months after the market crashes," Joe replied. "Sell her off today, Johnny, and put it in my account. I'm going over to Sam Dahl's and trade cars and then buy a radio with the profits. And put that thousand back into Maggie's savings."

"Okay, Joe, but just because you lost your shirt buying that Schumacher place, you needn't be as gun shy as a sheep-chasing dog when it comes to investments. This was a damn good deal, Joe."

"Johnny, I may be a lousy farmer, but I feel it in my bones that there's gonna be a crash and a depression that'll close up this bank of yours and send you packing for the Sahara desert."

As Joe drove away from the bank, headed for Sam Dahl's Ford dealership he wondered why he put so much faith in the words of that queer old geezer, Chicken King. What could a man who lived in a rundown shack with a bunch of chickens really know about national finances? Still, Joe traded his 1925 Chevrolet sedan for a shiny new 1929 Model A Ford. He didn't get much for the Chevy because it was still bent up from the time he watched a muskrat sitting by the side of the road instead of watching where he was going. The old Chevy had gone off the road and tipped over into the three feet of water in Liepold's slough, landing on its roof. Joe was trapped inside, but he had a couple of feet of air to breathe until a passer-by called a wrecker and pulled the old crate out of the slough.

Joe also got an eight-tube Atwater-Kent radio from Davis and Hager's grocery and hardware store. Joe congratulated himself that for once he might have been a wise old owl instead of a blind coyote.

One Friday night in the middle of January, even though the temperature dipped to ten below, the Pesches entertained the neighborhood, giving a card party. Most of the guests came by sleigh, and didn't have to worry about their cars freezing up during the party.

Entire families came to these neighborhood parties, and the children were shunted upstairs to play because they made too much noise and disturbed the adults who might find it difficult to make nine no trump in 500 with a lot of racket behind them.

Paul took charge of the upstairs kids and announced they would play funeral for a while. That prospect seemed to interest everybody present. He said he would be the priest, brother Edgar would be the dead person, and the rest would be mourners.

The steamer trunk in the hallway would be the coffin, and some of the mourners emptied it of quilts and sheets. Edgar was commanded to crawl into the coffin, now containing only a pillow. He lay down, closed his eyes, and a wake service began. The mourners walked past the open trunk and said how natural he looked. They stood around with sad faces when the "priest" arrived from the boys' bedroom wrapped in a quilt to serve as a vestment. Part of the vestment dragged along behind him. Paul had picked up an arithmetic book to serve as a ritual, and he used a stick that had been used to prop up a window as a holy water sprinkler.

"Ain't we s'posed to say the rosary at the wake?" piped up Lennie Liepold, the neighbor boy whom Paul had appointed undertaker.

"Yeah, I guess so," answered the priest. "Now all we have to do is say the 'Hail Mary' twenty times." That sounded like a good idea as the regular rosary seemed too long. "Now we ain't got no lunch to eat so we might just as well get on with the funeral."

Paul mumbled and mumbled like he was saying Latin, shook the stick at the coffin a few times to sprinkle it with holy water, and Lennie, the undertaker came to close the coffin. He had picked out six boys to be pallbearers, and called them into action.

"Where is the grave?" piped up Margie Pesch. Paul looked around and then pointed to the stairwell.

"But we ain't got no ropes to let the coffin down to the grave." Lennie said.

"Tie some of those pieces of cloth in the closet together," Toots suggested. "That'll make ropes." Maggie had stored bits of cloth in the closet for a quilting bee, and the undertaker and some pall bearers went to work making some ropes out of them.

Edgar, in the coffin got worried and started hollering to open it up.

Lennie lifted the lid a crack and said, "Shet ap, you are supposed to be dead."

"Let's get this over with," complained the corpse, "it's getting pretty stuffy in here, and I'm all cramped up."

"Keep your shirt on, Eddie," said Albert Mitchell, "we're gonna getcha buried in the shake of a lamb's tail."

Paul grew impatient too and uncomfortable with the heavy quilt hanging around his shoulders. "Bring that coffin over here to the edge of the grave, and then I'll bless the grave." He remembered the procedure at the cemetery when his grandmother had been buried.

The pallbearers shoved the trunk alongside the stairwell and waited for the priest to bless the grave. Paul mumbled some more and shook the stick at the stairwell, blessing the grave with holy water.

"Okay, get those ropes under the trunk, and we'll let her down," commanded Lennie. The six pallbearers had only two ropes of cloth pieces knotted together. A fight started among them as to who would handle the ropes.

"Shet ap, you guys!" commanded the priest. "Pallbearers ain't supposed to let down the coffin in the first place. Yer s'posed to stand by the grave and look sad. Albert, Evelyn, George, and Toots will let down the coffin."

"They ain't let no girls ever let down no coffin in the whole world," protested Lennie. "Clayton, you take Toot's place. Now you guys grab those ropes and get ready."

The four took solid hold of the ropes and edged the trunk closer and closer to the edge of the stairwell as quiet descended upon the assemblage. Soon the trunk hung in midair over the stairwell.

"Now slowly let down the coffin," commanded Lennie while Paul gave out with some more mumbling. The kids sensed the dramatic moment, and the silence was complete after Paul got through.

The knotting together of the cloth left something to be desired, however, for, when the coffin had been suspended over the stairwell no more than a minute, one of the knots gave way. The coffin catapulted down the steps. At the bottom it crashed and went sideways into the dining room where the elders played cards.

Immediately the corpse came back to life, and his muffled screams from inside the trunk could be heard by all. A couple of card players got up and released the corpse from bondage, and Maggie waded in to attend to his bruises.

Up in the cemetery, consternation registered upon all the faces of the mourners as they viewed the tragic turn of events. Then they quickly scattered, hiding under the beds or in the closets in fear of the General Judgement they knew was about to take place.

Paul stood his ground the longest, like the captain of a sinking ship and was soon the center of an interrogation followed by a thorough tongue lashing.

    This was Paul's first funeral, and instead of a stipend he got his ears pulled.

5

Paul walked to town to altar boy practice for Holy Week services when Andy Hanson, the rural mail carrier, sped by in his mud-caked, two-door, Ford V-8 and splattered Paul with dirty water. Paul called him a few nasty names, and then wondered if he'd have to go to confession again before Holy Thursday.

Hank Bullock's horses stood in the pasture by the road snipping up the first tender blades of grass on the higher ground above the slough, now full of water, which Paul called the "Lake of Galilee" after Sister Genevieve rolled down the map of the Holy Land one day and taught her charges a few geographical features of the Holy Land. Some of Hank's hens scratched out on the gravel road filling their crops with sand, and one rooster stood on the edge of the stock tank while another one celebrated the coming of spring by crowing lustily.

It was a good day to be alive after that long hard winter, Paul thought. Hank Bullock, aboard his old 1924 Dodge with the rag top, pulled out of his driveway in first gear, and must have been going a good three miles per hour. He yelled at Paul. "Ya wanna ride?"

"You betcha!" Paul replied and leaped aboard before Hank shifted into second.

"How did you get her started, Hank, after she's been setting all winter?" Paul inquired.

"I dunno. I thought I'd spin her a few with the crank for the heck of it, and I'll be doggone if she didn't pop off. Where you wanna go?"

"I gotta go down to the church, but I'll get off anywhere."

"I'm going to the blacksmith shop and see if Pewter has my disk done," Hank said. "Field work might start next week if we can get some drying weather."

"Thanks for the lift, Hank."

Paul got off at Pewter William's blacksmith shop and beat it up the street right away because he spied Fat Hunkle loafing in the shop. Fat had been laying for Paul ever since Len Tomfords and he had thrown a dead squirrel into his kitchen with a shipping label tied to its hind leg reading, "You will be next."

Fat had ratted on Len and Paul to Father Joachim after they had lifted a few pieces of charcoal and some incense from the Catholic church, and Len, who went to Sunday school over at the First Methodist Church, smoked up the place just before Palm Sunday services. Fat, who was a member, caught Len adding some more incense to the red hot pieces of charcoal in an old pie plate and assumed Paul, an altar boy, was also in on it because he would know where in the sacristy that stuff was kept, and Len and Paul were close pals.

Father Joachim made Paul haul ashes out of the basement of the parochial school for a week as punishment, but he didn't dump Paul as an altar boy because he secretly got a kick out of the idea of Catholic incense smoke filling up the Methodist church.

But it was Holy Week before Easter, and as Paul walked up the street in Lake Hebron to the church, he resolved he would try to be holy for a few days.

During the Holy Saturday services, which at that time took place on Saturday morning, a few shingles on the roof of the school ignited again. The siren started screaming as the venerable priest and his servers, in the back of the church, blessed the new Easter fire and fixed up the big Easter candle with wax nails and so forth.

Father Joachim interrupted the service and said to Paul, "Look out the door and see if that school is on fire again."

Paul welcomed a chance to peek out the door. He noticed a small column of smoke coming off the same place where fires had started before. Of course, Father Joachim had refused to fix the chimney, hoping the school would burn down so he could collect the insurance and build a nice modern brick academy of learning to match his magnificent church.

"Yes, Father," Paul responded, "she's on fire again."

"Good! I hope it burns down this time," Father grunted, but he knew it would not. He felt guilty praying for it to burn down. Father Joachim, who loved the liturgy of the Church, now lost his enthusiasm for the ritual he was performing.

"Go, get me a white cope," he commanded Paul. Apparently the Sister Sacristan had forgotten to put it out in the vestibule of the church.

"Yes, Father," Paul responded brightly, glad of another chance to get away from Father and all that Latin he was mumbling.

But Paul's heart sank. What was a cope? He hadn't the slightest idea. And if he came back with the wrong item he'd get his ears pulled by the pastor, who was not in a good mood at all since the school obviously was not going to burn down. Paul had had his ears stretched before at the hands of the priest and feared if that kept up he would grow up with ears as large as a mule's.

In the sacristy, Paul saw something lying on the vestment case. That must be it, he thought, grabbing it and heading back to the vestibule.

"Du dumkopf!" snarled Father Joachim eyeing Paul with a stole in his hand. Paul knew his time for punishment would come after the service was over and they were back in the sacristy. He could feel his ears burning already.

Meanwhile, Sister Agnita, the sacristan, guessed what Father wanted and trotted back with the correct vestment, the cope.

After the three-hour ordeal finally ended, and the retinue retired to the sacristy, Paul was tempted to bolt out the door to escape the ire of the celebrant. But right away Sister Agnita came in and started apologizing for forgetting to put the cope out. Father Joachim turned to her and said a most unusual thing. He smiled and said, "Sister, I think maybe that young feller will be a priest some day."

On his way home to taste the first candy since Lent began, Paul, remembering what Father Joachim had said, concluded he would rather be an airplane pilot instead.

The Holy Spirit, however, instilled the idea of becoming a priest in Paul's subconscious and waited for an opportune time to bring it to the surface again. Paul, of course, had no idea that the Lord was calling him.

When Paul was in the seventh grade the idea of becoming a priest emerged once more in another unusual manner. The Lord writes straight with crooked lines.

This incident had to do with Sister Genevieve. Paul thought she was worse than a tornado hitting that school the way she leaned on those kids and made them produce. Her strict discipline made Paul wish she would disappear into a cloud. There was just no fun in school. You couldn't get by with a thing. Paul thought maybe if he could get to be her pet things would ease off a bit. But how to become her pet?

Paul brought up the subject to Maggie one evening. All Maggie offered was to wait until Sister showed her weak spot. All people have them, Maggie said.

Paul's opportunity came a few days later. Sister had been thundering again and making the windows rattle, scaring the poor lambs in her room half to death. Then suddenly she piped down, got a bit off the subject and softly murmured, "I just love little boys who are going to be priests."

Paul stopped chewing on his pencil, and a light came on in his brain. He received a vocation right then and there.

The next day after school he edged up to her desk and in an embarrassment manner he put on, told her he was going to be a priest. She bit hook line and sinker. Paul had it made for the rest of the year.

"She lets Paul get by with murder," complained Lucille one day to Toots. "How does he twist people around his finger like that?"

Toots shrugged her shoulders. "You never know what he's up to next," she replied.

When the year ended, and the news came that Sister was being moved to another school, Paul breathed a sigh of relief and again set his sights on becoming an airplane pilot.

6

On a mild sunny spring day in April Paul, now age eleven, sauntered into the kitchen upon his arrival home from school and grabbed a butcher knife from the drawer by the kitchen sink to cut himself a slice of bread from one of Maggie's freshly baked loaves.

"For Pete's sake, Paul," Maggie said, "let me cut that bread. You'll ruin the whole loaf. You got the wrong knife, for one thing. What was that commotion out there by the road a while ago with Boots barking so much?"

"I sicked Boots on the Junger boys, that's all," Paul answered.

"What on earth did you do that for!" Maggie yelled. "He might have bit them."

"He did. That's what I wanted him to do. During the noon hour today them big eighth-grade boys started the whole thing by beating up on me for not buying them any candy."

"For land sakes, Paul, what are you talking about?"

"Shucks, Ma, we little kids gotta buy them candy during the noon hour, or we get beat up behind the bridal wreath bushes so Sister can't see what's goin' on. I told 'em I wasn't gonna do it, so they dragged me over behind the bushes to let me have it, when Fr. Joachim suddenly showed up and pulled Hank Junger off me and gave him a good lickin' cause he was beating the tar out of me. That Fr. Joachim is a wonderful man. I think I want to be a priest some day.

"Well, they said they was gonna get me after school and give it to me good then—that was them two Junger boys who always walk past here goin' home from school who said that. But when school was out I snuck out before the final prayer was over and got a head start on 'em, but they was gainin' on me. First thing I did when I got here in the yard was to call Boots and sic him on them. Boots tore up their pants some. But I betcha they ain't gonna try beatin' up on me no more, 'cause I told 'em if they did, Boots will be waiting for them when they walk past here again on their way home from school."

"Land sakes, Paul, you always get in trouble of some kind. Lemme see, did they hurt you when they tried to beat up on you? No, I guess maybe all you got was a bloody nose, I can still see some blood stains on your sleeve."

Paul still wolfed down a slice of bread with jelly on it when Maggie grabbed a big bowl and a paring knife.

"Now, Paul, you go out and dig some young dandelions for supper salad," Maggie commanded.

"Good grief, Ma," Paul protested, "that stuff ain't no good."

"Be on your way, Buster," Maggie patted him on the seat of his pants. "After no greens all winter, we have to have some now before we get scurvy. When you get done filling up that dish with dandelion plants you can go out and gather eggs."

By this time in the spring, Maggie had ordered garden seed from Henery Field's of Shenandoah, Iowa. "He always croaks over the radio about his garden," Paul commented to Lenny Liepold, the neighbor boy. "Ma listens to him all the time in the afternoon, and he drives me crazy."

"Yeah, I know," said Lenny, "my Ma listens to him too, and one of these days all those seeds like Swiss chard, spinach, lettuce, carrots and stuff will be comin' up. All that silage, 'specially spinach, should be sold to Popeye or fed to the hogs."

While digging the dandelions, cutting them off at the surface of the ground as instructed, Paul hummed a tune his older sister, Toots, liked when she heard it over the radio, "Flat Foot Floogie with the Floy Floy." This novelty song drove Joe Pesch up a wall, so the kids always switched stations quickly if it came on when he entered the house.

Danny Hughes, with his usual torn pants, came loping along the road past the Pesch place, and Boots ran out to sniff Danny's mixed-breed hound, Boxer, that looked a little like a bulldog.

"Hey, Paul," Danny called, "I'm going down to the lake to see if I can raise a duck boat now that the ice is out. Wanna gimme a hand?"

"Can't get away, Danny, but you go down and spot a couple of good ones, and when the lake goes down a bit we'll raise them. 'Sides, the water's too dern cold for wading around."

A year before, after Danny, Lenny, Edgar, and Paul had raised a couple for summer cruising, Herman Volkman, the Lake Hebron constable, came snooping around to inspect the fleet after "Snooty" Morton, the banker's son, tipped him off. Snooty's uncle, one of those who came down from the Twin Cities every fall to hunt ducks, had sunk his boat until the following fall. Herman sank the boats again, and Paul and company had to lay off boating until Herman forgot about the Duck Lake navy.

Meanwhile, Snooty got himself a bloody nose one night behind the Hughes Produce Station for ratting.

Danny went down to the lake, which was high with spring runoff and looking like an honest-to-goodness lake with the wind raising waves on it, instead of the half marsh it usually was.

"Danny won't even find any boats with the water so high," Paul muttered to himself as he delivered the bowl full of dandelions to the maitre d' and began his chicken chores, which included gathering eggs. Now that the hens roamed the farmstead at will on the mild spring days, they had started hiding their nests up in the haymow of the barn or under the granary, making Paul's job a lot harder.

Still, he enjoyed seeing those white leghorns bustling around the yard and dusting their feathers in the ash heap. Paul, a bit puzzled as to why the roosters took to chasing the hens around the yard now and then, saw that when they caught a hen, would jump on its back and ride for a minute. Maggie never explained that to him when he asked and changed the subject, but eventually, he began to see the connection between what the chickens did and the bull jumping on a cow. Dad had explained that there would not be any calves born if the bull didn't do that. By the time he was fifteen, a farm boy has acquired the rudiments of sex education.

The melted snow formed a little lake in the low spot of the pasture of the Pesch farm which King called, "The Belvedere," the Hapsburg palace in Vienna.

"Ach, vy don't you forget about dis Hapsburg business once," Joe Pesch growled at King one day. "I'd jes' as soon be married to a one of Abe Lincoln's tribe as to one of dose Hapsburgs, and Maggie sure as heck ain't one of dem."

"Do not deprecate royalty in anyone's heritage, Joe," King gravely replied. In other times and places Maggie would be addressed as 'Your Royal Highness.'"

"Vell, Your Royal Highness," Joe said to his wife, "It's time for supper, ain't it?"

"Oh, quit teasing me, you big dumb ox!" Maggie hurried to call the girls to come to the kitchen and set the table.

Paul gazed at the little lake in the pasture with the waves created by the wind, heard the frogs in it croak in the evening, and felt good about the coming of spring.

"You boys have to fan six sacks uff oats after supper before you can do yer homework," Joe announced during supper to Sir Edgar, as King called him, and Paul. "I'll need that much seed for drilling tomorrow."

The west forty on the creek farm had raised corn the year before, and the corn stalks had been disked, ready for the oats to be drilled into it.

After supper, Paul and Sir Edgar, went to the granary to operate the dusty fanning mill. Edgar turned the crank and Paul shoveled the oats from the bin into the top of the machine. The oats went through the shaking hoppers, cleaning it of weed seeds and making it ready for sowing. But fanning grain was an extremely dusty job, and the two boys soon coughed and sneezed.

"You two sound like horses with the heaves," observed King, who came out to watch the operation for a while.

Lenny Liepold showed up, and suggested that they go down to the slough in the pasture where the frogs were croaking, catch a few, and put them in a sack to take to school where the boys could sneak them into the desks of the girls.

"Sounds like fun," said Paul. "Where's Pop?"

"I saw him drive up the road going somewhere," Lenny observed.

"Let's finish that fanning later," Paul suggested, "and get those frogs."

They grabbed a gunny sack and headed for the slough, but forgot to close the gate. While down in the pasture capturing a few frogs, Tom, one of the horses, wandered into the barnyard and soon stood at the open door of the granary dining on oats.

Joe returned home and found Tom still munching oats at the granary, and was very displeased. He sent Marge down to the slough to break the news that the master of the estate had arrived home and found one of the horses helping himself to the oats. The frog hunt quickly broke up, and the boys slowly made their way back to the fanning mill prepared to face the music which turned out to be a severe scolding accompanied by cussing in German on the part of their honorable ancestor.

Pandemonium reigned the next day in the seventh and eighth grade room of Sacred Heart School when Paul's sister, Toots, lifted up the lid of her desk and found herself staring at a large bullfrog. Evelyn Haberman had the same experience, and she let out a blood-curdling scream. Sister Genevieve then proceeded to inspect the rest of the desks occupied by girls and found two more frogs, looking particularly miserable. She gave the frogs to Paul and told him, Lenny, and Edgar to walk out to the Pesch farm, release the creatures back into the slough and return to school. The time it took them to make the round trip would equal the duration of the boys' stay after school.

"Golly, I wish I knew how Sister knew right away we did it," grumbled Paul as he walked home with Edgar and Lenny where further chastisement awaited them.

Spring was baby chick hatching time, and to augment the hatch from the setting hens in the upper floor of the granary, Maggie told King to help her get the kerosene incubator out of the woodshed where it was stored. She set it up in a corner of the dining room, filled the trays with eggs, started up the burner and announced to the family that along about Easter the hatching of all those eggs on the trays would begin.

"On Easter Jesus rose from the dead from his tomb," she said to her assembled offspring. "He came out of the tomb. Also around Easter you'll see little baby chicks pecking through the eggshells and coming out too."

The Pesch children kept an eye on those eggs in the incubator all during Lent just in case one pecked out ahead of the others.

"Quit shoving, Paul," was Maggie's frequent complaint because only two or so at a time could get a view of the trays through the glass, and Marge often monopolized the viewing stand. "Get outa here, Egger, and let me alone! Hey, Ma, Paul and Eggar are pulling my hair!"

"Hey, Ma," wailed Sir Edgar, "When them chicks start hatching she and Maggie will be there day and night, and none of us will be able to see." Maggie was the baby of the family named after her mother.

Just in case the kerosene burner went out during the night and ruined all the eggs in the incubator, Maggie insured that at least two hundred baby chicks would be on hand by ordering some from Gurney's in Yankton, South Dakota. They arrived in flat cardboard boxes full of holes for ventilation.

Andy Hanson, the mail carrier, hated the baby chick season because it meant he had to drive into the farmstead and deliver the baby chicks to the house lest they freeze out by the mailbox.

"I don't want none of those damn baby chicks yirping in my car all the time," he growled at the postmaster, Al Smith. "They drive me nuts. And it takes too long to make my route if I have to lug them crates to the houses."

"Stop complaining, Andy," Al retorted. "How would you like to have to hang around here where boxes of these chicks are chirping all the time? Hell, I must have a couple dozen boxes of 'em stacked around here after the train comes in. You only have to lug three or four crates of 'em around."

That time Chicken King happened to be in the post office and overheard Andy and Al complaining about baby chicks.

"You are both callous creatures," he called out. "You can't appreciate the beauty of God's creation anywhere. Those chicks make beautiful music."

"Hell, King, you're no judge of that," said Al. "You sleep with the dang birds all year long."

7

As Paul entered the eighth grade, Sister Jacoba operated as the queen bee in Sacred Heart School. She had to be the "Lion of Judah" when one considered the "Philistines" she had in the eighth grade. Strapping farm boys fifteen years or older, many had flunked a couple of grades for staying home too often and helping on the farm. But their dads insisted they somehow graduate from the eighth grade. So some of them were truly "giants on the earth," and were fond of throwing their weight around, especially at the "sons of Ephraim" as the Queen called the smaller boys like Paul.

The Lion of Judah kept the Philistines in check. Like everyone else in the class, the big boys were afraid of her, and so they behaved most of the time in the Lion's classroom. During recess, however, they were, as Father Joachim sometimes called them, "Visigoths from Saxony."

And when he had to, Father Joachim, who stood six-feet-three inches tall and was well-endowed with muscle, dealt them chastisements reminiscent of that given out in a castle dungeon during the Middle Ages.

For example, on one wintry day during recess, the Philistines besieged the girls' outhouse back of the school, peppering any female with snowballs who tried to exit the comfort station. The snowballs fractured many lathes on the shielding wall in front, and the screaming of the trapped girls could be heard even in the rectory some distance away. Prince, the massive bulldog that had followed aged Schultz, the German shepherd, growled restively as he lay on the rug in Father's office when the distant din of the Battle of the Outhouse reached his sensitive ears.

"Prince, what ails you, grumping like that?" Father inquired and peered out the kitchen window where he could easily perceive the flying white missiles bombarding one of the outhouses. His first thought was that damage might be inflicted on the laths, which cost money.

"Come, Prince, it appears the Philisitines have attacked Israel again," he announced. "We shall scatter the enemy."

He quickly moved into the field of battle with Prince generously exhibiting his fangs, and commanded instant cessation of the Philistine attack.

"Every one of you big boys assemble immediately upstairs in the Cage," he commanded. "The rest of you return to your classrooms."

Following the opening prayers after recess, there was silence as young ears awaited proceedings from the Cage, a small area, formerly a tiny office, in the hallway upstairs. From it soon emanated sounds of blows descending on buttocks as Father wielded a section of a bike tire on the guilty Philistines. They were thrown one by one upon a table as Prince stood guard. A brief reign of terror descended upon the other members of the holy institution of learning.

Thus it was that it only took one session in the Cage every two or three years to ensure perfect discipline among the Philistines in the parochial kingdom of Lake Hebron.

Exulting in the sound of this chastisement of his enemies, Paul smirked with satisfaction. Only the day before one of the Philistines beat up on him because he wouldn't buy him candy during the noon hour.

Paul's vocation received its biggest impetus in September when he was in the eighth grade. That's when prayer entered the picture, and prayer was to have a decisive role in Paul's vocation.

The Queen exhibited quite a surprise one day when in religion class she smiled sweetly—something which happened about twice a year—and surprised the Philistines so much they just sat there with their tongues hanging out of their mouths. She said she was going to talk about the Blessed Virgin Mary. The Queen's message that morning was that Jesus would never refuse anything His mother asked Him, and in that vein she taught the class the Memorare prayer and had them repeat it after her until they learned it by heart.

She concluded the lesson by saying, "If you really need something, no matter what, just stop in the church on the way home from school and say this prayer at the Blessed Virgin altar on the side. You will certainly have your prayer answered."

"Gee whiz," Paul said to himself, "Pa has been lamenting for weeks about how we are going to lose everything in this Depression unless we can get some cash someplace soon to pay interest on the home place. There's enough equity in the Hartneck place he owns across the road to fetch up the cash he needs. But who wants to buy the Hartneck place? Absolutely nobody."

"By golly," Paul concluded, "I'm going to take the Queen up on this deal and go over to the church and make that visit she's been gargling about."

After school he beat it over to the church. At least, the Philistines wouldn't look for him there if they had any plans to beat up on him. At recess he as much as told them to go and hang themselves from the willows by Jack Creek when they demanded he buy them some candy.

Paul plunked himself down on his knees at the side altar and said the Memorare as devoutly as a Carthusian monk on his deathbed. And then he added, "Blessed Mother, I'm counting on you in this deal so we don't lose everything. I'll give you a hint, though. I heard Pa say that the only one around here who has the cash to buy the Hartneck place is George Gehling, but he's so tight it would take a Caterpillar tractor to pull a dollar out of his pocket. Thanks for listening, Blessed Mother."

Paul scooted out of the church and trotted home to feed the chickens, gather the eggs, and then disappear into the orchard so they wouldn't think of giving him something else to do. It was September and the plums were ripe. He liked to perch himself in a plum tree and dine contentedly.

When Paul arrived home, he noticed George Gehling in a huddle with his dad. George usually showed up once or twice a week to borrow something, so Paul paid no attention.

At supper table, Joe Pesch seemed very jubilant as he produced a gallon jug of Uncle Thorval's illegal moonshine that the bootlegger had hidden in the oats bin the night the minions of the law were hot on his trail.

Joe poured some apple cider into glasses for Maggie and himself and "spiked" it with some of this 180-proof alcohol.

"What's got into you, man?" Maggie cried. "Why are you bringing some of Thorval's filthy hootch into this house? What's got into you?"

"Today we've cause to celebrate," Joe said as he raised his glass. "We've sold the Hartneck place."

"Are you drunk already?" Maggie voiced her concern.

"No, I'm not drunk," Joe declared. "George Gehling bought the place this afternoon for our price, believe it or not! 'Tis cause to celebrate."

He took a sip of the cocktail, and his whole body shook from the power of the mixture, and he realized he had put too much hootch in the apple cider.

Paul, in his place at the supper table, calculated that the answer to his prayer had taken less than an hour to arrive. From that day forward, without his realizing it, he began a steady march toward the priesthood since he had adopted Mary, the Mother of Priests, to be his chief intercessor. As long as he pursued this devotion, she would not fail him.

8

A half mile up the road from the small Pesch farm lived the Liepolds—Otto, Lena, and son Leonard.

On this particular July day Paul, thirteen, and Leonard, ten, were down by the shore of the shallow Duck Lake, which they called the "Dead Sea" because that was how King referred to it once. King read the Bible a lot and was familiar with more biblical places and terminology than his brethren. The Pesches and their offspring, for example, were too wrapped up in their agricultural pursuits to cultivate Holy Writ.

Though drawn to the shore of Duck Lake that morning, Paul and Leonard did not contemplate going fishing like Peter and the sons of Zebedee. They knew that a miracle was needed for Jesus to produce even a pailful of bullheads and suckers from this body of water, to say nothing about catching game fish.

Instead they looked at the fleet of sunken duck hunting boats at the eastern shore of the lake.

"Them rich bastards from the Cities come streaming down here in the fall to shoot ducks, and then when it's time to go home, they sink their boats and leave them here for the next season," said Paul when they were poling the Liepold scow among the reeds one morning looking for duck nests and spied the sunken boats. "What we wanna do is raise one of these boats, paddle it around all summer and stuff, and then sink it again in the fall before those fat slobs come around to shoot some more ducks."

"That sounds like a great idea!" exclaimed Leonard. "When we gonna raise her?"

"Well, we'll go back to your dock and see if we can't scout Egger up to give us a hand."

Sir Edgar was Leonard's classmate in school, and both three years younger than Paul. Neither Leonard or Sir Edgar were classified as serious students by the teachers at Sacred Heart. Both boys giggled too much, and Sister Ruth had to slap them on the hands a lot with her ruler to try to impress them that the academy of learning was not an amusement park.

The rotting Liepold dock rested below the end of the lane, which channeled the Liepold cows from their farmstead to graze along the bank of the lake. Paul and Leonard trotted up the bank, up the lane, and a

26

quarter mile down the gravel road to the Belvedere where they found Sir Edgar in the hog yard engaged in making the old sows mad by catching little pigs and causing the young porkers to squeal.

"C'mon, give us a hand to raise the Titanic and fit her out as a gunboat this summer," commanded Paul.

"Huh?" said Sir Edgar, "where you gonna get a boat to raise?" Paul explained about the sunken fleet in Muskrat Bay of Duck Lake.

The trio returned to the boat graveyard, raised one, and paddled it to the Liepold dock where they christened it *USS Piss Boat* or *PB* by taking turns pissing on its prow instead of breaking a bottle of water over it.

At this point, "Fatty" Hunckle showed up. Fatty was a stocky town lad of thirteen. Like town boys in Lake Hebron and other country villages, Fatty didn't have much to do most of the summer and on Saturdays, and he often wandered down to Duck Lake a mile north of the village, to pole the Liepold scow around and look at duck nests and muskrat mounds. Fatty had blonde hair above his fat face, "a typical Prussian countenance," once said his teacher, Miss Carlson.

Fatty's problem was that he was not accepted into the Maloney gang because Johnny Maloney, the leader, said Fatty was too fat and couldn't move fast enough and gave the gang a bad image. For instance, on the previous Halloween night when the gang moved a lot of farm machinery up to Main Street and thus blocked it off, Fatty was the last one to make himself scarce. Oscar Peterson, the village constable, caught sight of him waddling away from the scene of the crime when he made his rounds that perilous night, and grilled him some.

Fatty had to seek acceptance elsewhere, then, and, in the meantime, spent a lot of time down at Duck Lake.

Paul gazed at Fatty's bike leaning against a half-rotten fence post on top of the bank and got an idea.

"Hey, you guys, you know we could make our new boat really move over the water with the help of Fatty's bike."

"Whaddya mean?" spoke up Fatty as he cast a concerned look at his bike up there on top of the bank.

"Well," explained Paul, "we could fasten the bike frame in the middle of the boat and hook the sprocket chain to a shaft propelling a couple of paddle wheels. Then somebody gets up on the bike and starts pedaling. Man, I think the *PB* could really move with that arrangement."

Paul had some doubts that the bike could be secured to the middle of the boat in the first place, and secondly, he knew the arrangement would be too top-heavy to be practical. What he had in mind was to have some fun seeing Fatty madly paddle away, then the bike frame separate itself from the boat, and Fatty go headlong into the drink.

But Paul sold the idea to the consortium, which by then had increased by one—lanky Danny Gullickson from town showed up looking for something to do. Handy with tools but a little short on brains when it came to thinking things through, he had built a tree house and forgot to fasten it securely to the branches of the tree. It fell down with him in it, and he broke his arm. Danny was all for powering the *PB* as Paul suggested.

Leonard was dispatched to get some of his dad's tools from the garage while the other three rustled up a couple of old buggy wheels and an axle plus some wooden shingles to form paddles to be fastened to the buggy wheels.

The new shipbuilding firm worked for six hours under the guidance of Danny Gullickson, fitting out the *PB* with its new source of locomotion oblivious to the damage being done to somebody else's duck boat when they drove nails into the gunwales and keel.

The refitting of the *PB* finished up by about 4:30 in the afternoon, and things seemed ready for the initial cruise of the flagship of the Pesch-Liepold Line. Paul looked at the schooner and became certain that the vessel would not survive its maiden voyage without disaster. Therefore, he would have to make certain not to be among the crew for that maiden voyage.

"Tell you what, fellas," Paul said, "since Fatty and Danny have actually done most of the work in fitting out our boat, it seems no more than right that they be privileged to try out this swift destroyer of His Majesty's navy. Lennie can go along if he likes, but Sir Edgar and I have to go home and get the cows for milking. Lennie, what are you going to do?"

"I guess I gotta find those cows of ours and see if I can't get them home for milking," Leonard smirked. He knew that the *PB* was not long for the sea, and wanted no part in the maiden voyage.

"Okay, Fatty and Danny, the boat is all yours. Good luck," said Paul.

While quite certain that the ship would capsize sooner or later since it was much too top heavy with that bike frame mounted above the gunwales, Paul didn't fear anyone drowning, since the water in the lake was no more than five feet deep in its deepest part. He looked forward to seeing the occupants of the craft getting pitched into the drink, and took up a post on top of the bank to watch the proceedings.

Leonard started after the cows but couldn't resist the prospect of watching what happened to the *PB* and positioned himself on the bank some distance away to enjoy the show.

Fatty and Danny pushed the boat out into the "deep" with an oar, and Danny mounted the bike and started pedaling.

In the western sky hung a curtain of deep blue signaling the onset of a summer thunderstorm. In fact, the rumblings of thunder could already be heard. The storm, a fast moving one, in a short time pushed a greenish roll cloud ahead of the blue curtain in the west, which sent a heavy wind coming.

The *PB* had its moment of glory, however. No doubt about that.

Danny pedaled vigorously while Fatty stayed aft and tried to steer the boat with an oar. Fatty could never have undertaken the task of pedaling, for the bike mounts would have immediately given way under his weight. As Danny pedaled, the paddles dug into the water, and the boat picked up speed, soon sailing fifty yards out on the lake while the two sailers joyfully whooped it up. Then it happened.

The first gust of wind from the fierce wind cloud threw a high wave at the boat just as Danny felt the bike frame separating itself from its mounts. The two sailors were thrown out of the boat into the water along with the separated bike frame, and they were thoroughly doused with the wind-whipped water.

In the meantime, Paul sought shelter in a rotting boat shed near the shore as the storm struck. He chuckled as the boat tipped over, and Fatty's stocky frame rolled into the lake.

The rain, coming down in sheets, was soon accompanied by hail. Paul could make out Fatty and Danny crawling back into the boat only to be flailed by the icy white pellets. But the storm and the hail soon subsided, and the wreck of the PB entered the cattails on the other side of the lake.

Soon the soaked sailors crawled back onto shore. They faced a three-mile hike around the lake back to town.

Paul gave a weak wave of his hand to the unfortunate crew of the PB, and headed out for home to help Sir Edgar milk the cows.

Just then Lena Liepold hove into view coming down the lane to the lake.

"Where's Leonard?" she inquired in a quavering voice full of concern.

"I guess he's looking for the cows somewhere," Paul replied.

Just then the wind switched direction and blew the PB off the shore, and it could be seen drifting on the lake.

"You're lying!" Mrs. Liepold shrieked. "He was in that boat, and he fell out in that storm and drowned!" She was nearly hysterical.

"Naw, Mrs. Liepold, Leonard wasn't in that boat at all. Even if he was, he couldn't drown anyway. The lake ain't deep enough for that. Shucks, Mrs. Liepold, ain't no use a you carryin' on like that. I tole you Lennie was looking for the cows."

Mrs. Liepold gathered her wits about her and finally remembered that the lake was indeed very shallow, and that Lennie bragged about walking across it several times. Her face hardened as she said, "I'll beat the hide off that kid when he gets home, so help me! What was he doing by the lake in a storm in the first place!"

The sun broke through the clouds and formed a lovely rainbow on the other side of the lake.

"Ain't that rainbow nice, Ma'am?" commented Paul. "Lennie should be coming down soon with the cows." And he started trotting homeward.

After the chores and supper, Paul noticed two forlorn-looking creatures plodding down the road toward town. Their soaked shirts had already dried as had their mud-caked trousers which slapped against each other as they strode along.

Paul moved up to the fence by the road, and inquired politely, "Now what in the world happened to you fellas anyway? I thought you both were still out there on the lake putting the *PB* on her shakedown cruise." He had to stop talking at this point to try to stifle his laughter.

"You goddam son of a bitch," snarled Fatty. "You knew perfectly well that your goddam idea wouldn't work, and that's why you didn't go along. You bastard."

"Oh my, oh my, Fatty. Tsk, tsk, the way you swear! You gotta go to confession for swearing like that," Paul cautioned.

"Piss on you!" was all the acknowledgement Paul got from the fat Prussian.

Fatty completely dissociated himself from Paul and company for a time after the fateful voyage of the *PB* and made new efforts to ingratiate himself into the Maloney gang again. That gang, among other things, swam naked every afternoon in the gravel pit south of the village, while some of the village girls sneaked down and peeked at them from behind the gravel ridges.

But Fatty again didn't get anywhere with the Maloney gang. He swallowed his pride and returned to studying aquatic life down at Duck Lake with Paul and company. He even agreed to ride in the *PB* again without the bike frame after Danny repaired the boat fairly well. Danny, however, hardly uttered ten words throughout the entire *PB* incident and became known around the village as Silent Beanpole.

9

On an ideal spring day in early May in Paul's senior year at Lake Hebron High School, he began the mile and a half trek home to do his chicken chores.

"Hey, Paul, hold up!"

Paul swung around to see Calvin Ford running to catch up. As Paul turned around, he looked at the high school, a three-story square building made of red brick. A small bell tower capped the facade over the front door, and the structure resembled a courthouse built in the last half of the nineteenth century in mid-America. With its high windows Paul remarked once that if they were all bricked up except for small gun ports, the building could pass for Fort Sumter. The happy high schoolers who did their part to wear down the oak flooring inside simply called their alma mater, "The Fortress."

Attached to the ancient bastion on the right side was a spanking new addition housing an auditorium-gym and some classrooms. Completed in April 1937 in time for Paul's class to sit on its new stage at commencement, the new building sported beige-colored bricks, straight lines, and modern windows, and matched the mother building "like a trim racehorse matches an old elephant." So said Harris Amundson, the science teacher.

The new building had been erected by the WPA (Works Progress Administration) to provide jobs, but most of the country folk thereabouts were not very enthusiastic about receiving "charity" from the government.

Hermon Volkman, the village cop, who was slightly prejudiced against youth of the town because he was occasionally the victim of their tricks, looked on the new addition as a waste of money.

"That damned Roosevelt spends money like water, and sends out his WPA to build us a new school. Shucks, those kids never learned nothin' in the old one."

Cal came puffing up and gasped, "How about fixing me up with Toots Friday night?"

On Friday night one of the big bands, Clyde McCoy, played at the Roof Garden down at Lake Okoboji, thirty miles south. Every kid who wanted to rate with his peers went down there to dance to the big band music.

31

"Now look here, Cal," Paul said, "I tole you before a dozen times that I don't want no dang communist in the family."

In social studies class one day a month earlier, Cal had risen to defend the Loyalists in the Spanish Civil War, and Paul got up and yelled, "The Loyalists are supported by the Communists, and they slaughter priests and nuns. What the hell is the matter with you Cal? Are you a Communist?"

"Boys, quit swearing . . ." bleated Miss Barnes, the teacher who was more suited to mothering babies than dealing with teenagers.

Cal admitted to Paul later that he was a Communist. He reminded Paul, "I told you when we wuz shooting mudhens in the Big Swamp last Sunday afternoon that when we Communists take over the country, I'll see to it that they leave the Catholic Church alone."

"Piss on you and all the Communists!" Paul shot back.

Despite their idiological differences, Paul and Cal remained friends and usually walked home from school together since they were neighbors. And Cal knew he would never get a date with Toots anyway. She simply didn't like him and had more offers from others than she could accept.

Of medium height, Cal had a square face with a wide mouth and straight black hair. He wasn't handsome but not the worst looking chap in the class. It was just that he did not appeal to Toots. Paul, on the other hand, was very good looking with light curly hair and could have any girl he wished despite the fact that he was a sloppy dresser.

Cal and Paul did have one thing in common. They were the founding fathers of the "Cafe de la Chicken Coop," a small night club they had set up on Cal's place.

The previous year Paul and Cal put together the setting for the junior-senior prom. The theme was "A Gypsy Serenade," and they constructed a gypsy camp. While they worked on the project over at Cal's place, the two decided to get dates and attend the affair, but neither knew how to dance.

"Why don't we clean up that new chickenhouse over there as long as you don't use it," Paul had suggested. "We'll turn it into a night club, invite some girls over to teach us how to dance. For music we'll use a radio. The big bands, you know, come on after the ten o'clock news."

The Cafe de la Chicken Coop originally had been built as a brooder house for baby chicks and, therefore, had a wooden floor, which the two boys scrubbed and prevailed on the girls to wax. The building was about twenty feet long with a row of small windows on the front and a door at each end. Cal put up a shelf at one end for the table radio. With no electric lights in the building, Cal tapped power from the house and strung wire out to the Coop.

"Good grief! It's a wonder you didn't electrocute yourself," commented Paul. "Good thing your dad is gone most of the time, or he would have crowned you with a fence post."

The Coop's ceiling reached barely high enough for the kids to stand up, but they weren't interested in that nor in having the sole light bulb burning while they danced to Guy Lombardo broadcasting from the Roosevelt Room or Harry James triple tonguing from the Trianon in Chicago.

The project became a success. The girls taught the boys how to dance and thus assured themselves of prospective dates to take them down to Lake Okoboji. Toots came for a while but left when Cal started squeezing her too tight on the dance floor. She returned, however, when invitations to the Coop became very much sought after.

The dances continued on Friday nights all summer in the Coop.

Leila Sorenson came to the first session of dancing instructions and remained one of the elite invited every Friday night. Very pretty with a sensuous figure, she liked Paul very much. When she and Paul skipped a dance or two to sit on the bench outside the Coop and look over the Liepold slough reflecting the moonlight, they ignored its smell and imagined it was Lake Louise. Leila squealed that there was a caterpillar in Paul's hair. That gave her an excuse to run her fingers through his curls, pretending to eradicate the worm.

Paul had a difficult time keeping his concupiscence in check when in Leila's company, but those strict nuns whooping it up on the subject of impurity, mortal sin, and hellfire had made too much of an impression on him to risk much with Leila. He took her to the movies a couple of times because she was a good listener when he rambled on and on in the Corner Cafe afterwards.

Going out with the same person twice in a row automatically meant "going steady" in the youthful parlance of late Depression America. But Father Joachim looked darkly upon the practice.

One evening at high school religion class Father Joachim dissertated on the subject. "That's a terrible thing—this going steady in high school. A poor girl goes out with a boy a couple times, and she's trapped with the coyote. Nobody else will ask her for a date, and she is stuck with the lug who might not be the greatest thing God has created to fulfill the dreams of a maiden. And, of course, the boy is trapped too. They are stuck with each other and eventually they start messing around until they have to get married. After they get married, they spend the rest of their lives pining for that dreamboat they missed dating. Ach, this going steady in high school is for der dumkopfs."

Paul looked at Leila, turned red, and smiled weakly. Leila looked like she was about to cry.

10

Two days before graduation, Paul walked home from school on a lovely day in May when he suddenly stopped abreast of the village park and turned right.

"Now what in the Sam Hill am I doing going this direction?" he asked himself. "Oh yeah, the rectory is up ahead. Is that where I want to go? Well, it won't hurt to ask Father Joachim about the seminary. Doggone, I've got to do something this fall after graduation, and it won't be pitching hay as a hired man on some farm. I gotta get to college somehow, and maybe the old boy can come up with something."

Paul mounted the steps to the porch and rang the doorbell. Father Joachim came to the door in his shirt sleeves and suspenders. It was rare to see him without his Roman collar.

"Yes?" he said. "Oh, it's you. What do you want, laddie? Is school out already today? Come in."

Paul was a bit nervous, a situation in which he rarely found himself. "Father, I was just wondering. Is the seminary tough?"

"Seminary? Well, no, it isn't bad. Got to study pretty hard, of course. You wanna go to the seminary?"

"Naw, I was just on my way home from school, and, I don't know, I thought I'd make an inquiry. Well, I gotta get home and do my chores. Thanks, Father."

"Shucks, I don't wanna get involved in no dang seminary," Paul growled, as he walked away at a rapid clip. "Dunno what in the Sam Hill I stopped in there for. Jiminy Crickets! I must be getting absent-minded."

Paul had left Father Joachim standing in the open door. The priest closed it and went back to his desk and addressed his dog on the settee. "Get off that thing, Prince! You leave hair all over it. Lay on the floor like you're supposed to. Now that Pesch lad who was just here. Can't figure him out. Here he was inquiring about the seminary—the last place I'd expect to see him land in. Been a bit of a scoundrel at times, I hear. Prince, pay attention and quit going to sleep on me, you good-for-nothing dog."

Prince opened one eye and wiggled his tail a few times to satisfy his master, and resumed his nap.

After graduation Paul was quite content living a life of a country gentleman on the Belvedere. He read library books, mowed the lawn and kept the farmstead neat and tidy. But the farm was not going to be known as the "Belvedere" anymore since Chicken King had died a couple months before. Paul missed the old man very much.

It had happened like this: One day after Easter, Maggie hadn't seen King around for several days, and became quite worried. It was not like King to be absent from her kitchen for almost a week. She sent little Maggie over to check on him. Little Maggie found him lying on his crude mattress "sleeping with his forefathers" as he himself described death. Little Maggie was afraid of dead people, and she thought he looked quite dead; so she rushed home with the news and was all out of breath when she got there.

Maggie grieved King's death and dreaded thinking how much she would miss him. It had been such a relief from the struggle of making do in the Depression to have King around spinning his tales and expressing grand illusions.

After his visit to the rectory, Paul had given little thought to going to the seminary, and nobody in the family hassled him about what he planned to do in the fall. However, Maggie hinted one day that he would have to get a job on a farm as a hired man to start making himself some money pretty soon rather than living like a member of the House of Hapsburg in his palace. Just the thought of becoming a hired man gave Paul a pain in his duodenum, a term he heard Dr. Chadbourn use once, and wondered ever since where the duodenum in the body might be located.

One summer day after he had spent a couple of hours in the afternoon reading *A Tale of Two Cities* Maggie called his attention at supper to an ad in the Lake Hebron News that John Weisenkamp was looking for a hired man for the rest of the summer.

"That I," said Paul, launching into a discourse, "a cultured young man of noble tastes, born for higher things than working as a peasant on the land, should be subject to the role of a Chinese coolie on the land of John Weisenkamp—well, even the thought of it is revolting."

"Would Your Majesty mind passing the bread," said Sir Edgar.

"I wonder how your superior culture comes out when you get Leila in the car after a movie," said Toots.

Maggie frowned. "None of that talk at the table. I preached enough to you kids about carrying on with members of the opposite sex as you got older. And I don't want to hear even the word necking mentioned around here. Now Paul, I trust you are not laying hands on that Sorenson girl."

"Oh, for Pete's sake," responded Paul. "We always talk about things above the flesh and the earth. We discourse on things spiritual and noble."

There was a chorus of laughter from his siblings, and even Pa Pesch smiled a bit, something he rarely did around the table.

Meanwhile, Father Joachim decided just before the Fourth of July that since Paul had not shaken the community yet with some choice scandal, it was time to inform the Pesch family that he had lined Paul up to begin college that fall, and he thought he would advise them to begin praying that the Holy Spirit direct the lad to more things consonant with the holy priesthood.

"Prince, I bet they don't even know Paul is a little interested in the seminary. I'll surprise them good, heh, heh. Guess I'll go out there this evening, but, Prince, you got to stay home. I understand they got a dog out there who gets into a lot of dogfights, and I don't want you to chew their hound to pieces."

Prince wiggled his tail stump.

That evening as twilight set in, Father Joachim drove out to the Pesch place. He noted Maggie's colorful morning glory vines covered the fence separating her garden from the lawn, and he was quite favorably impressed since he loved flowers and gardening.

After he shut off the engine of the big Chrysler, he heard a chorus of crickets chirping their vesper song. A bit early for crickets this year, he thought, but maybe that was because it had been so dry this summer.

Boots sounded the alarm, but no one emerged from the house, so he honked the horn. Father Joachim could have gone up and rang the door-bell, but he wasn't much for standing around doors and knocking. He preferred that the peasants come out to his car where, enthroned on the cushion, he would conduct his business.

Boots, a nondescript mutt, whose ancestors started out as Airdales, but had mutated new bloodlines through promiscuous breeding, trotted over to the Chrysler and proceeded to sniff the tires.

"Scram, dog! Don't you dare go pissing on my tires," hissed the priest through the rolled-down window. Undeterred, Boots selected the left front tire, and raised his hind leg.

In the house, Margie, fourteen, and little Maggie, eleven, had been engaged in a verbal battle as to who put the spot on Margie's new blouse. When Boots sounded the alarm, Margie withdrew from the field of battle to see who was outside. Taking her time, she smoothed her tan gingham dress, fluffed her hair a bit before emerging from the house. It was then she recognized the occupant of the black Chrysler.

"Good evening, Father," she said. Then she remembered she had forgotten to include the preliminary phrase, "Praised be Jesus Christ," which the Sisters had taught the children at Sacred Heart to include in addressing a priest. She amended her greeting to: "Praised be Jesus Christ! Good evening, Father."

"What's your name, girl?" the priest growled as he peered at her.

"Marjorie, Father."

"H'mm, not so sure that's a saint's name. I wonder how you got by with it if I baptized you. Are your mother and father home?"

"No, Father, they went out to Johnny Pelzels to get some rhubarb for canning."

"Is Paul home?"

"No, Father, he's . . ." She thought better of it and didn't tell the pastor that Paul was over at the Chicken Coop, dancing. That was not the kind of information which would serve to cheer the heart of a straight-laced pastor.

"Well, anyhow, tell your folks that I lined Paul up for St. Mary's College this fall. Also tell your Pa to come in and see me tomorrow. Good night, girl."

Father Joachim turned the switch and kicked his foot down to the floorboard where the starter button of the Chrysler was located. The big six rumbled into action. Boots emerged again from his lair under the porch to give the priest a barking send-off. With Boots this time was Ole, Sir Edgar's pet pig, now about the same size as Boots. Ole had been trained to stay under the porch when visitors came lest they "get strange ideas about the Pesch family," as Maggie put it. However, Ole was allowed to assist at the departure ceremonies of guests because he would not likely be noticed by the visitors.

Margie ran into the house and, somewhat breathlessly, gasped, "Have I got news! Oh boy, have I got news for Dad and Ma."

Little Maggie rose from the chair where she had been listening to the "Lux Radio Theatre" and cried, "C'mon, tell me! What did Father want?"

"Father said that Paul was going to St. Mary's College this fall. I think he meant that Paul was going to study to be a priest. Can you feature that? Boy, if Father only knew what Paul was up to right now! Gee, I almost let it slip that Paul's over at the Chicken Coop, dancing with the girls."

Both Paul and Toots were at the Coop engaged in swinging and swaying to Sammy Kaye broadcasting from the Aragon Ballroom in Chicago. The orchestra played Paul's favorite on the Hit Parade, "Deep Purple," and he danced with Delia Munson, a very nice, cultured girl but not one to inflame his concupiscence like Leila did with her curvy figure. Leila was out of town on vacation with her folks.

Toots had been captured by Cal Ford who turned his pimpled face toward her, trying to maneuver himself into a cheek to cheek situation. Toots looked desperately for someone to cut in.

Toots noticed that Bob Fernham, her favorite boyfriend, was missing from the floor, and so was Queenie McNallan. In her mind that spelled trouble for her Bob. Queenie was full of life and romance and loved to pet. She went to the Methodist-Episcopal Church in town where the preacher thundered against drinking and dancing, but he never spelled out what was wrong with dancing. He was just against it. Queenie wrote him off as an old fashioned grandpa who didn't understand young people, and she felt free to dance to her heart's content at the Coop or down at Okoboji.

Toots complained it was "too hot" to dance and went out to sit on the bench that had been propped against the side of the former chicken brooder house. The youthful occupants of the bench gazed at the Leipold Slough, a morass of grass, cattails, and the habitat of mud hens and muskrats.

On the bench Queenie was about to move in closer to Bob, hoping to get in some necking, when Toots and Cal appeared and caused Bob's rising blood pressure to subside.

Generally speaking, the Friday night dances over at the Coop were nothing to cause parents and preachers to lose any sleep. Queenie was about the only one who posed much danger, and she never had enough privacy to throw her web over any of the boys. Paul was always her favorite target, but he didn't like to get shriven from sins of the flesh down at church very often. So he backed away whenever she started cuddling up on the dance floor or the bench.

Father Joachim had never heard of this private night club some of the kids operated in his parish, and, if he knew about it, he probably would have thundered from the pulpit sooner or later about the "den of iniquity," a term he used to describe anything he thought an occasion to sin.

When Ma and Pa Pesch arrived home with Sir Edgar that evening and had unloaded the rhubarb, Margie told them about Father Joachim's visit.

"Father Joachim was here? Tonight?" Maggie was incredulous because the priest rarely visited any parishioners. "What on earth did he want?"

Margie finished relaying the message.

"Well, I declare!" Maggie exclaimed. "Paul never said anything about being a priest. I don't believe it! That boy is up to something again. Besides, he's too lazy to be a priest."

Pa Pesch, who said very little about anything on most occasions, sat there cracking his knuckles like he always did when he tried to figure out a problem. Finally, he spoke up. "We ain't got no money to send Paul to school."

"Where is Paul tonight for heaven's sake?" Maggie asked.

"Him and Toots are down at the Chicken Coop again."

"Chicken Coop? What on earth would kids want to do down at a chicken coop?"

"For Pete's sake, Ma. You heard us talking about the Chicken Coop over at Ford's. They put a radio in there and dance."

"They do?"

"Well, for Pete's sake, Ma, what do you think they are doing? Watching chickens hatch?"

"That's a fine place for a future priest to be spending his time, I say!" declared Maggie. "Sounds like there might be some sinning going on there too. You go there right now, Margie, and tell Paul to come home. I wonder if that boy isn't trying to put one over on Father Joachim. Land sakes, I don't know what to make of all this."

Marge trotted off down the gravel road toward the Ford's, and, in less than five minutes, she could hear the smooth sound of Tommy Dorsey's trombone emanating from the speaker of the Emerson radio in the Coop. But nobody was dancing. All the teenagers sat on the bench or on the grass overlooking the slough, listening to the music drifting out of the open window and probably imagining that the slough was Lake Louise and they were whispering sweet nothings into the ear of a lover instead of munching hot dogs and sipping nectar.

Marge tripped upon the scene and announced, "Paul, yer s'posed to come home. Ma wants to talk to you."

"What about?" Paul sat near Queenie and enjoyed her scratching his ankle with her big toe.

"Father Joachim stopped in and said something about you going to college."

"Holy cow! Say no more. I'm on my way." He was conscious of the glances of adulation from the group. Not very many young people went to college in 1937.

On the way home, Paul said, "Marge, what else did Father say when he came out tonight?"

"Nothin.' But we think he's putting you up to be a priest."

"Naw, I never told him anything like that. Boy, I'm glad you didn't say nothing about me becoming a priest to the kids there at the Coop. They'd think I was a holy joe."

"Naw, you ain't gonna be a priest, Paul," Margie said. "You're too lazy. All you wanna do all day is sit around and read library books."

As they trudged along, Paul remembered the stop he had made at the rectory the previous May. He figured Father Joachim should have forgotten all about it, but instead he lined him up at St. Mary's, which was a priest factory in Paul's mind. Paul wanted to go to college, that was for sure, and it looked like he might make it at that. Things were looking up. Paul thought, "You farmers around here can take your manure forks and milk pails and give them to some other hired men. I ain't about to eat my bread by the sweat of my brow. I'll see what I can squeeze out of my noodle instead."

11

The Pesch family usually assembled in the dining room to listen to the radio after supper. Homework was done there (with the radio off), and Pa often sat there staring into space, cracking his knuckles while trying to solve a problem. The dining room also served as the location for saying the family rosary in Lent, and the place for family tribunals when one of the kids had to answer charges brought up against him or her. The family sat there awaiting Paul's appearance. In the meantime Toot's curiosity had gotten the best of her, and she swiftly trotted home to get in on the proceedings.

Paul stood in the dining room, fiddling with one of the buttons on his shirt, all eyes on him.

"Now what's all this about what Father Joachim said tonight?" asked Maggie, usually the chief spokesperson at these gatherings. Secretly, she liked the idea of Paul's becoming a priest very much; she just couldn't quite make herself believe that he was sincere about it. You never could be sure about Paul. He was a crafty customer.

Pa cracked his knuckles, and thought that it would be great to have a son in the seminary. It would boost his standing in the community, for, amongst the faithful there in Sacred Heart parish, it was a great honor to have a son in the priesthood. Pa never bothered about Paul's vagaries except he did not approve of the lad's hostility to earning his bread by the sweat of his brow.

Paul launched into his side of the story "I never said anything to Father Joachim about going to the seminary. I just stopped by to see him last May on the way home from school and asked him what a seminary was like, and then got out of there as fast as I could. But I sure would like to go to college, and it kinda looks like he's got that arranged."

"Now see here, young man," Maggie protested, "You can't be spending hard-earned money in college just sitting around reading library books with no intention of becoming a priest."

"Well, gee whiz, Ma!" answered Paul. "I'll bet the Pope wasn't so sure he wanted to be a priest when he started college. Quit pestering me."

So nothing definite came out of the family pow-wow that night, but Paul smiled as he waited for sleep to come and recited another "Memorare." It looked like he was going to college. Hooray!

The next morning Joe Pesch drove the family's Ford V-8 into town to deliver a can of cream to the Farmers Cooperative Creamery. While they tested the cream and made out his check, Joe went over to the rectory to see Father Joachim. The only two times people of the parish ordinarily went to the rectory was to make arrangements to get married—and they dreaded this confrontation if they had a Protestant on the string—or to pay their annual pew rent. They liked the latter visit because the pastor was always in a good mood to receive money.

"Joe, do you think Paul would make a good priest?" Father Joachim asked.

"I dunno, Father," replied Joe, cracking his knuckles.

"By the way, where was he last night when I came out to your place?"

"He was over at the Chicken Coop, I guess."

"You mean he was out feeding chickens?"

"No, Father, the Chicken Coop is a place over at Ford's where some of the young people dance, I guess, on Friday nights."

"What! Do I have a den of iniquity right in my own parish? And Paul was over there prancing around and necking on the floor?" Father Joachim always called dancing, "necking on the floor."

"Well, yah, I guess so," said Joe. "I never knew about the chicken house till last night."

Father Joachim tapped the top of his desk with a fountain pen, looked at Prince lying at his usual spot on the right of the desk, stood up, and said, "Joe, we'll send Paul to St. Mary's College anyway, and see what happens. The Lord can do a lot with sinners, as the example of St. Augustine shows. Keep Paul busy on the farm the rest of the summer, but make the chicken house off limits for him. How much of the freight can you pay the first year?"

"I don't know. I'll have to see, Father," said Joe.

"Well, Joe, it's going to cost around $500 a year. But I'll throw in some if you run short."

That afternoon Joe found Paul in the messy garage and tool shop, trying to adjust the blades on the lawn mower. The only job Paul liked around the farm besides driving the new John Deere tractor was mowing lawns and tending the trees and flowers in the yard. He detested pitching bundles into threshing machines as a hired man for Harold Stumpf, husking corn by hand, and helping his dad butcher pigs. In fact, it was during his tenure at Stumpf's a couple of weeks previous, that he felt the Lord was hinting at him to become a priest.

Paul had been sweating profusely as he pitched bundles of grain into the threshing machine when again the thought came into his mind: "Oh, my goodness, this business just ain't for me, that's all there is to it." There flashed through his mind the scene he had witnessed the week before of Father Joachim standing under the shade of a tree on that hot day, directing a stream of water from a hose toward his flowerbed. Now that was more like it! He stopped pitching bundles to dwell on this pleasant scene, and his side of the feeder became empty. Joe Hullerman, the threshing master, hollered at him, and Paul resumed pitching into the machine but at a slower pace.

That evening after supper, Harold started making fun of his "lazy hired man," and Paul told him to take his job and shove it. The way he put it was, "Take your job and give it to Jesse James, for you will no longer have the pleasure of gazing upon my pleasant countenance around here." Paul walked home to the Belevedere and resumed mowing lawns the next day.

In the garage, Joe Pesch said, "Now listen, Paul, I was talking to Father Joachim this morning, and he and I will try to get you to college this fall, providing you mean business. That means you gotta stop telling these farmers to go to the devil and also stop girling around, see?"

"Okay," Paul assented.

It wouldn't be too hard for him to ease up with the girls. Leila was the only one he dated, and she never made his heart thump anymore when she sat across from him at Mattison's Cafe after the movie, gazing at him with adoring eyes as he carried on a monologue. He thought he might still sneak over to the Coop for the next two Friday nights left of the summer and dance with some of the girls who gave him bad thoughts— like Queenie McNallan.

In the meantime, Maggie lost no time getting on the phone to gossip with her cousin, Mary Winkler, who lived on a nearby farm. Mary had a good view of the Ford place from her living room window, and she could never quite figure out why the Ford chicken house was always lit up on Friday nights. She knew they didn't raise chickens.

Maggie cranked the wall phone by the pantry door and asked "central" to ring up Mary Winkler.

When Maggie told her Paul was going to college in a few weeks, Mary was quite surprised.

"What's he going to college for?" Mary gasped. In the Depression it was too expensive for the average poor lad around Lake Hebron to go to college.

"He might try for the priesthood, I guess."

Mary opened her mouth wide like she always did when she received some astounding news and said a few "Ahs" like she did in Dr. Chadourn's office when he examined her throat to see if her tonsils were growing back. She always insisted they were, but Dr. Chadourn knew they weren't. To satisfy her he peered down her throat every few months.

"Of course, Mary, you know how things are when boys say something about becoming priests," said Maggie. "You just never know what they really have in mind, especially my Paul."

"I heard he likes to dance," said Mary. "Is that right?"

"Well, yes," replied Maggsie. "He goes over to the Chicken Coop with the other boys and girls on Friday nights."

"What do you mean? Chicken coop?" Marie said.

Maggie explained, and then Mary understood why the chicken house over at Ford's was always lit up on Friday nights. She decided to focus her husband's bionoculars on the Ford chicken house on Friday nights in the future and see what those young people were doing.

After Mary hung up she decided that Siena, her only offspring, now twenty-four, should go to the convent so she could keep up with her cousin, Maggie, in furnishing a vocation to the Church and obtaining some prestige, which was automatically given when an offspring became a priest or a nun.

The news about Paul got around the parish very fast, and the following Sunday, when some of the parishioners came into church for the ten o'clock high Mass, they noticed Paul in the stairwell room to the right helping Cedric, the janitor, ring the bells. As usual Paul hung on to the rope of the largest bell, "Big Bong," and was dragged off the floor at the top of its cycle. Ellie Juster said to her sister, Nora, "He's not a serious enough boy to be a priest, don't you think so, Nora?"

Juster sisters noticed that, after helping ring the bells, Paul went on upstairs to sing in the tenor section of the choir; they didn't know his motivation was that the balcony gave him a splendid view of the congregation below and a good peek at some of the girls all dressed up for church.

‡　　‡　　‡

The following Friday night had the usual dance at the Chicken Coop, and Paul sneaked over after pledging Toots not to squeal on him.

Cal looked at him with considerable disapproval. If Paul went holy on him he'd never be able to get Paul to help fix him up a date with Toots. Besides, communists had no time for priests, who always peddled religion, the opium of the people.

Queenie McNallan went up to Paul, took him by the arm and spoke softly. "Paul, you're too good looking to become a priest. What you're doing is pulling a fast one on old Joachim so he'll help you get to college. After that you'll take off and get married. C'mon, let's dance."

Paul thought her not only a curvaceous cutie but also a smart cookie, good at sizing people up.

The lighted radio dial providing most of the illumination inside the Coop, although some light came in through the windows from the yard light. Both the Ford and Pesch farms lay inside the city limits of Lake Hebron and were able to hook on to the city lights, although most farms at that time had no electric power yet. Sammy Kaye and his orchestra played from the Aragon in Chicago and broadcasted over Chicago's WBBM which came through very clearly at night via the table model Emerson.

The orchestra played "Harbor Lights," high in the hit parade at the moment, and the weeping steel guitar sounded very romantic. Queenie snuggled up to Paul as they slowly shuffled around on the waxed pine boards, and Paul felt his "passions beginning to rise." That was the way Queen Jacoba the Fierce put it and solemnly warned that, when that happened, "you have to get away from the occasion of sin right away, for the devil is moving in fast."

Paul moved away from Queenie a bit to keep his temperature down, and then suggested they go outside. Queenie thought he meant going outside to sit on the back of the old wagon in the grove and neck, and she was eager to accept that invitation.

Instead Paul seated her on the bench along the Coop and said, "Queenie, you're too doggone exciting to be alone with. Shucks, I'd be rolling in the leaves with you in less than a minute."

Queenie snuggled up to Paul on the bench and whispered, "Paul, sweetheart, let's do it."

Just then Toots and Bob emerged from the Coop and sat down on a log to watch the moon rising over Liepold Slough. Paul moved away from Queenie a bit and started to discourse about the life cycles of the muskrats in the slough and the reasons why cattails were so prolific in wetlands like that. Queenie started to pout until Paul began tickling her ears with a stalk of pigeon grass.

Eleven o'clock was closing time at the Coop by order of Abigail Ford, Cal's mother. Queenie and Paul, Toots and Bob piled into the Pesch Ford V-8 and drove to Okabena three miles south for a hamburger at Ma's Place. This was a hangout for high school kids who delighted in heckling the proprietor, "Ma" Keisling, a large buxom woman with a voice like a foghorn. The heckling consisted of begging her, sometimes on bended knee, for a bottle of beer, knowing full well she wouldn't even think of yielding to them. Instead she would yell with enough volume to vibrate the rivets on the nearby water tower, "Get off the floor, you pocket gopher, and beat it!"

The kids in the booths whooped with laughter and waited for the next one to beseech her. It was a lot of fun until one o'clock in the morning, at which time Ma drove out the remnants of the youths with a broomstick.

The next morning Joe told Paul to take the tractor down to the creek farm and finish plowing the east forty. But Paul had not had enough sleep the night before and became drowsy, finally falling sound asleep on the tractor. When the tractor reached the end of the field, it kept going on into the haymeadow. Here the two-cylinder engine barked considerably louder, since plowing sod put a much heavier load on it. Still, the laboring engine did not awaken Paul.

Sixty yards further was the bank of Jack Creek, a drop-off of fifteen feet or so to muddy water, but Paul's guardian angel steered the tractor into the path of a haystack. The tractor engine, not capable of moving the haystack in addition to pulling the plow, quit. There was silence broken only by the tinkling call of a meadow lark.

When Paul finally woke up he found the tractor half buried in hay and sized up the situation. He realized that, had he plunged off the bank of the creek up ahead, the tractor and engineer would have sunk into the muddy waters and had bullheads and mud turtles for company. He likely would have fared worse. Paul raised his eyes and prayed: "Thanks, Lord, for dispatching my guardian angel to get that haystack in my way. Does that mean, Lord, you might still want me to head for the priesthood?"

12

The evening before Paul was to leave for St. Mary's College, Alvina, alias "Toots," was thinking about her future too and announced at the supper table that she was going to be a nurse.

"The only nurse you'll ever be is a mother nursing babies of which you'll have about a dozen," taunted Paul.

"Shaddup before you get slapped across the puss with a wet floor mop," Toots snapped.

Paul who had experienced the application of one such weapon wielded across his fair countenance one time when he barged into the kitchen from the barnyard without removing his overshoes, had to admit to himself that the threat posed a great deterrent force. But he continued to tease her.

"Ah, Toots, why don't you just stay home and mop floors while waiting for Cal to come over and take you out? Naw, I got a better idea. Cornelius Schwartz is the one to wait for, and he pines away day after day for just a glimpse of you."

"I told you to shut up! Ma, make that good-for-nothing be quiet."

At the mention of Cornelius the rest of the siblings at the table joined in the merriment. "Whee, Cornelius and Toots!" chanted Sir Edgar. High pitched laughter came from Margie and little Maggie, formerly the baby of the family until Darlene, now two, had arrived.

"All right, you kids, keep quiet," commanded the matriarch of the household. "Toots will make a good mother some day, and there is nothing wrong with being married to a plain-looking man as long as he is a devoted husband. Paul will be leaving us tomorrow, so let's try to be good to each other on this last evening together."

In the silence that followed, Paul became uncomfortable and excused himself to go upstairs and finish packing.

Maggie had found some extra egg money to buy a few new items of clothing for Paul as well as a new suitcase. Suitcases were in very short supply in the Pesch family since they couldn't afford to travel.

The next morning after the chores were done, everyone piled into the Ford V-8, the four girls and Maggie in the back seat and the three males in the front, the usual seating arrangement for family travel from the beginning.

46

About 180 miles to Winona, the trip was the longest ever undertaken by the family together. Having never left the prairie, they were awed by the bluffs of the Hiawatha Valley and "ooo-ed" and "ahhhed" a lot.

St. Mary's College nestled on a mesa at the foothills of the bluffs and commanded a view of the Hiawatha Valley. Paul was enamored by the natural beauty surrounding this small institution of learning and concluded he could probably stand it there okay.

St. Mary's had been established as a minor seminary by Bishop Heffron, but he didn't quite have enough seminarians to fill the campus, so he invited regular collegians to the college, and soon the seminarians were far in the minority. Even so, the college couldn't make ends meet, though the Bishop sent a good number of his priests to travel the highways and byways to the villages and towns of the diocese to beg for funds from the faithful. Eventually, the Bishop turned the institution over to the Christian Brothers and divested himself of a headache.

The seminarians, in the meantime, enjoyed four years of regular college life. After a year in the place, Paul opined that this arrangement was preferable to being "roped down and brainwashed in a minor seminary."

Rome still looked darkly on her future priests being thrust into the "worldly" environment of a regular college with all its dating, dancing, and occasional hell-raising. Before Paul came upon the scene, the ecclesiastic who wore the purple and ruled the diocese had decreed that his seminarians were to be shipped off to a major seminary after two years of college at St. Mary's. Paul later said that he had two years of freedom before going to the "ecclesiastical penitentiary."

The forlorn-looking company from Lake Hebron alighted from their humble conveyance in front of St. Mary's Hall, and, thoroughly awed, crept into the building where they were directed to the registrar's office in the adjacent Kelly Hall.

Here they met Brother I. Leo, encased in a long black soutane with two white wings floating out parallel to his chin.

A smile spread over his ruddy countenance as he spied the new student from whom the institution could extract somewhere in the neighborhood of $500 a year, in return for which the farm lad could soak up the liberal arts.

"Your son looks like he will be a great student," beamed the good brother to Ma and Pa Pesch who stood in the hallway looking a bit sheepish as if they were in the presence of the Pope.

The Pesch clan wasn't much for emotional greetings and farewells. "Goodbye, Paul, study hard and don't forget to write to us all," said Maggie giving Paul a quick hug. As usual Pa said nothing, and the others scurried out with their heads bowed, trying to hide their tears. All got back into the Ford and headed for Rochester to visit with Aunt Emma and family there.

Paul climbed five floors to his assigned dorm on the top floor of St. Mary's Hall. Before he took time to contemplate his new situation in life, he went over to the window. Leaning his elbows on the sill, he gazed over the vast Mississippi Valley and the rugged hills flanking it. Suddenly a wave of homesickness engulfed him. But, being a child of the Great Depression and accustomed to taking life's rough punches on the chin, he didn't dwell very long on his homesickness. He pulled out a package of Wing cigarettes (eleven cents a pack) from his pocket, lit up, and searched for something interesting in the vista below. He soon found it—the college for women about a mile and a half away—the College of St. Teresa.

"Shucks," he said to himself, "with a good pair of binoculars, a fella should be able to catch some good scenery down there now and then."

In due time one, of the more affluent freshmen from Chicago, who also occupied the "Penthouse," as the occupants called their humble dormitory, did procure a pair of binoculars, and the boys took turns scanning St. Teresa's for something more interesting than girls walking around the campus—things like the windows of the residence hall and sunbathing beauties toasting the epidermis on the second story patio, but there were few gratifying results from these scanning sessions.

"Jeez!" spat out Mel Beltrami, who owned the glasses, "those well-feathered chicken hawks who run the place must be warning their chicks that we are putting the glasses on them. Every damned window has the shades pulled down at night and, hell, this climate's too cold for sunbathing except in July. Phooey!"

All freshmen were invited to the Cardinal Room in Kelly Hall for a "smoker" the first evening. Brother Elzear, the public relations director of the college and debate coach, was on hand to get the somewhat bewildered frosh into the swing of things. He was full of dynamism and good cheer.

"This is the greatest little college in the world," he emoted, "and you have the privilege of occupying its hallowed halls. The spirit among the St. Mary's Redmen is the envy of the Midwest," he continued while his double chin vibrated above his Adam's apple, which moved up and down like an elevator gone wild in the Foshay Tower.

"Bullshit!" said Mel Beltrami softly.

Paul was mildly scandalized at the remark as he was somewhat awed by Brother Elzear.

"The big fart looks like an overgrown penguin," continued Mel.

"To get you into the spirit of St. Mary's, and as part of our freshmen orientation," continued the effervescent Brother Elzear, "we'll take you on an outing tomorrow to the Farmer's Park in the hills and you'll get to know one another better and have a big feed around a campfire in the evening."

"He looks like he's been on too many of those feeds already," commented Mel. "He must weigh close to two hundred."

Mel was a slim six-foot-three with a heavy mat of curly black hair which almost reached to his eyebrows and looked like it might cut off his vision if allowed to grow.

"You look like a black sheep dog," commented Brother James Alfred, the dean of men, to Mel one day. "Get a haircut. The woolen mill downtown buys the kind of moss you grow on your head."

Not very handsome either, Mel's mouth was too wide, and his complexion, pockmarked from past skin disorders, resembled the surface of the moon. His ears flared out like air scoops on a jet fighter plane. But Mel soon became the best-liked occupant of the Penthouse.

At the evening picnic out at Farmer's Park the next day, Brother Elzear bellowed, "And now we will sing the rousing school song of St. Mary's. All join in."

He opened his mouth and a powerful bass voice erupted from the depths of his throat. "St. Mary's, it's up to you. . . ."

The eighty or so freshmen present were still too homesick to sing anything, and furthermore, they didn't know the melody. Brother Elzear gave up.

"Anybody see anything unusual this afternoon in your hikes around the hills?" he inquired. "Did you run into anything you hadn't seen before, maybe?"

Paul said to Mel, "You Chicago lads must have seen a lot of things you never saw before. All you see in Chicago are buildings, cars, and streets and gangsters shooting up the place."

"Bullshit!" responded Mel. "Whaddya you know about Chicago?"

Just then one short-statured boy with red hair who identified himself as Homer Wells from Chicago piped up, "I saw a cow licking a calf out in the meadow. The farmer came over and said the cow had just had the calf. Gee, I never saw nothin' like that before."

"See, what did I tell you, Mel?" said Paul.

"Bullshit! The pipsqueak should have his old man take him down to the zoo once in a while."

Paul raised his hand and yelled out, "I was climbing up a bluff and, just as I got my head over the edge of a rock on top, I stared right into the eyes of a rattlesnake sunning himself."

"My goodness, what did you do then?" gasped Brother Elzear.

"I said, 'Good afternoon, Snakepuss,' and went right back down where I came from."

"You're a damn liar," growled Mel in Paul's ear. "You're just trying to scare some of these dumb bastards. You never saw no rattlesnake. Boy, we're gonna have to watch you, you slippery son of gun."

13

Back at the Penthouse Paul took particular notice of the plump lad who occupied the bed next to his. About five-foot-ten and a bit overweight, he had a crew cut and a plain-looking face. He had briefly introduced himself as Ed Riley after declining to go along to Farmer's Park. He immediately went back to bed.

"Whatsa matter with the guy?" Paul commented to Mel. "Is he going to sleep all day? Looks like a lazy old tomcat to me."

As time went on, Paul and Ed Riley became fast friends, spending most of their time together arguing. Ed, who went out for the debate team, liked to get lots of practice by always taking the opposite view of almost anything Paul said.

"Ed, how come you study so hard?" Paul asked one day, "but physically you're so abominably lazy. Man, you're on that floggin' bed every minute you're not studying."

"That stinking food around here is so bad that I can't eat it, and without eating I have no stamina and have to rest in bed."

"Aw, Ed, that food isn't so bad," countered Paul. "Why are you always bitching about it? You're just spoiled because you were the only little critter in your family, and your Ma must have been a pretty good cook. If you'd been raised like us poor old coyotes on the prairie, you'd be more contented with the grub. Furthermore, don't you know that you're supposed to offer up your pains and inconveniences for the poor souls in purgatory and push on with a smile on your face? Some lousy Catholic you turned out to be."

"Aw, go flog yourself! That's the trouble with you slaves of the Church, you're all brainwashed. They even brainwashed you into becoming a priest and living without a woman. Jeez!"

"Spoken like a true slave of the flesh. Look at you. You're as fat as a hippo," taunted Paul. "And as a future priest, maybe, I have no alternative but to warn you of the perils of coddling the flesh. St. Paul said, 'He who lives by the flesh will die with the flesh' or something like that. Doing penance through violence to the flesh sometimes is necessary for entering the kingdom of heaven. Beware of those who go into hell with two hands instead of one."

At this point Ed must have imagined he was on the debating stage again and countered, "Did not the Lord create the wheat, the sugar cane, the fat cattle, and other sources of food in order that we might properly nourish our bodies? Did He not also plant in our bodies an appetite for the food prepared by other mortals in order to meet the needs of the body? Why, then, do you condemn me because I take enjoyment in carrying out the will of God?"

"Bullshit!" Mel Beltrami had quietly walked into the dorm and listened to Ed's oration. He made his usual comment on what he considered a phony declaration. "Aw, hell, Ed, you're just a lazy bastard. Why not admit it? And you eat too much and don't get enough exercise, and so you're too fat. Now don't give us that crap about the Lord sanctioning it."

"Mel," Paul intervened, "you have to keep in mind that our patient is only practicing debating and doesn't believe what he puts out. What puzzles me, Ed, is how come you are so physically lazy but you study like a demon and pull down high grades?"

"Well, I goldbricked all through high school, and, when I graduated, the principal told me I was wasting my talents and would end up cleaning toilets to buy some cheap wine. That made me mad, and I told the bastard that after my first year at St. Mary's I'd come home with the Bishop Heffron prize for having the best grades in the joint and I'd jam that certificate down his gullet. And, dammit, I'm going to do it!"

"Well, blow me down!" exclaimed Jim Lawler, another inhabitant of the Penthouse who had been lying on his bed monitoring the verbal exchanges. "I believe the fat old walrus is about to make good his boast."

Jim Lawler, a lad of short stature, with a small face not too unpleasant to look at, and black hair in a crew cut, had parents who were very wealthy, and he possessed an extraordinary talent for learning. He could take the textbook of any course, speed read it in thirty minutes the night before the exam and easily pass it the next day.

Riley propped himself into an almost seated position in his bed by repositioning the pillows, raised his right arm and launched into another oration. "Now there's an example of laziness! Hereafter, don't any of you swarthy hypocrites of the Sanhedrin point your stubby fingers at me. There is a lad who is really lazy. . . ."

"As a budding prophet of the Lord," shouted Paul, "I must say I concur with Brother Riley's charge and warn thee, Brother Lawler, that the day will come when, at the throne of Judgement, thy sins of omission shall swarm down to haunt thee."

"You must not be too severe in judging me," said Jim. "All of you Pharisees have never trod in my moccasins for a moment. I must reveal to you a deep dark secret which I have never revealed to anyone before. I threw all ambition to the winds because my father treated me so atrociously when I was in my tender years and literally destroyed my purpose for living."

Jim assumed a very sad look on his face and seemed to be at the edge of tears.

"What did he do to you anyway?" inquired a solemn-looking Mel.

"You don't know how much I hesitate to reveal this," answered Jim, "I know you are all gentlemen of honor and will never violate my confidence." He hesitated for a moment and dabbed his eyes with a handkerchief, swallowed, and continued. "My dad made it a regular practice when I was but a tender youth to wrestle me to the floor and cut notches in my spine. . . ."

The room immediately filled with flying objects—pillows, shoes, and anything handy—all sailing towards Jim's bed.

The mood of the group now favored more horseplay.

"Let's give the sheepdog a haircut! Whaddya say?" someone yelled.

The "sheepdog" in question was, of course, Mel Beltrami. Before Mel could escape, many pairs of hands grasped him and forced him into a chair where he underwent a rough haircut at the hands of "Goofy" Gillespie, who had just arrived, and insisted he had considerable barber talent. But when the gang released Mel, it was obvious that a professional barber would have to give him a close-cropped crew cut to rectify the damage of Goofy's crude operation.

To relieve the heavy strain on the Pesch exchequer, Paul worked off $100 a year by sweeping the halls of Kelly Hall each day and by working as a sacristan. The latter job consisted in laying out the vestments for all the priests offering Mass in the morning. Sister Theodosius, one of the sisters working in the kitchen, taught him how to do this, as well as how to prepare the cruets, candles, and linens.

One day Father Julius Haun, the eldest of the three priests on the college faculty and a keen observer of the human species as well as being quite learned in church history, came into the sacristy while Paul performed his duties.

"The day will come, young man," he said to Paul, "when priests will have to lay out their own vestments because they won't have the sisters to do it."

"What's going to happen to the nuns?" Paul inquired.

"A good share of them will go on a rampage and do their own will after the next Ecumenical Council."

Julius always predicted another Council, which, he said, would drastically change things in the Church and give the devil a golden opportunity in the resulting confusion to rip apart the Church, but nobody paid much attention to him.

One evening after Paul finished preparing things in the sacristy for the next morning, he decided to stay around in the chapel and have a talk with the Lord.

"Dear Lord," he prayed, "I kinda like it here, but I don't want to waste any of Pop's money. He thinks I'm going to be a priest and is shelling out cash to keep me here. What I want to know is: Are You calling me or not? And I gotta know at least by this time next year. I'm going to get Your Mother in on the act because You just don't ignore her nohow. I found that out when I asked her to put in the good word for me so we could sell that Hartneck place and keep from going broke."

As Paul sauntered out of the chapel, he reflected that Brother Ludwig, his Greek and German professor, had made it clear to everyone in the class that he felt Paul had no vocation. Brother Ludwig gave as his reason overhearing that Paul had attended the Freshman Tea Dance at St. Teresa's College, and there had not only mingled with members of the opposite sex, but, worse, he had held several in his arms and danced with them. This picture of Paul's betrayal of a possible vocation made Brother Ludwig shudder.

Brother Ludwig seemed to be afraid of women. He held an exaggerated opinion of their powers of seduction. In fact, he seemed to think they had no other purpose in life but to seduce priests and brothers. With fearful tones, he recounted an event that had happened to him in Austria where he had grown up. He had taken a girl out for a buggy ride, and, apparently, she had made an advance. To save himself from sin he said he whipped his horse into a gallop homeward to rid himself of this proximate occasion of sin sitting by his side.

He seemed to like recounting this event and would gladly do so if requested by a member of the class. A student soon learned that if he was not prepared he could always request the professor to tell them about his fateful "buggy ride."

After about the tenth recitation of his deliverance from temptation in the buggy, Brother Ludwig turned his bloodshot eyes on Paul and said, "So I hear you have been stepping out, Mr. Pesch. What have you got to say for yourself? And you presumably a candidate for the holy priesthood who places himself in serious occasions of sin with members of the opposite sex!"

"Shucks, Brother," Paul replied. "I just decided to go over to our sister college and bring some joy to the heart of a lonely Christian over there for an evening."

Brother Julius looked steadily at Paul and prophesied in a grave tone, "Ach, Mr. Pesch, you will never be a priest. The Lord hath cast thee out to stand shamefacedly in the ranks of the unrighteous." And he resumed his attempt to teach some Greek.

What had happened was that Paul, hearing that a "Tea Dance," as they were called, was in the offing for the following Friday night, approached one of the upper classmen for more information knowing he was risking some verbal abuse since the period of freshmen hazing was still in progress.

"What are these tea dances, honorable member of the celestial intelligentsia?" Paul asked.

Freshmen had to address upperclassmen with extreme civility in order to escape being reported to the "Kangaroo Court." The latter tribunal involved itself primarily in blistering the rear of a frosh with a wooden paddle if the lowly freshman made an "indiscretion" toward an upper classman.

"You toad full of warts," the upperclassman answered, "why do you want to know?"

"Because," Paul replied, "I would like to attend, thou honorable Prince of the Zodiac." ("You horse's ass," Paul whispered under his breath.)

"Just get on the bus and go, scum of the river bottom, and see what it's like for yourself. Don't bother me with childish prattling," concluded the high and mighty classman.

"Aw, go piss up a tree," softly whispered Paul.

14

There were two tea dances held for the freshmen of both schools, and the one in question was the first. The purpose of these socials was to facilitate the getting-acquainted process for the students of both schools. Then they would be more likely to date each other rather than students from the State College across town, which increased the danger of mixed marriages. Catholic pastors deemed mixed marriages the evil of the age, and some of them blew their stacks talking about it from the pulpit. This made the audience in the pews involved in mixed marriages very uncomfortable.

On the appointed evening, Paul with his frosh beanie on his head as per regulations, climbed on the bus with forty or so other St. Mary's freshmen, and the bus sped down the hill from the men's college on Terrace Heights to the "sem," as the College of St. Teresa was called by the St. Mary's Redmen.

Enroute, Paul spied "Dizzy" in the front of the bus, and lurched forward.

"Dizzy, you're a pre-sem. You're not supposed to be attending these social events designed to apply some glue for a possible wedding march later on. You, as a seminarian, have to write off any possibility of a trip down the aisle."

"Speak for yourself, John Alden," quote Dizzy, "Since when did you quit the holy ranks of those destined for eternal glory?"

"Okay, Dizzy, but old Ludwig better not get wind of our expedition tonight, or we'll get more than a buggy story in class tomorrow."

The male youth in their prime piled out of the bus and streamed into the reception parlor of Lourdes Hall and immediately started looking for some girls. Sister Constantine, in her flowing brown habit and immaculate white coif, seemed to be in charge and informed the assembled lads that the girls would be down shortly. She added, "As the girls come down the open stairway leading to this room, you boys select anyone for your partner this evening."

"Jeepers, that could be rough on some of the broads," observed Dizzy, "If they don't get picked off right away, they'll wish they were dead. Wassa matter with the old girl anyway?"

Dizzy seemed perfectly right. Sister Constantine, not more than forty but still classified as an "old girl," was not using her head. And she seemed to realize this because, before the girls appeared, she announced, "Remember, boys, there are exactly the same number of girls as boys, so line up and take the girl who arrives at the bottom of the stairs as your turn comes."

Paul considered himself very fortunate. His girl was just the right size, five-foot-two (Paul was five eight), well proportioned, had chestnut-colored hair growing down to her shoulders, and a very attractive face speckled with freckles around the bridge of her nose. Paul looked at her and congratulated himself that he had indeed picked a fair blossom from the rose garden. But she was very shy and spoke so softly Paul could hardly get her name at the introductions. This only made her more attractive to Paul. He raised his eyes to heaven for a second and whispered, "Lord, this one is liable to pull me right out of the seminary. Give me strength to survive this angel's attraction."

Paul bowed and said, "Mademoiselle, may I have the pleasure of your company this evening?" All the boys had been instructed to say that by the social director of St. Mary's, Brother Elzear.

Everyone was ushered downstairs to the college dining room for "tea," which was a light supper. During the tea Paul extracted the following information from the girl: 1. Her name was Eleanor. 2. She was a farm girl from Nebraska. 3. She came from a very strict home, which forbade dating in high school. (I might well be her first date, Paul thought. Ah, she will remember it for the rest of her life as being as close to achieving ecstasy as she ever will—at least, that's what I'm going to tell Dizzy.) 4. She had never attended a dance before and confessed that she did not know how to dance. Eleanor delivered all this information in the softest voice, her eyes cast down.

Not at all thrilled with the knowledge that his little petunia did not dance, Paul determined he would rectify that situation somehow. He, a graduate of the "Chicken Coop," could dance the light fantastic with some grace and would qualify also as a dance teacher. No, he was not going to sit along the sidelines all evening discussing farm life in Nebraska.

The recreation hall in the basement was large, but had a low ceiling. Folding chairs lined its walls where young people sat when not dancing. The music came from a juke box in one corner.

Paul turned to Eleanor and said, "Won't you let me teach you how to dance?"

"W-e-ll . . . but certainly not there on the floor with everybody looking!" Eleanor spoke up with full voice for the first time. Paul thought that maybe this gal had a bit of spunk in her at that.

"No, Eleanor, not here. We'll go out in that dark hallway, and, in ten minutes, I'll have you doing the fox trot. Whaddya say?"

The girl was a bit hesitant, but Paul took her by the hand and led her out through the French doors into the hall situated opposite from where they came in. Eleanor must have been warned by her mother about being in the dark with a boy, but maybe she decided she was a big girl now. Without hesitation she went with Paul. Soon the dance lesson was in progress. "One, two. One, two. You're doing fine, Ellie," Paul purred. He was pleased and a bit stimulated to have the soft body of a girl in his arms.

"Just what's going on here!" A dark figure advanced upon the couple. Sister Constantine was most unhappy to find a couple of supposedly well-instructed young people engaged in what she thought was very sinful handy-panky in the dark on the holy premises of a Catholic institution founded for promoting virtue as well as knowledge.

"This is simply scandalous!" the nun hissed. "We try to arrange a proper social for you people, but no, some have to sneak away into the dark where Satan beckons, to engage in sinful activities. Now get back into the recreational room or I shall have to report you to your deans."

Eleanor was so embarrassed she was at the verge of tears, and Paul put an arm around her shoulder to comfort her once they got out of sight of the wrathful servant of the Lord.

"For crying out loud!" Paul muttered. "That dried up old prune has to see evil everywhere. Don't pay any attention to her, Ellie. We'll dance a while and then go back and finish the lessons."

"Oh, we can't do that," Eleanor protested. "If she catches me again, she'll have me expelled."

"No, she won't," said Paul. "Because she won't catch us next time. See, we're going to dance right in front of that door there while keeping an eye out for the old witch. The second she pops up—whish! back into the rec room we go. Okay?"

Eleanor began to savor the adventure of it all a bit, and she giggled as Paul led her back into the semi-darkness of the hallway. She easily picked up the rhythm of the music filtering out of the recreation room and followed Paul's lead through a fox trot, "Red Sails in the Sunset," and a waltz, "When My Dreamboat Comes Home."

Then it happened again. A dark figure rounded the corner at the end of the hall. In a split second Eleanor and Paul were inside the room. They quietly closed the door and waited with bated breath as the patrolling female slowly walked by, the rosary hanging from her cincture softly slapping against her thigh as she walked.

In the room Paul held Eleanor close and sighed under his breath, "Dear Blessed Mother, this is beginning to test my powers of resistance. I'd better let go of this creature."

"Now, Ellie, I think it's time you showed them how well you can dance."

Eleanor danced in perfect harmony to Paul's lead, all the time looking with adoration into his eyes.

"This girl is falling for me," Paul said to himself. "That's nice, but what's she gonna think when I don't call her for another date? Old

Mangan (Father Bernard Mangan, spiritual director at the college and deputized by the Bishop to keep an eye on the preseminarians) will get wind of my dating and start raising hell, and they'll throw me back to Lake Hebron to pitch bundles into threshing machines again. Oh, cripes! Ellie is such a sweet young thing too."

Paul's unhappy thoughts at this point were interrupted by Dizzy Gillespie who barged in with his girl and said over the music, "Hey there, Paul old boy, you sure can cut the rug. Who's that cute babe you got there?"

"Never mind, ya old sinner," Paul replied. "I can see you won't be with us long in Brother Ludwig's classes the way you were dancing with your chick. Old Prune Face over there is watching you and is about to step in to cool you off. You gotta leave some space between you and your girl or the old witch will be riding in on her broom to give you the word. She caught us out in the hall a while ago and preached up quite a storm."

The tea dance ended at 10:30 p.m., a bit early for Paul and Dizzy, but they had no choice but to go back to the barracks on the hill.

Paul bid Eleanor a gallant adios, and felt terrible for not asking her for another date because by then she was obviously infatuated with him.

"She's stuck on me, I'm afraid," Paul confided to Dizzy on the bus. "I'm quite a charming old bugger, you know."

"You big, inflated, pumpkin head!" retorted Dizzy. "Say, why not have a double date next Friday night with the same girls?"

"Nothing doing, Sir Lancelot. I'm not getting involved with girls at this stage. Say, Laddie, you know what I think? I think you are about to turn in your ticket for Greek and Latin in favor of becoming an old married bookie or something."

And Dizzy did change his course that same week in favor of pre-law.

Back in Greek class, Brother Ludwig raged, "Paul, you Pharisee, not only were you stepping out, but you led astray one of our young men of good will. You dragged him into an occasion of sin last Friday night, and he lost his vocation. Paul, you are a snake in the grass!"

But Paul, unperturbed at the reprimand, knew full well that Dizzy had had no real intention of becoming a priest but was trying to please his mama. Still, he felt the need for pleading his own defense in the presence of his roly-poly judge.

"Brother Ludwig," Paul began, "a man of such high virtue and sanctity as myself would never try to dissuade anyone from a true vocation to the holy priesthood. My august presence at that social sponsored by our sister institution of Catholic learning down the hill was my little contribution toward establishing amicable relations between our colleges and set up high standards of conduct among these good young people on the dance floor. I'm sure you will agree that I am truly an exemplary Catholic gentleman as well as an excellent Greek scholar."

Brother Ludwig grabbed his cane, which he kept under his desk and used to assist him in and out of the classroom, rose and advanced on Paul branishing this weapon as if to bring it crashing down upon the skull of his tormenter, but he gave a hint of a smile on his ruddy countenance as he swung around to resume class.

15

The next dance scheduled for students of both colleges was the Halloween Prom, a more formal affair than the tea trots had been. Paul was sorely tempted to sign up for this affair but began to suffer scruples about running to all these dances when he was supposed to be serious about adjusting to the celibate life. Maggie Pesch back home would be saying an extra rosary each day if she had known her offspring at the preparatory seminary contemplated another dash into an occasion of possibly falling for the charms of a female of the species.

After he completed his sacristy work one evening, Paul dropped on his knees to talk the matter over with the Lord.

"Dear Lord I would like to go to this Halloween dance, but that does not mean that I am deserting all ideas of going to the seminary. Not at all. The only thing I worry about is that alligator Mangan might find out and squeal about me to Bishop Kelly. And I'm sorry about calling him an alligator, Lord."

After Greek class the next day Paul hailed Melvin Helmbrecht's vanishing figure ahead of him in the hall. "Hold up, Melvin," he called.

Melvin Helmbrecht was one of the two surviving levites besides Paul in the class pushing toward the priesthood. The other was Anthony Odenbrett, a plump short-statured young man wearing a perpetually serious countenance who would never think of going to a dance any more than he would think of burning down the Papal Palace. "Now, Paul, if you were more like Anthony," Brother Ludwig said once, "you might possibly make it to the priesthood."

Melvin, on the other hand, was a tall, thin boy with a drawn face who had been carefully sheltered on a farm by a pious mother who kept him away from girls and other temptations of the world in order that he might successfully become a pious priest some day.

"Melvin is a hothouse plant, I'm afraid," said Paul to Dizzy Gillispie one day. "He needs a girl in his arms at least once in order to return to the human race. I'm going to take him along to the Halloween dance."

"Say, Melvin," Paul asked him in the hallway that day after class, "how would you like to go to the Halloween Prom with me next week?"

"Oh gracious, no!" Melvin gasped. "I've never been to a dance in my life! Oh, no, no. It's out of the question."

"Tell you what, Mel, just try it once. That's all, just once. You can go with me, and I'll fix you up with a girl. What d'ya say?"

"Oh, I dunno. . . ."

In the meantime, Paul used his noodle a bit to get his hands on a car for the dance. Taxis cost too much and were not like having one's own car to transport his "Queen of the Ball" to the Castle of the Dreams where the affair was held, the castle of dreams being the Cotter Gym, a mile or so from St. Teresa's College.

What Paul did was to ask Father Julius Kuhn if he could wash and wax his black Plymouth. Father Kuhn was all in favor of his chariot being restored to pristine condition. Paul had had some experience in waxing cars at home on the old Dodge and Ford, and he knew when Julius beheld his shiny Plymouth after his treatment, his ego would expand to the point where he might offer Paul half of his kingdom.

Paul simply asked for the loan of the car for a couple hours that evening, a request readily granted by the Professor of Shakespeare. Clutching the keys of the car in his hot hand, Paul chuckled over the happy outcome of his plot.

In the meantime, Paul had called up Eleanor and she quickly accepted Paul's invitation. He asked her to please line up a girl for Melvin, and Ellie said it would be no problem.

As Paul hung up, his heart was heavy. This would be the last date he would have with Ellie. This also would have to be the last dance he attended while at St. Mary's.

However, getting Melvin to agree to it took every last bit of persuasion Paul could muster up. On the night of the prom, Melvin looked very miserable when he got into the Plymouth as if he were getting aboard a tumbrel heading for the guillotine.

Ellie appeared in a pink chiffon dress without shoulder straps, and she wore a sort of matching scarf to cover her bare shoulders, otherwise, she would not have passed Sister Constantine's inspection. Paul looked at her and said to himself that he was a goner in the presence of this beauty. Still, he would have to tell her it had to be over between them.

Lucille, Melvin's date, was, if anything even more attractive than Ellie, and Paul thought that she would slay Melvin that night for sure. He felt a bit guilty for his part in eliminating another candidate for the altar.

The young people frolicked away the evening under the pumpkin decorations and the leering faces of goblins overhead. At first, Melvin was very shy, but before long his eyes began to sparkle a bit as he beheld the sweetie in his arms and was ushered into a world he had never known before. Of course, Paul had given him a few dancing lessons before the affair.

Just before the last dance, Paul sat Eleanor down on the sidelines and softly spoke into her lovely ear. "Ellie, sweetheart, they're putting the squeeze on me up on the hill. I'm afraid I can't go to any more of these dances, or I'll be disqualified for the seminary. So, with a breaking heart, I must tell you I must withdraw into my hermitage and deprive myself forever of your lovely presence and turn you over to the eager arms of some Sir Galahad who can offer you marriage."

Eleanor's fair countenance fell, and Paul detected a few tears glistening on her lovely eyelashes. As the orchestra began the last dance number, "Goodnight Sweetheart," Paul drew Ellie on the floor where she cried on his shoulder to the sound of the sentimental saxophones of Hal Leonard's orchestra. Paul thought it better this way where she wouldn't be noticed in the semi-darkness as much as if she were on the bench. When the last strains of the sentimental ballad drifted away, Ellie dashed for the ladies' room to powder her red eyes.

While she was in the ladies' room, Paul, in a somber mood for a moment, reflected that it should be a lesson to him to leave the members of the fair sex alone from then on. This resolution, like so many made by weak mortals in this vale of tears, was due to be broken again and again. And he thought he should tell her what a weasel he really was. Then she would be glad to get rid of him.

Paul took Melvin and Lucille back to Lourdes Hall in the shiny Plymouth, and, after they left the car, he had a painful parting ceremony to complete with darling Ellie. He gathered her in his arms and intended to deposit a quick kiss upon her lips when she threw her arms around his neck and pressed her lips to his in a manner Paul only had observed in the movies, an osculation which Father Joachim had denounced in the pulpit and in CCD classes.

Paul now felt new sensations arising within him and remembered a passage from the Gospel, ". . . it is good for us to be here," although it was way out of context. But the bliss Paul enjoyed was shadowed a bit by a vision of a priest giving a mission at home, howling denunciations at those who committed sins of the flesh. He separated himself from his adoring companion, quickly bolted out the door on his side and dashed around to her side. With tears welling up in her eyes again, Ellie quickly dashed from the car and ran to Lourdes Hall without looking back.

Paul, his heart still palpitating, sat for a moment behind the wheel of the Plymouth, contemplating the state of his immortal soul and decided he'd better go to confession the following Saturday.

Melvin, likewise experienced an exciting evening. He fell hopelessly in love. His girl, Lucille, however, was not yet at the stage where she regarded him as the man of her dreams, but he did extract from her a date for the following Friday night.

‡   ‡   ‡

For days after the Halloween Prom, Melvin walked around with a glaze over his eyes and could no longer seem to concentrate on Greek or anything else except Lucille. Brother Ludwig noted the change in Melvin and was concerned.

"Melvin," he asked one day in class. "did you step out last Friday night to that witch's brew they called the Halloween Prom?"

Melvin blushed like a Darwin tulip in May. "Yes, Brother," he said and cast his eyes down.

"I'll bet it was Paul over there who was responsible for roping you into that den of iniquity. Am I not right?"

Melvin nodded sadly.

Brother Ludwig turned his bloodshot eyes in Paul's direction and launched into another impassioned oration about the evil machinations of women and added that when occasions of sin are presented, aided, and abetted by a "snake in the grass" who still regarded himself worthy of the priesthood, it was time that action be taken to prevent another Judas from entering the ranks of the holy priesthood.

Paul decided not to rise up and defend his innocence this time for the wrath of the ruddy-faced mentor indicated that silence was the better part of valor. Brother Ludwig, in that very bad mood, just might use his cane instead of brandishing it.

Soon after that, Melvin, still with that lovesick look in his eyes, informed Paul he was changing his course in midyear to business administration. Since he realized that God was not calling him to the priesthood, he thanked Paul for helping him become properly oriented at last.

The following week his chair was vacant in Brother Ludwig's Greek class. The sight of the vacant chair prompted another outburst of pious rage from Brother Ludwig. He turned his red eyes again upon Paul.

"It is written in the Holy Bible," he rasped, "'that anyone who scandalizes my little ones, it would be better that a millstone be tied to his neck and that he be drowned in the depths of the sea.'"

Paul patiently endured the diatribe because he was thinking of Eleanor and sorrow pervaded his heart. He experienced sorrow also at the thought that he had just danced his last. Paul reflected on his face enough of the grief in his heart that Brother interpreted it as true remorse for his sins and eased up on his oratory that time, lapsing back into the Greek lesson of the day.

When Paul mentioned to Riley later on that day that he had attended his last dance, Riley turned out to be a true prophet when he said, "hell, Paul, don't give me that horse manure about you giving up dancing. Many is the time yet when thou, hypocrite, shalt swing and sway across the floor with a broad in your arms."

16

As fall turned into winter, Paul's homesickness returned and worsened. Occasionally he hiked along rural roads in the valleys surrounding the campus. When he came upon a farmyard containing cows standing by the barn, pigs grunting in the hogyard, and the laying hens scratching about in the stubble for insects, it was those chickens especially that pulled his heart down almost into a depression. After all, he used to take care of the chickens at home. If only he could get back to the home farm just once before Christmas vacation!

Came Wednesday before Thanksgiving, and most of the Chicago students, (the majority of the student body at St. Mary's) boarded the streamlined train *The Hiawatha*, for a long Thanksgiving weekend. Riley left too, and the dorm was deserted, which made Paul feel like a wood duck perched on a sand dune in the Sahara.

Paul thought of Eleanor over at St. Teresa's, who was probably as homesick for the farm as he was. The temptation to call her plagued him, but he knew if he and Ellie got together then, they might both lose their heads and swoon with romance into God knows what.

But on Thanksgiving day Paul could resist no longer. The phone in the Cardinal Room, normally in use day and night, was now abandoned. Paul dialed the number of St. Teresa College. But, before someone answered, he hung up and sighed, "Shucks, what in the hell am I doing? The way I feel now I'd probably ask her to elope with me. Suffer it out for your sins, you confounded clodhopper," he savagely growled to himself.

The long awaited Christmas vacation finally began, and Paul caught a bus on Highway 14, which ran past the college. For the rest of the afternoon and evening he rode it west until it arrived at Windom where his dad awaited him at the bus depot. What bliss to be back on the Belvedere for a couple of weeks!

Paul paid a courtesy call on Father Joachim. The pastor of Sacred Heart of Lake Hebron said some kind words to him and gave him a five-dollar bill. Prince, who always considered Paul an unwelcome intruder at his master's manse, gave him a few menacing growls. Paul pocketed the fiver and began to regard the pastor in a new light, a potential golden goose worthy of his careful attention.

Back at St. Mary's after Christmas vacation Brother Ludwig finally got over the loss of Dizzy Gillespie and Melvin Helmbrecht from the ranks of the pre-seminarians. But occasionally he became steamed up on the subject. One day he opened class with the prayer, "Thy ways, God of all Creation, are indeed incomprehensible. Why should that rascal Paul be kept in the ranks of the pre-seminarians when he, by his wicked ways, leads other lads down the road to perdition in dance halls? But truly, Lord, I seriously doubt if the rascal will ever make it to Thine altar. Amen."

Paul put his Greek book up in front of his face so Brother Ludwig could not detect his giggling.

The Greek classes went on more peacefully after that, and Brother Ludwig no longer recounted his buggy story more than once a month. Paul ceased trying to bait him into doing so because Brother Ludwig no longer paid much attention to Paul's requests.

The only other pre-seminarian in the class was quiet Anthony Odenbrett, a short-statured, serious student who never did show much interest in any extra-curricular activities. Neither did the "geese," three of four Christian Brother scholastics, nicknamed from their custom of slowly walking in single file around the grounds of their novitiate, reciting their divine office.

The semester exams came, and Paul, who, despite his vagaries, did labor mightily in his studies, felt he should make the scholastic honor roll and maybe get his name in the Lake Hebron News, maybe encouraging Father Joachim to come forward with a tenspot next time.

But, alas, Paul failed to make the first semester honor roll, and when he received his report card he soon found out who tripped him up. Paul had earned Bs in every subject except Greek. Brother Ludwig had seen fit to award him a C in Greek.

Paul legged it down to the two-room suite occupied by Brother Ludwig and rapped on the door.

"Come in," rasped Brother Ludwig. Paul addressed the rotund professor of Greek, who was seated at his rolltop desk in the outer room.

"Brother Ludwig," began the curly-haired little Teuton, "How I have slaved in your Greek class these many weeks, applying myself diligently to the subject at hand, have performed brilliantly when called upon to recite in class, have shown a unique talent for translating the writings of the Greek master, Xenophon, and have been a model student certainly worthy of receiving an A on my report card. But to my horror, I noticed you have given me only a C, which I must say seems to be a grave rupture of justice toward such an admirable student as I."

Brother Ludwig reached for his knotty walking stick leaning against the side of his desk, and Paul was not quite certain whether he intended to use it, so, in favor of preserving his fair skin intact, he began backing out of the room. The last view he had was of the great hulk of the professor rising up and brandishing the stick while his face was about as red as Paul had ever seen it.

However, once outside the danger zone, Paul started giggling as he strode down the hall.

Back up in the penthouse, Riley, as usual on his bed, inquired about the outcome of the protest Paul had said he was going to lodge with the intransigent professor.

"Shucks," said Paul, "I got nowhere at all. The old hippo even threatened me with his cane. However, if I'm ever to get on the honor roll, I have to face up to the necessity of smoking the peace pipe with old Ludwig. We both have Austrian blood sloshing in our veins, and if he recognizes that, a reconciliation should be quite feasible. And I suspect the old geezer sort of enjoys my antics, only he doesn't wish to let on."

17

Spring came early during Paul's first year at St. Mary's, and on St. Patrick's Day the weather became very balmy. It seemed that at St. Mary's College the Feast of St. Patrick was observed with great joy and solemnity, but the celebration was something new to Paul. Back in the Sacred Heart parish of Lake Hebron, the people, whose forefathers worshipped Wotan and the Sacred Oak in Germany, manifested no apparent interest in the monk who converted the wild Druids of Ireland. The German Catholics of Lake Hebron had been led by their pastors to give the nod in March to the feast of St. Joseph on March 19 instead of the feast of St. Patrick on the 17th.

Paul remembered being dragged to Mass on March 19th by his father, to honor his distinguished namesake in Heaven. He could not recall, however, a word being said about St. Patrick back in Lake Hebron. As a matter of fact, they didn't even make much of a fuss over St. Boniface, their spiritual hero, who Paul found out later had hacked away at the Sacred Oak with impunity, which impressed the pagan Saxons so much they decided to lend an ear to Boniface talking about his God. Thus the Germans became converted.

Come the eve of the feast of St. Patrick, however, Paul became very much aware that most of the students at St. Mary's College, were either Irish or very sympathetic toward the Irish, and made a lot of noises around March 17th. In fact, the Hibernians and their fellow travelers staged a pow-wow down in the Cardinal Room on the eve of St. Patrick's day to make fitting preparations to celebrate the feast on the morrow.

Riley even got up enough ambition to arise from his bed to attend the Hibernian howler, impressing Paul with the great loyalty St. Patrick must command among his followers to persuade Riley to get out of bed. When Riley later staggered back to the penthouse and his bed, he informed Paul what the Irish had cooked up for the morrow.

"Paul," he said, "descendant of the ancient Goths, you will be called on to honor good St. Patrick tomorrow by appearing in something green."

"What happens if I decide not to wear something green?"

"They'll clean your clock."

"Well," said Paul, "the hell I'll wear green. Why should I? Let those peat burners and potato eaters wear all the green they want, but they've got no right to issue decrees that krauts like me have to wear green. I'm not about to follow the antics of these leprechaun lovers who use the feast of a saint as an excuse to raise Cain every year."

"I'm telling you, Paul, if you want to preserve your carcass in one piece tomorrow, you'd better do as we say."

"Aw, go piss up a tree, Riley," Paul growled and went to bed.

Before falling asleep Paul determined that not only would he refuse to wear green because it was being forced upon him, but would instead appear in the color he heard made the Irish tempers flare—orange.

The next Morning Paul put on an orange tie.

"Oh, boy, Paul," Riley warned. "You're asking for it. You leave this room with that tie on, and you're likely to be hanging from a light fixture within the hour."

Paul grabbed his books and headed for class. A few yards down the hall a knot of green-garnished males spied him, and before he could beseech St. Joseph for some assistance against the descendants of the Druids, Paul felt himself being deposited into the shower room with cold water spraying down upon him.

Paul straggled back to the penthouse and changed into dry clothes. "Those bastards are indeed a mean bunch," he sighed and decided that discretion at the moment was the better part of valor and pinned on the shamrock Riley had left on the dresser for him. However, at the same time Paul began to plot some counter action, but before he got very far, some Slavs in the student body approached him and said," "Hey, Paul, we heard about the shower, and we gotta make a stand. Here's the plan. At noon you come down to the cafeteria and bring your orange tie along. When you get inside the dining room, put it on. Nobody can touch you in the dining room, but when you come out they will be waiting to tear you apart. But we'll be waiting, too, and we'll come to your defense. Could be a big commotion outside the cafeteria this noon. You game to go along?"

"Sure thing, Literski," Paul said.

At noon after he had finished eating, Paul slowly put on his orange tie. As he marched out he saw the Irish lined up on one side of the hallway, and the big Poles, other Slavs, and burly krauts on the other. However, before Paul arrived in their midst, the two phalanxes hurled themselves at each other. Paul then sought another route out of the trouble spot, and escaped without a hand being laid on him.

In the meantime, the Battle of the Orange and Green raged on, and was finally quelled after one of the Brothers turned the fire hose on the troops.

After the battlefield had been cleared, the wearers of the green became aware that the Orangeman wearing that blasted orange fabric had melted into thin air, and they made inquiries about his whereabouts. They learned that he had ducked into a lavatory down the hall.

Paul indeed hid behind the door of the men's room and peeped out through a crack to watch the results of the battle. When he observed that the pressure hose had cooled the ardor of the combatants, and the Irish chieftans were inquiring after his whereabouts, Paul elected to hightail it upstairs and find a new refuge. A son of an O'Brien spotted him bolting up the broad stairs and sounded the alarm. The pursuit was on— hounds barking at the heels of an orange-colored fox.

Paul knew he had only seconds to find another refuge. At the head of the stairs on the next floor was the office of the college nurse, its door open. Paul shot into the nurse's office, slammed the door and clicked on the night lock from the inside.

The college nurse, a short girl about thirty and very curvy, had large breasts, a small cute face, blonde hair upswept and piled on the top of her head upon which her nurse's cap perched. Because of her attractiveness, the boys at the college became sick quite regularly and fondly had their temperatures taken and pulses noted by this dreamy female, whom they called, "Tina, the Titmouse."

Brother Ludwig regarded her with holy indignation. "She is the Helen of Troy in our midst," he raged. "The gallant Greeks in our holy institution will weaken in virtue before this creature wielding her seductive wiles."

If Paul dreamed that he was now situated in the secure protection of the Tower of London as the Irish gathered in force to destroy him, he was wrong. Tina's last name was Callahan, and she emerged from the inner room demanding an explanation from Paul about the commotion outside, and why he had made his abrupt entrance into her chambers without knocking.

"'Tis an emergency, Tina," Paul whispered between his heavy inhaling and exhaling. "Mine enemies are about to encompass me."

"What's going on" Tina piped in a high-pitched voice. Then she noticed the orange tie gracing the neck of this bloody heretic.

"Oh, now I see!" she exclaimed, "You traitor to the old sod, you! Don't come to my office expecting protection!"

She moved to the door to release the lock and allow the mob to capture their quarry. Paul grasped her wrists to forestall her action, and a struggle began during which Paul found his arms encircling her soft body, her large breasts pressing against him.

"Holy Mother of God," he whispered as waves of concupiscence engulfed him. "I'm no match for this situation. Lord, come to my assistance. Make haste to help me." The latter prayer he had heard the nuns chant as they recited their Holy Office before Mass back in Lake Hebron.

Meanwhile, the IRA increased in troop strength outside the door, and their shouts for the prisoner to be delivered to them increased in volume. This demonstration attracted some members of the Brother of the Christian Schools founded by St. John the Baptist De La Salle to come to the scene of what sounded like a brewing insurrection. Brother Matthew, a tall, big-boned man with the rugged countenance of Attila at the gates of Rome, issued orders for the mob to disperse and, finding his efforts in vain, unrolled a portion of the fire hose, turned the valve, and initiated another dousing of Hibernia.

Once securing his command, Brother Matthew crisply ordered the cooled-down followers of St. Patrick to proceed to their classes, demanding whoever was inside that door to open up!

By this time Paul's lips had found Tina's, and she hung limply in his arms. The nuns in Sacred Heart School had always pictured such a scene that, when giving into a temptation one's weeping Guardian Angel retreated as the devil moved in. Paul happily began waving goodbye to his Guardian Angel when Brother Matthew thundered his demand that the castle door be opened. This rescued Paul from his ever-steepening spiral into fleshly delights. He released his hold on Tina, who stumbled back into her inner room to straighten her disheveled white uniform and put her cap back upon her somewhat disarrayed blonde hair.

"Just what is going on in there?" blazed the irate Brother Matthew. His black soutane glittered with beads of water—powder burns, so to speak, from the water cannon he had manned moments before.

"Brother, I was only protecting the integrity of my body against the assaults of mine enemies," declared Paul.

"I'm not so sure that your so called bodily integrity should have been protected. Anyone who wears an orange rag on St. Patrick's Day should be thrown to the wolves. Now get that damned thing off your neck!" Brother Matthew yelled.

The good Brother stomped his feet a couple of times and pointed a burly finger at his cornered Austrian fox, "Now you listen to me! You're going to pay for the extra labor involved in mopping up all this water, ya understand! Which means you'll dust mop this entire corridor of St. Mary's Hall every day in addition to your job in Kelly Hall until you have worked off the expense, and I don't want to have to repeat it again. Get that damned tie off your neck!"

Sans the orange tie, Paul trudged over to the library and remained there in obscurity the rest of the day in order to assure that his fair skin and well-knit bones remained intact. "I think old Matthew was a little heavy with his sentencing," he thought. "It's a heavy burden on my weak shoulders, but I will offer it up in behalf of all the persecuted souls in Holy Mother Church."

Paul looked out of the library window at the green grass and robins skipping around, seeking their suppers, and gave glory to God for the early spring that year which farmers always welcomed. And while he was in the prayer mood he beseeched the Almighty to be merciful to him for disturbing the peace among the Irish that day, which, among other things, had resulted in his suffering grave temptations of the flesh.

Shortly afterwards, having lost his prayer mood, he resolved to darken the doorstep of the nurse's office a bit more in the future. He would have to ask some of the more frequent visitors to Tina's domain how they artificially boosted their temperatures to gain Tina's tender solicitude. Of course, she might still be angry at him and tell him to get lost if he showed up in her office again. But he decided to take the risk.

18

Twighty O'Toole, whose baptismal name was Theodore, stood six feet tall and was a neat dresser. He had a wide mouth and thin lips usually parted in a smile, revealing a perfect set of teeth except for a gold filling on the edge of one incisor. With straight, black hair and skin slightly olive-tinted "because of an errant gene which slipped in from somewhere," Twighty was one of the many Chicago students at St. Mary's.

On a lovely Saturday morning in May Twighty suggested to Paul that they hitchhike to Rochester, some forty miles west. After a short stroll, they reached U.S. 14, which passed through the north edge of the campus.

The first vehicle to come along, a battered pickup truck, labored up the hill toward them. When Twighty raised his thumb and flashed his attractive smile, the vehicle with its brakes squeaking, came to a stop.

"I'm going as far as Stockton," said the driver, a bewhiskered man wearing a battered felt hat.

"My good man," said Twighty, "we would be honored to ride with you as far as Stockton." The two collegians crowded into the seat beside him. An Airdale pup didn't like the idea of being crowded by two strangers and whimpered its disapproval.

"Shet ap, Luke," the driver commanded his dog. "You don't own this truck." He scooped up the pup into his lap under the steering wheel.

"My good man," said Twighty, "what do you do for a living?"

"I raise worms," replied the driver, "Just delivered a batch to a bait store in Winona. Ya know, some dang fools can't even dig their own worms when they wanna go fishing." He directed a stream of tobacco juice out the window, and it landed in one of the empty worm boxes in the pickup's cargo area.

The delapidated truck labored up the long Stockton hill as the highway curved upward through the wooded area with the valley visible below on one side. Very scenic, thought Paul. "I love hills and woods," he observed.

"Hell, I don't," said the driver. "Too hard for my truck to get up them hills." By now the engine, overheating from a defective cooling system, belched steam through a crack between the radiator and the hood. However, the vehicle had reached the top of the ridge and began coasting down toward Stockton. Paul noted the rapidly increasing speed of the pickup, and the tires squealed as they hurtled around curves. He began to suspect the vehicle had no brakes.

"I ought to get those dang brakes fixed once't," remarked the driver, who was now hanging tightly onto the steering wheel. "We just went around the last curve. She's straight in to Stockton now, but we ain't gonna be able to stop till we get way beyond town 'cause there ain't no brakes. Gotta get those dang brakes fixed once't."

Although the speedometer also did not function, Paul estimated the pickup's speed at sixty as they streaked through the hamlet.

"A couple of miles further, and we should be able to stop and turn around," said the driver, who expressed relief that the crisis had passed by spitting some tabacco juice out of the window where a lesser wind velocity caused the brown stream to miss the worm boxes.

"You fellers wanna go back to town or get off when we stop?"

"We'll get off when we stop," said Twighty. "You must have a rough go of it in the winter coming down that hill if the road is a little icy."

"Hell, we don't deliver worms in the winter," replied the driver. "Where was you raised anyway, young feller?"

Paul giggled and poked Twighty lightly in the ribs.

"Thanks for the ride," Paul said as the truck came to a stop by the side of the road. "May your worms multiply and make you rich."

"T'aint likely," grumbled the driver. "Worms ain't bringing much of a price these days. So long."

After the pickup rattled off, Paul exclaimed, "Jeepers, Twighty! Seems to me if a fella is going to hitchhike, he'd better stay in the state of grace."

"It ain't usually that bad, Paul. You don't run into crazy palookas like him very often. Man, I didn't know if we were going to make it down that hill in one piece. Well, let's get the old thumb up and pick up something better."

Their luck was amazing. The next vehicle to come along stopped. The black Cadillac convertible had two girls in the front seat, an attractive blonde and a beauty with light brown hair. Paul and Twighty eagerly leaped into the back seat.

"Where are you boys going?" the blonde driver asked.

"Rochester," said Twighty. "Are you pearls of great price going there too?"

"Yes, we are. My daddy's in the hospital there, and we're going to visit him. By the way, my name is Sue, and this is Sandy. What's yours?"

"My name is Abelard," Twighty said, remembering it from his history of philosophy course," and this handsome lad beside me is Dun Scotus. We go to college back there in the hills, and we're both learning to be bums."

"Oh, you're funny!" giggled Sandy, the one with the light brown hair. Your friend Don Scotus is cute. Why don't we trade seats so I can sit by him? What's your real name, Don?"

Before Paul could think of another fictitious name Sandy rolled over into the back seat so quickly she was cuddling up to him in a couple of seconds. Paul was relieved she wore slacks executing the maneuver.

Sandy helped Twighty flop into the front seat where he slid close to Sue and whispered into her ear that she was as beautiful as Helen of Troy.

Sandy, cuddling up to Paul, began to excite him erotically, and he wanted to fold her into a tight embrace. "But a future priest must steer away from the pleasures of the flesh," he thought. "At least that's what Brother Ludwig always says. Why do I always remember what he says, the old woman hater. Nevertheless, the devil is laying siege to me at this moment, I can see that."

To get his mind off the temptations assailing him, he decided on a bit of conversation.

"My name is not Dun Scotus, as the alias Abelard there says," he declared, turning to Sandy and holding her a little closer. "It's Oglethorpe von Suppe. My dad is the only gangster in Chicago of Prussian descent. He shoots girls who fall in love with me—all except Emma von Guggenheim whom he wants me to marry."

Sandy squealed with laughter. "Sue," she called out, "aren't these two just the berries?"

She wore pink slacks and a white sweater, the latter accentuating her curves. Her wavy hair fell loosely to her shoulders, framing a very attractive face.

"This gal is about as great a temptation as I've ran across," Paul thought, and he decided that any more romantic conversation would only make the situation there in the back seat worse. He felt he was on the edge of a cliff. He would have to start a conversation about something scientific or religious. And that would also distract Twighty from his amorous pursuits in the front seat.

"How come you girls took the chance of picking us up this morning?" Paul spoke loudly enough to bust in on Twighty's monologue going into the ear of one Susan B. Anthony, or whatever her name was.

"We knew you were college boys, you know, from that college back there," sweetly answered the vision by Paul's side. "We knew it was a Catholic college, and that we could trust you."

"But it's still a bad idea for girls to pick up men on the highway. You were still taking a big chance," Paul preached.

"Aw, come here you cute one," whispered Sandy and drew him to her. Paul went falling into space and, in a very unenthusiastic manner, implored Mary, the Mother of Jesus to rescue him from a moral catastrophe.

"S-c-r-e-e-c-h!" The tires of the Cadillac protested the sudden application of brakes. The large convertible came to a halt at the stop sign and rocked on its springs. Paul and Sandy were thrown against the back-rest of the front seat and fell on the floor. Paul pulled himself back up onto the seat and assisted Sandy. Up in the front seat, Sue giggled, "Boy we almost missed that stop sign. Twighty, you got to stop pitching the woo so much when I'm driving."

Paul turned to Sandy and said, "Sandy, thou art a seductive creature, to be sure, and you most certainly would have borne me away to a fleshly paradise and consequently might have been executed by the Mafia were it not for the sudden stop of this vehicle."

Sue burst into laughter and said, "Boy, talk about a comedian. Scotus, you ought to be on the stage."

"Hey, stop, Sue. We got off here by the nurses' residence," called out Twighty. "Gotta see my sister there."

He gallantly kissed Sue's hand and, once out of the car, bowed from the waist to her. "Many sentiments of gratitude to you for this pleasant ride in your chariot of the gods, dear one."

Paul struggled out of the back seat, bowed to Sandy with his hand over his heart. "Fair daughter of Eve, you have conquered me and left me in the pit of desolation. I bid thee, adieu."

The Cadillac slowly drove off, and Paul noticed that Sandy maintained a serious countenance all through the parting banter.

"What's the matter with her all of a sudden, I wonder," Paul mused.

"She just fell for you, that's all." Twighty said. "You don't know much about wimmin, I can see that."

"Twighty, who do you think those creatures were, anyway?" Paul asked. "They certainly weren't ordinary girls."

"They're both from the state college in town," Twighty said. "I saw them cruising in that Caddie downtown once. I'd say they are a little wild and might get into trouble some day. At any rate, I wouldn't be surprised if they showed up on our campus one of these days. You sank an arrow into Sandy's heart, you Romeo."

"Well, what are we standing here for?" asked Paul. "You don't have a sister here, do you?"

"Hell no. Let's get out of here."

"On the other hand, let's not," said Paul. "Remember there is a ratio of five girls to one boy in this town with all these nurses, waitresses, and clinic secretaries. We'll stand outside and give a wolf call and watch all the heads pop out of the windows of this building. Then we'll give them a big line and make this a day they will treasure in their memories."

19

Meanwhile, Riley and Brother Xavier, the dean of men, whose empire included the Penthouse, had not developed a good relationship. Riley couldn't keep his mouth shut in the presence of the dean, saying unflattering things to the Brother that caused him to smolder inside.

The crux of the conflict seemed to be Brother Xavier's habit of conducting a bed count almost every night "like we were inmates in the Joliet penitentiary," as Mel Beltrami put it. Riley put it in much more graphic language.

Paul had tried to stay out of the conflict but was drawn into the fray a week before summer vacation began. Riley, because of his ability to "hemorrhage from the mouth," as Paul put it, had been chosen the toastmaster for the annual Freshmen-Sophomore Banquet, held one evening during exams. Riley selected Paul to represent the freshmen and also give a speech at the banquet.

"Good grief!" said Paul, "Whaddya want me for? I can't give a speech a dog would listen to."

But Riley remained adamant. When the banquet came up, Paul had no idea what to talk about. When called upon, he stood up and, at the very last second, decided to talk on women's hats.

He looked as solemn as he could and, maintaining a deadpan expression, launched into his subject. His sober appearance and serious delivery and not the content of the speech struck the funny bones of his peers in the audience.

"Nobody knows why women buy hats," he began. "They don't buy them to keep their heads warm, of course, because they usually have as much hair to provide insulation as polar bears. . . ."

The audience roared with laughter throughout the entire speech. The banquet turned out to be a great success, and Riley, who masterminded it, was exuberant. "Paul, let's go out and have a beer to celebrate," he suggested.

As they checked out, Brother Xavier reminded them that it was not Friday night, and, therefore, they would have to be in by 10:30 p.m. "It's 9:30 already," he said. "You haven't much time. And Riley, you fat walrus, I'll be checking that you are back on time."

"Brother, go and drill a hole in your front tooth," said Riley's, un-diplomatic.

"Riley, you really asked for it this time," Paul commented as they left.

They took a bus downtown to the "Hurryback" and ordered a pitcher of beer. Soon they engrossed in an argument.

"Roosevelt spends money like it grows on pine trees in our national forests," said Paul, echoing his dad, who listened to Father Charles E. Coughlin every Sunday. "Still FDR can't get the country out of the Depression, and the bastard is starting us out on the dangerous road to socialism."

"He has compassion on the poor," retorted the Democrat Riley. "It's time somebody stopped the Hoover starvation."

"Compassion, huh? That's the line used by every vote-buying Democrat these days, and it sounds real good to somebody who doesn't have a job. What the Democrats are doing is teaching the people that they can vote themselves largesse from the public treasury. And once that virus sets in, there's no stopping the gimme-something-for-nothing disease until the country is broke."

The two of them argued and argued as was their custom until the beer ran out. The proprietor came over and said he was closing up, and the two collegians looked at their watches. It was one a.m.

"We were supposed to be in by 9:30, thou demagogue," said Paul. "How will you plead before the judgment seat of one Brother X, pray tell?"

"I'll let you do the talking, your reverence, I'd only dig myself deeper into the quicksand," replied Riley.

They commenced the early morning journey of three miles on foot since the buses had stopped running. An evening spring shower had freshened the atmosphere, and the warm late spring air carried the perfume of lilac blossoms.

"Riley," said Paul, "this is indeed a lovely night, which should make you give praise and glory to your Creator, but I'll bet all you're thinking about at this moment is wrapping your licentious arms around a broad."

And that precipitated another argument that lasted until they were within a mile of the college. At this point Mr. Larson, assistant professor of biology, returning home from a lecture in the Twin Cities stopped and offered them a ride.

It was 2:00 a.m. when Paul and Riley reached their beds in the Penthouse. Both found notes on their beds: "Report to me at breakfast in the morning. Brother X."

"Sure enough, the bugger made his usual bed check," mumbled Riley, "I suppose he'll lower the boom on us tomorrow."

Both had quite a surprise awaiting them when they reported at the faculty breakfast table the next morning. Riley received the bad news first since Paul had his sacristy chores to do before breakfast.

Brother Xavier, his straight brown hair impeccably combed, and his handsome face smoothly shaven, spooned corn flakes into his small mouth when Riley approached the faculty table. Brother said to Riley, "Pack up and be out of here by nine o'clock this morning."

Robert D. Riley's distaste for Brother Xavier was greater than any regrets he had about being expelled. His face flushed in anger, he stated with some emphasis: "Hell, Brother, I'll be out of here by eight!" And he strode out of the cafeteria.

Meanwhile, Paul, after finishing up in the sacristy headed for the cafeteria, thinking to himself, "I'll bet the cocker spaniel is going to bark a bit loudly because we got in late last night."

He marched up to the faculty table and stood at attention without speaking. Brother Xavier stuffed a portion of sausage into his mouth, chewed on it, and finally looked up at Paul standing in front of him. In a matter-of-fact tone he said to Paul, "Pack up your belongings and be out of here by nine o'clock."

"Huh?" croaked Paul.

"You heard me. Be out of this place by nine o'clock. You and Riley are expelled."

Paul was troubled, deeply troubled at the news. Although he possessed a happy-go-lucky nature, being expelled from college seemed a bit more serious than getting stuck in a snowbank with his dad's Ford.

"Expelled?" he mumbled to himself while bolting down breakfast. "Hell! the weasel can't do that! I'll appeal this decision, that's for sure."

Paul dashed up to the Penthouse. Riley had his bags packed, ready to move out.

"Hey, Riley, what's with that weasel casting us overboard? You were expelled too, I'm thinking."

"Yeah, and I told him I would be out of here by eight, and by the snuffbox of St. Columbanus, I'll make it."

"Now, Riley, keep your pants on. He can't throw us out just because we were late coming in this morning."

"Paul, I don't give a damn about what grounds he has. I'm getting out of here right now. Yep, I'm shaking the dust of this place off my sandals, and I'll not be back until the birds quit shitting on the statue of General Grant. And I hope Brother Elzear, the debate coach, hangs Xavier up on a meat hook."

Paul extended his hand to Riley and said, "Goodbye, you fat walrus. Remember my sermons warning you to keep out of mortal sin. With your flabby carcass and your habit of coddling it, the state of your soul will always be in a precarious condition, but with my pull in the presence of the Most High, I'll rescue you from the fires of Hades. Adios, Demosthenes."

"I'm going to miss you, you handsome little bastard," Riley said and grasped Paul's hand, then swept up a valise and a beige topcoat, and left.

Paul parked himself on his bed to think about the distressing turn of events. "I shall have to take steps to get this unjust expulsion reversed, but first I'll hightail it down and finish my last two exams."

His exams done, Paul swung into action to assure he would be welcomed aboard the good ship Lollipop come September.

"Now, let's see. Maybe I'd better try old Ludwig first. We've been smoking the peace pipe lately, and I suspect secretly he likes me even though he swings his cane at me now and then."

Minutes later, Paul tapped on the portal of Brother Ludwig' apartment.

"Come in."

Paul walked in to find the expansive body of the professor perched on his chair in front of his rolltop desk, correcting exam papers.

"Brother Ludwig," Paul began, "I bring you tidings of great sorrow. Brother Xavier expelled me from college this morning."

Brother Ludwig quickly raised his head and swung around on his swivel chair.

"Ach, du Lieber!" he hissed lapsing into a German accent. "I knew it would happen sooner or later. And I varned you! Und now you haff tipped over the buggy anyvay. Ach, du Lieber, vat did you do?"

"Riley and I went out for a beer last night and got back pretty late because we had to hoof it all the way back."

"Did you get drunk?"

"Nein, mein Fuehrer."

"Ach, you don't get kicked out for yust being late. You must be hiding someting."

"Nein, Herr Professor. Riley and the dean have been feuding all year, and I got caught in the crossfire."

"You haff some vitness to testify dat you vere not drunk, ya?"

"Yes, Brother. Professor Larson picked us up and gave us a ride the rest of the way to the campus, and he knows we weren't loaded."

"Okay, I go to see der President. Come back dis afternoon. But if you vass drunk, I can't help you."

By three o'clock that afternoon the matter quietly had been settled, and Paul whistled as he packed his things for the hitchhiking trip back to the "estate of his honorable ancestors," as he put it, for a relaxing summer during which he would dodge as much work in the heat of the day as he could.

And the summer was quite pleasant for the exalted collegian. So few of the lads from Lake Hebron queued to college that Paul felt elevated to patrician rank in the community.

When Paul was not mowing lawns, trimming trees and shrubs, weeding flowers—work he liked to do—he sat at the base of a maple reading Thomas Hardy novels.

But Maggie, who knew her son better than anyone, suspected Paul was putting one over on his family. "Paul," she said one day, "how can you expect to sit around here and live like a king? You know, you're costing us a lot of money to send you to college and, therefore, you should be lending a hand instead of sitting around reading books."

"Ma," Paul said, "I do realize that there's work but first things have to come first. During college years, one has to do a lot of homework in the summer preparing for the fall courses, and so I beg to be excused from the ordinary things of life while I prepare for the priesthood."

"Paul, you're going to have to repeat that speech to Pa," Maggie replied. "He's getting fed up with you laying around all summer."

The speech didn't work with Pa. He told Paul he had to help out with farm work the rest of the summer, that's all there was to it, and Paul decided he'd better pitch in and do some work anyway.

One afternoon in early June, Robert D. Riley walked into the Pesch farm after hitchhiking over from his home town of Beaver Swamp.

"Greetings, ex-collegian," he sang out to Paul, who sat under a tree on the lawn. "How does it feel to have been ejected from the college world?"

"Welcome to the humble estate of my honorable ancestors, Riley." Paul extended his hand and advanced to his guest. "But I'm a bit puzzled by your mode of greeting for I am no longer a member of the low caste of expellees. Verily, I want you to know I have been reinstated among the righteous."

"The hell you say!" shouted Riley. "Brother Elzear made a special trip out to Beaver Swamp to invite me back this fall, but you're not one of his star debaters nor are you a stellar student like me, so why should they want a mangy kraut like you infesting the campus again? By the way, Paul, did your folks find out you got canned?"

"Not so loud! No, they didn't, and what they don't know won't hurt them. Ma would throw a fit and get another upset stomach and have to take some more bicarbonate of soda. She must have taken a half ton already over the years. You didn't tell me—are you going back to St. Mary's this fall?"

"Nope, not for all the moonshine in Tennessee. Brother X really cooked the goose that time. I'm going to St. Thomas."

And Riley faded out of Paul Pesch's life except for occasional visits twenty and thirty years later when Paul stopped in Arizona to visit him and preach to him some more about the dangers of wealth, which Riley was rapidly accumulating.

20

B ack at St. Mary's in the fall, Paul had the same jobs he had had the year before, except he had worked off the water damage incurred when the Sons of Erin went after him the previous March 17, and no longer had to mop the extra hall of the St. Mary's buildings.

Each evening Paul laid out the vestments for the priests who would be celebrating Mass the next day and got other things ready. Then afterwards he knelt in the quiet deserted chapel for a few minutes to have a chat with the Lord concerning his vocation to the priesthood or lack of same.

He told the Lord his dad had fetched up a hefty sum of scarce cash to keep him there at college, and Father Joachim likewise had invested a hundred dollars in him that term. However, the old pastor could afford it. Still Paul, who rarely felt guilty about anything, experienced some such pangs for being probably a poor investment since he was not certain whether he even had a vocation, and secondly, whether he successfully would make it through the seminary even if the vocation was genuine. His merry adventures with the few pretty maidens who had crossed his path did not bode well for a lifelong commitment to celibacy, and he felt certain more encounters with members of the fair sex would come. In his prayer, he petitioned first of all to find out whether he had a God-given vocation. Once that issue was settled, Paul told the Lord he would chart a course for the holy priesthood, but offering nobody any assurance he would persevere. "Therefore, Lord, increase your kilowatts in transmitting this message since I have a poor receiver, that is, a thick skull."

A few weeks later came the annual retreat for students, and Paul decided to keep quiet for a change so the Lord could get a word in edgewise. One evening after the conference, which had nothing to do with vocations, Paul walked out of the chapel with the conviction that the Lord was calling him.

It seemed to be a quiet whisper in his ear, but as the days went on he felt a firm conviction that he did indeed have a vocation to become a priest, and it didn't go away.

For Paul it seemed to settle the question, and he knew he would begin a long struggle to remain in St. Mary's without getting bounced out again. But an even more serious problem involved remaining in the good graces of the authorities of the seminary, where discipline was akin to that of West Point.

Paul, who had developed a great faith in the power of Mary's intercession with her Son, started to call upon her regularly for help. After all, she had saved the family when they were faced with being bounced off the farm unless a certain piece of property sold pronto.

"Well, dear spiritual Mother," Paul prayed, "you are in charge of me for the next six years to keep me from getting the boot, or I just won't get ordained. By the holy prophets of Gilead and Jerusalem, you got quite a job here, dear Mother of Jesus."

Paul resumed his career at St. Mary's without worrying about anything anymore, which was his usual way.

The next afternoon after class, Paul ran into Brother Ludwig taking a walk around the campus on that mild autumn day.

"Brother Ludwig," Paul murmured, "how fortunate for you that we meet on this gorgeous day. How fortunate, too, that your eyes, misting with age, should once more be able to look upon the countenance of the finest young man ever to cross your path. Give thanks to the Lord for this great favor."

Brother Ludwig blubbered with frustration and raised his cane presumably to bring it crashing down on Paul's skull, but Paul, quite agile, quickly stepped out of range and waved his fingers at the good Brother and peeped, "Toodle doo!"

"Judas Priest!" Brother Ludwig spat, "if by some miracle that scalawag ever gets ordained, I most certainly will never go to confession to him."

Brother Ludwig expressed the same sentiments to Paul later on when the young man exasperated him in class. Paul found himself taking the second year of Greek from the old gent, but whether Paul shortened the old man's life or secretly cheered the cockles of his heart will never be known.

The second year at St. Mary's went by swiftly, and as Easter vacation approached, Twighty O'Toole, seated across the table from Paul in the college refectory gulped his peach dessert and said, "Hey, Paul, whaddya say we spend the Easter vacation touring the State of Minnesota?"

"Ya mean on the thumb?"

"Yeah. Be a lot of fun, huh?"

"You know it's colder than a pickeral's tail up there in the north even at this time of the year," Paul commented. "But I s'pose it might be worth a gander. Lessee, we get out of here at noon on Good Friday. We can take off then."

Paul had a few misgivings about bumming around on the day Christ died for "you ungrateful good-for-nothings," as Brother Ludwig put it.

On a chilly Friday afternoon they stood beside Highway 61 awaiting a ride. An old Essex came along, and Twighty flashed his irresistible smile, revealing pearly white teeth that always seemed to stop motorists, though it could hardly have had much of an effect on the driver of the delapidated Essex, an old man with a thin face. He wore a crumpled gray felt hat which covered a generous crop of white hair. Still, he stopped to pick them up.

"Where are you young whippersnappers going on this holy day?" he inquired.

Twighty, always ready with an answer, said, "We're going to my grandmother's in St. Paul for Good Friday Evening Watch services tonight."

"Damn liars," grunted the farmer. "You loafers are from St. Mary's College. Can tell it from the 'M' on your sweaters." (Both Twighty and Paul had received letters for playing in the band.) "As loafers from that college, you're probably Catholics, and Catholics have the Stations of the Cross on Good Friday evening and not Watch Services like you was talking about. If the truth be known, you bums ain't going to no church at all tonight."

"You're perfectly right, my good man," replied Twighty who could adapt to a new situation faster than a camouflaging lizard. "It's the good God-fearing citizens of the Republic like you who go to church on Good Friday and keep the nation from incurring divine punishment for its sins." Twighty had switched to his flattery mode.

"Well, I can say this much for you," the farmer replied visibly gratified, "you'd make a good politician. FDR could use you in Washington to sell the American people some more of his horse manure that's putting the country deeper into debt. But getting back to you loafers, where in the Sam Hill are you going?"

"My good man, let me introduce myself first," Twighty offered his hand, "I'm Dwight J. O'Toole from Chicago, and in the back seat is Paul J. Pesch. My dad is a lawyer, and Paul comes from the farm. We're touring the state of Minnesota during our Easter vacation."

"I see," grunted the farmer. "My name is Paul Devers, and I'm going as far as Wabasha. That feller in the back seat might amount to something if he comes from the farm. But you city slickers from Chicago are more likely to become gangsters, especially if your old man's a lawyer. I got no time for lawyers except for Abraham Lincoln."

The "loafers" got off at Wabasha and raised the thumb again.

By dusk the two knights of the road arrived at Pine Bend, and they noticed a small hotel downtown. It advertized cheap rates. But Paul said, "I, who am suffering in the dregs of poverty at the moment, can afford only free housing at this juncture, but in view of the fact that we're the two most distinguished gentlemen ever to grace these city gates with our presence in five decades—I, being the member of the House of Hapsburg no less—the city council should be presenting us with a key of the city right now, including the key of a nice hotel too."

"Dream your little dreams, Sir Pesch," said Twighty, "but yonder little hotel beckons to be conquered by us Knights of the Road before we freeze to death."

The cloudy day had turned bitterly cold at eventide. Paul and Twighty stumbled into the tiny lobby of the hotel and hovered over the small coal heater there. They blew into their cold hands, stretched their palms over the stove, and stamped their feet.

"Stay at it, Twighty," Paul said, "we gotta impress the old girl who runs the place that we've been exposed to the rigors of the weather for a long time and are in grave need of succor. When she appears, give her your line, and maybe she'll keep us free for the night."

At that point the landlady appeared, and a new interest lighted up the eyes of the collegians. She turned out to be a very attractive woman of short stature and was, at the most, thirty-five years of age. She wore a dark gray dress covered with a lighter gray apron with a full bib. Her dark hair hung down halfway to her shoulders, and her face still showed evidence of youthful beauty which muust have caused a stir among the swains at that time. Paul could see that Twighty would have little difficulty coming up with poetry to match the occasion.

"My good lady, your inn is truly a godsend to us cold and tired travelers," began Twighty, bowing low. "You are indeed a most pleasant sight for our weary eyes. Helen of Troy, whose beauteous face was reputed to have launched a thousand ships, could not have surpassed thee, thou gracious Queen of the North. May we be so bold as to warm ourselves by your cheery fire?"

"Aren't you the gallant one now?" said the woman. She spoke in an Irish brogue. "Come into my living room where you can be seated. Take off your coats. Perhaps you would like a cup of tea?"

"Your kindness surpasses that of the saints of the Emerald Isle from which thou has come apparently," replied Twighty. "Permit me to introduce ourselves. I am Dwight J. O'Toole and am too descended from the old sod. From Chicago I am. At present, I'm absorbing the wisdom of the ages at St. Mary's College down in Winona and pursuing a degree which will allow me to administer justice before the bench. My worthy companion here is Paul Joseph Pesch, a devout Catholic from the same institution of learning. He hopes, I might add, to be the mouthpiece of the Lord some day as he faithfully ministers to a flock entrusted to him by his bishop."

"Oh, you're college boys. Isn't that nice? Paul, your companion who wants to be a priest, is very welcome."

Paul blushed and gazed down at the rough oak floor of the ancient building. She introduced herself as Sheila and promptly excused herself to get the tea.

"You sure got a good start in getting us free room and board," whispered Paul. "Keep it up."

"And she thinks you're cute," whispered back Twighty, "and that'll help too. Better start buttering her yourself, Paul. I suspect you're in the driver's seat in this carriage."

In a pinch Paul could come up with some poetry. He occasionally gave Brother Ludwig some rather outrageous examples of it, but he wasn't very comfortable dishing out sweet talk to females yet, with the exception of Eleanor on one or two occasions. However, in view of his distressing lack of money at the moment, he gathered his wits about him to initiate a campaign with Sheila, who returned with the tea.

"Behold the goddess of the pine country," Paul began. "This little city up here among the forests shelters a beautiful queen at whose castle the forest wolves must gather and howl."

Twighty gave him a dark look of disapproval at his imagery so Paul decided not to pursue the wolf angle any farther.

"Sheila," he said, "when you came into this room bearing refreshments for us pilgrims, I was reminded of Queen Guinevere appearing in the banquet hall before King Arthur and the Knights of the Round Table. The Knights gasped in astonishment at her beauty and stately bearing. The heart of Sir Lancelot in particular was wounded with love at the sight of her much as the hearts of Sir Dwight and myself just now. . . ."

Paul continued on the theme of Camelot, although he wasn't sure of all the names of the characters, but he felt she would not know the difference. As she sat with them sipping tea she blushed at the gallant words tumbling from Paul's lips.

The campaign paid off. Sheila invited her two guests to stay for supper and occupy one of the empty guest rooms upstairs, and she seemed to be quite pleased that the two knights of the road accepted her invitation.

After supper and some more words of flattery and endearment directed at Sheila, the two tired travelers begged to be excused and went to their unheated room upstairs. They were very comfortable under the warm down quilts. Twighty murmured, "You did okay, Paul, old boy. Couldn't have done better myself. Appears to me you have a way of appealing to the maternal instincts of women. It's about the only way I can figure it out. . . ." And he sank into slumber.

The next morning Sheila prepared a hearty breakfast of pancakes and sausage during which the two lads dished out some more sweet talk. Sheila tried to persuade them to stay awhile longer, but they said they had to leave, promising to return again, "when the maples were flaming with color." They hugged her and kissed her on the cheek, and a tear or two appeared on her pretty eyelashes.

A clear day, the sun rapidly warmed the chill morning air. As Twighty raised his thumb, Paul asked, "Say T, old boy, where was Sheila's husband, do you suppose?"

"'Tis a good question, pal. All I can say is I'm glad he wasn't around.

If he had heard you pitching the line to her like you did, you'd probably be giving up the ghost right now from a wound inflicted by a deer rifle."

The motorists were generous that spring morning, and the vaga-bonds arrived at the outskirts of Duluth by mid-afternoon. They decided to continue on to the Iron Range and skip Duluth. However, from their vantage point on the heights overlooking the city they both gazed with some awe on the mighty Lake Superior, which stretched eastward to the horizon like the Atlantic Ocean.

Along Highway 53 going north, the pair waited an unusually long time before a car stopped. The air became very chilly after the sun set. Finally a car stopped. A young couple sat in the front seat. They said they were heading for Virginia, a very acceptable destination for Twighty and Paul. During the ride the couple up front ignored their guests in the back seat, preferring to do a little necking and nuzzling.

"They aren't married," observed Paul. Twighty solemnly nodded assent.

The road cut through second growth forest, and soon darkness came. Suddenly the couple stopped and decided to have a beer at a roadside tavern. "We'll be back in a second," they said.

But it soon became apparent that this Lothario and his lady love were having more than one beer. The hitchhikers took a stroll up and down the road, and finally Paul said, "Leave us enter this den of iniquity into which our hosts have gone and observe what transpires therein."

"It looks like just another one of thousands of these beer joints clut-tering the highways and byways of America, eroding the beauty of moth-er nature," said Paul, more sensitive to natural beauty than Twighty, who was raised amidst the miles of ugliness of Chicago.

Because it was Saturday night, the tavern was crowded and smoke-filled. To the left a bar stretched along the entire wall, and around it were tables and booths. The jukebox pumped out the current novelty hit, "Three Little Fishies."

Twighty and Paul surveyed the scene. "Paul, comrade," Twighty said, "should we draw out a couple of unattached shy maidens from yonder booth and demonstrate to these woodsmen the art of jitter-bugging?"

"Okay by me," said Paul.

They approached a pair of dark-haired girls in a booth. Twighty, in his usual flowery manner, invited them to dance.

"You dark-eyed beauties from the forest primeval, it seems such a pity that you are obscured in the shadows when you should be decorat-ing the center of the floor. May the two of us have the privilege of danc-ing with the two of you?"

Twighty was a good dancer, as flamboyant as his personality, and Paul was not to be counted out in demonstrating terpsichorean art, hav-ing won a jitterbug contest during the previous Christmas vacation at

Rochester's Rainbow Pavilion. The girls were easy to lead, and soon the two couples became the center of attention. Trouble came soon enough.

The two young men who had brought the girls now performing on the arms of the two collegians, emerged from the restroom in the back of the room and saw their dates in the arms of two other men. They didn't like what they saw. Pangs of jealousy seemed to expand the surplus of muscles on their arms and chests, muscles developed from swinging axes and working crosscut saws. They looked quite formidable, clad in their plaid woolen shirts, their thick black hair shining from a liberal application of Briliantine. Several ounces of alcohol, recently consumed, inflamed their jealousy even more. Each picked up an empty beer bottle and advanced upon their dates' fancy dance partners.

Both Twighty and Paul saw them coming and wisely chose not to attempt to calm down the juggernauts with diplomatic overtures. Instead they quickly disengaged themselves from their partners and beat a hasty retreat out the door as the jukebox struck up the lively strains of the "Beer Barrel Polka."

The mighty woodsmen followed them out but soon lost sight of their adversaries, who had quickly melted into the darkness of the surrounding forest. The mighty swingers of the ax stood in the center of the road by the tavern and cursed.

Twighty and Paul made not a sound as they stood behind a tree in the darkness, and presently they saw the enemy return to the tavern.

"What we termed a den of iniquity, comrade," whispered Paul, "verily hath turned out to be a den of gorillas and a most unhealthy place for two peace-loving pilgrims like us."

"You have spoken well, Great Medicine Man," replied Twighty. "And I for my part suggest we vamoose from these precincts post haste. Let's get our bags out of the car and pray a late motorist'll be coming along to pick us up."

They got their bags, and just then noticed a stout man emerging from the tavern. He lurched erratically toward his car, a 1937 Chevrolet. The drunk found his car but opened the rear door instead of the front one and struggled into the rear seat. Finding no steering wheel he seemed puzzled.

"Let's go over and ask him if we can drive him somewhere," suggested Paul.

"My good man," said Twighty, "may we assist you perhaps by driving you home?"

There was a long sigh from the back seat, and then the drunk fell upon the rear cushion and passed out.

"Let's move out in this chariot," said Paul getting into the driver's seat. He noted the keys were in the ignition.

"Yeah, friend, but where to?" croaked Twighty.

"Since the chap doesn't seem to be very concerned about the matter now," said Paul, "his destination becomes our destination. He could do worse. Some less honest folk than us would take his car and deposit him upon the rotting leaves in the ditch. But we good Samaritans will be merciful to this man who fell among the effects of alcohol. Let's drive to Eveleth and there decide his fate."

They arrived at Eveleth at 11:30 p.m. and, as they neared the center of town, Twighty spied the new city jail.

"Cast your eyes, Paul," he said, "upon that comfortable-looking hostel for the perpetrators of petty crimes. Whatsay we take up our quarters in there for the night to preserve our diminishing exchequer and deposit out guest on a hard mattress of the same inn, providing the gendarme in charge with the keys of his car."

The jailer was kind and sympathetic to the collegians and happily installed them in cells for the night along with the inebriated man. The jail was clean and warm. Soon Twighty and Paul were lost in the arms of Morpheus.

"Good morning, fellow convict," Paul greeted Twighty on Easter Sunday morning. "Let's find a church and go to Mass and then see whether the City of Eveleth might provide breakfast for us honest citizens as they do for ordinary breakers of the law."

After breakfast, courtesy of the city, the vagabonds continued on an all-day tour of the Iron Range, which still dug gaping holes in Mother Earth to extract high grade iron ore to supply munition makers getting ready for World War II.

At Grand Rapids as the mild spring day ended, they splurged for a dinner and a hotel room. But the next day they woke up to a snowstorm. The vagrants decided to push on anyway to Bemidji.

In the worsening blizzard a new Buick stopped, and a well-dressed man exuding perfume suggested they allow him to be their host at a nice hotel in Bemidji until the next day when the storm would cease. Twighty was very firm in refusing the offer and insisted on being let off at the intersection of Highway 71.

"Now what in the hell is the matter with you, T?" stormed Paul, as he buttoned his coat to the wind. "Why did you turn him down? I'm not exactly enjoying this onslaught of winter out here, ya know."

"For the sake of your sweet old grandma, Paul, can't you recognize a queer when you see one?"

"I dunno what yer talking about. Whaddya mean, a queer?"

Twighty explained.

"Well I'll be a snake curled up in the collection box! We never had people like that in Lake Hebron."

"The question now, farmer in the dell, is what do we do next for shelter in this ferocious storm?" groaned Twighty. "I am so cold now my toenails are peeling off."

"Elementary, my dear Watson," said Paul. "See those cabins up yonder in the woods? We break into one, start a fire, and bundle up for the night with what bed clothes we find available."

The cabin, the port in the storm for our enterprising students, provided sufficient shelter through the stormy night. The next morning the sun shone again, and an old lady, driving the first car to come along, provided them breakfast at the next cafe. Paul gave thanks to the Lord for the mercy He extended to his creatures.

A couple days later the vagrants were back in the halls of their academy of learning, happy to have toured the North Star State, which Paul referred to ever afterwards as the Land of the Frozen Carp.

21

Paul was finishing his second year at St. Mary's when, one evening in early May, Father Bernard Mangan, spiritual director at the college, called Paul into his office and told him to sit down. It was the first time Paul remembered being asked to sit down in that priest's office.

"He must think he's the Pope," Paul mused to himself, "and no one is supposed to seat himself in his august presence."

Paul suspected that something more important than the usual was up. Either he had been selected to be a Cardinal, or he was about to be thrown out of college for something or other. Paul leaned heavily toward the latter possibility.

"Paul," Father Mangan began, "you will please report tomorrow morning to the chancery office downtown for an interview with the bishop. After pre-seminarians finish their second year at this place, the bishop prefers to send them to the major seminary for the last two years of college, because he is wary of candidates like you who use the freedom of a place like this to raise Cain and lose their vocations.

"But first the bishop wants to look you over and see if the diocese should adopt you, which they usually do before sending a candidate on to the major seminary. That's what he'll do tomorrow. I, personally, don't think you got much to offer the diocese."

Father Mangan broke into one of his nasty laughs which Paul hated. Under his breath Paul whispered, "You pink-toed lizard! May you be suffocated by red pepper."

"Be there at ten o'clock tomorrow morning. Understand?" concluded Father Mangan, and Paul beat it out of his office.

Paul walked back to his room entertaining great misgivings. It was common knowledge that young men applying for the seminary had to translate all kinds of Greek for the bishop, the prelate being a classical literature nut. If the candidate was good in Greek, he was accepted for further training at a major seminary. If he couldn't handle Greek he was rejected.

"It's a hell of a way to run a diocese," commented one veteran priest one day. "What's so all-fired important about Greek anyway? The Curé of Ars didn't know a word of Greek and became the patron saint of parish priests."

90

Paul contemplated the next day as the date of his execution, being very deficient in both Greek grammar and vocabulary. No one was more aware of that than Brother Ludwig.

Paul went to the chapel to pray about the new turn of events. There he addressed Mary, the Mother of Jesus. "Dear Mary, Mother of Priests, I have been limping over here for some time to find out about my vocation to be a priest, and you sent me the word from the High Priest, your Son, that I might have a calling. But I'll need a miracle tomorrow to pass that Greek test."

The next day with his copy of Xenophen under his arm Paul took a bus to the chancery office, a large mansion, probably at one time the home of a lumber magnate. As he walked up the sidewalk, Paul felt like Anne Boleyn called in by Henry the Eighth to explain to him why she couldn't produce a male heir.

Inside the massive door of the house, the secretary told him the bishop waited for him in his office, and Paul walked into the august presence of the Ordinary of the Diocese of Winona, His Excellency, the Most Reverend Francis M. Kelly.

"Good morning, Your Excellency," croaked Paul as he advanced to grasp the bishop's hand and went down on one knee to kiss the bishop's ring, a required protocol then.

Bishop Kelly, a tall man whose full head of white hair was partially covered by a red zucchetto, a small skull cap, wore a black cassock with red piping. Around his waist he wore a red sash. His countenance seemed pale but kindly. Years before, when he came to Lake Hebron to confirm a class of which Paul was a part, Ma's cousin, Nettie, declared after the ceremony, "That man's not a bit healthy. He's always pale. He ain't gonna live long."

Paul, not much concerned with the bishop's longevity, worried over the possibility that he might be called upon to answer a question during the inquiry. At Confirmation Paul had been more certain he could give a definition of actual grace than he was about translating a sentence of Xenophen at the moment.

"Please sit down," the prelate murmured. "I'm sure the course you took in the splendid Greek language the past two years must have inspired in you a love for classical literature."

"Yes, Your Excellency," responded Paul. To himself he said, "I hate the damned stuff."

"I would have you open your volume of Xenophen to page sixty-seven and translate for me that magnificent first paragraph," the bishop said softly.

"Oh, oh, here it comes!" sighed Paul to himself. "I am about to meet my Waterloo. Mother of Perpetual Help, come to my aid."

The Mother of Perpetual Help did come to his aid, for the bishop immediately began a monologue on the Greek heroes of yore and commenced to stride up and down the office extolling the beauty of the Greek language.

All through this monologue, Paul nodded agreement to everything the bishop said.

"So far, so good," exulted Paul to himself as the bishop kept unwinding. "Gosh, I hope the old boy keeps up this chatter till he gets all dragged out and sends me home with my ticket to the seminary."

At this juncture the worthy prelate abruptly ceased his ruminating, walked behind his desk, sat down, and again picked up his copy of Xenophen.

"Now will you please open your book to page eighty-four, and we will examine that classic essay of Xenophen on discipline. You will begin translating that paragraph," ordered the bishop.

"Well, that does it!" Paul sighed, the deep sigh of a condemned criminal on the gallows. He thought, "As sure as the devil hates holy water, I cannot even begin to translate that gob of Greek. Well, they say the bishop of Rapid City is accepting almost anyone for the seminary as long as he hasn't robbed a bank or run off with a member of the church choir. After I get the boot out of here for my miserable job on this Greek, I will head for Rapid City."

Before Paul could open his mouth the bishop seemed struck again with a pleasurable vein of thought about Greek, and again he stood up and discoursed on the subject, striding back and forth across his office. And again Paul solemnly nodded in agreement.

He may have lacked the ability to act, considering they only gave him a one line part in the high school class play, but apparently he could put on a convincing display of his love for Greek by nodding in response to the bishop's discourse. The bishop glanced at Paul several times and seemed gratified by his empathy. He must have thought that he, indeed, seemed like a fine candidate for the seminary. He sat down at his desk again and said, "I suppose you are getting short of money these days as the academic year draws to a close."

Paul's heart exulted with joy. He thought, "What a stroke of good fortune hath come my way! From lousy Greek he turns to one of my favorite subjects," Paul nodded in agreement, this time not feigned but genuine.

"Father Hale," the bishop called to his secretary. "Please come in here." When the priest arrived, the prelate instructed him, "Make out a check for fifty dollars for this young man, He needs some spending money."

"Wow! Talk about an answer to prayer!" whispered Paul, "The frail old bishop is ending up taking me aboard for the Diocese of Winona, and even giving me an advance. Now I can do some bumming around this summer. And I didn't have to translate a word of Greek! I am indeed the choice of the prophet Samuel from among the sons of Jesse."

On the evening of May 31st, the first anniversary of the evening when Paul and Riley got into rough weather with Brother Xavier for drinking beer too long down at the Hurry Back, Paul finished his meal and remembered that day when he was expelled for a few hours.

Twighty hove into view and sat down opposite him. "Paul," he said, "it hath dawned on me this lovely evening in May when the sun hangs low in the western sky, that we are about to leave this campus without completing the tour of all the caves we planned."

"So what, Twighty? What's so all-important about some dang caves?"

On Saturdays during May that year they had decided to visit caves as an excuse to go hitchhiking. They had visited two: one near Spring Valley and another near Harmony. The third Saturday they bummed to Rochester to prowl around the nurse's residence behind St. Mary's Hospital seeking out a daughter dedicated to the sick with whom to carry on a bit of flirtation instead of visiting the third cave on their schedule—the one at Whitewater State Park.

"Whitewater's the one we should visit tonight," said Twighty. "The sound of that cave has a poetic ring to it that stirs my soul. It seems to connote the magic of a Sioux war dance."

"Well, who gives a damn about Sioux war dances?" growled Paul "You can go down to that brewery cave right here in town under the Sugar Loaf tonight and dance your heart out, if you want. As for Whitewater, hell's bells, man, it's close to thirty miles over there, and there are no more Saturdays left. We'd have to go tonight, and then get kicked out again for rumbling in at four in the morning? No thanks."

"No problem, Paul, about running afoul of the prime minister on this one. I got it all planned. We simply go to Brother Ladislas, the dean, and plead that we want to sleep out in the hills tonight because it's too hot in our rooms. I borrowed a couple of sleeping bags, and we can approach the good Brother with this equipment under our arms, and who knows? He might fall for this suggestion since he was a Scoutmaster once."

Paul thought the plan over for a moment. His adventuresome spirit couldn't resist Twighty's innovative scheme.

"Okay, let's try it."

They approached Brother Ladislas with the camping cargo slung about their frames.

"I don't know why you fellas want to sleep out in the hills. Lots of rattlesnakes out there, you know," was Brother Ladislas' comment.

"Brother, we are well aware of the presence of such reptiles out there in the lap of Mother Nature where we propose to rest our weary bones this eventide," gushed Twighty. "But we are not fearful of any of God's good creatures any more than you were when you led the lads out on camping forays during the glorious days of your scouting. We seek the cool fresh air wafting beneath the pine and the hemlock to refresh our lagging spirits now so thoroughly drained by the exhaustive exams of yesterday and today. We seek strength to cope with the last of the tomorrow."

"Somehow I smell a spoiled fish in your frying pan," said the dean, narrowing his eyes, "but there's no big harm in camping outside for a night if you're not up to something more than that. Report to me by 7:30 in the morning. Understand?"

With their sleeping bags slung over their shoulders, the two wicked pilgrims hiked down a country land in the valley.

"I'll betcha the dean has his binoculars on us at this moment," said Twighty. "If he has, he is to be commended for we are certainly not to be trusted."

"Amen," said Paul.

Once they were out of the view of the college, they cut sharply to the right through a meadow, and climbed to Highway 14, which circled the hill above. They deposited their gear in a thicket along the road and raised their thumbs.

Rides for hitchhikers were plentiful in those days, and they arrived at the cave hardly before dark. An owl up above them sounded an ominous warning.

"Twighty, comrade of my devious travels," said Paul as they stood before the mouth of the small cave, which neither was really interested in exploring, "behold yonder owl up there silhouetted in the moon rising in the east. He can see in the dark. We cannot, and we forgot to bring a flashlight."

"Well, we can't explore that cave tonight without a flashlight. What suggests ye at this point, Daniel Boone?"

"Very simple, pal," replied Paul, "we commence walking up yonder road back toward 14 and hope some local yokel gives us a ride to provide succor for our aching feet."

"But first leave us use our imagination a bit," said Twighty. "We must be able to tell our grandchildren that we explored this cave one night, this cave that might some day be the scene of a grisly murder. And we must be able to say we were there. Leave us crawl into the cavern for just a couple of feet anyway."

They dropped to their hands and knees, crawled in and promptly crawled out, rose to an erect position as befits anthropoids and began the long walk up the lonesome trail toward Lewiston.

No cars came along as they trudged for two hours in the moonlight, while Twighty quoted poetry and Paul practiced preaching, again bemoaning the crassness of men who exchanged the realm of the spiritual for money and the delights of the flesh. But Twighty, unlike Riley, wouldn't contest a single statement he made, and Paul, without a challenge, lost all his zeal for proclaiming the word.

An oil station at the east end of town was still open at two a.m. when the lads arrived at Lewiston, and the two exceedingly thirsty collegians ingested a considerable amount of pop to slake their thirst. Finally, Paul addressed his fellow traveler. "Put down that third bottle of the nectar, which frogs wouldn't be caught drinking while alive, and let us move on toward our alma mater before the sun comes up."

About three-thirty a.m. the nearly full moon had set in the west, which meant dawn would soon appear.

A car finally appeared and stopped. A new 1938 Chevrolet four-door, at the wheel sat a very bedraggled-looking man who hadn't shaved for days and was quite intoxicated. This fact should have caused the two pilgrims to shy away from entering the vehicle, but they got in anyway—Twighty in the front and Paul in the back.

The driver engaged low gear and fed full power to the engine, which screamed in high rpms. He managed to get the car into second gear, but seemed oblivious as to how to get it into high. Twighty motioned at the gear shift until he did so.

"My good man, you are obviously drunk," yelled Twighty. "Let me drive."

"The cops are after me," wailed the inebriated driver. "I stole this car in Rochesters off'n a new car lot. Somebody left the keys in it. I picked youse guys up so you could help me escape from the cops."

"I tell you you're driving too fast and swerving all over the road." Twighty yelled again. "Here, let me drive. Pull up, ya drunken bum!"

"Like hell I will!" the short, stubby tramp shot back. "You'll turn me over to the cops, that's what you'll do!"

By then the first of many curves appeared, as the road snaked into the valley. The driver swerved off the concrete toward the guard rails on one curve. Twighty grabbed the wheel and pulled the vehicle away from the rails but not before the fender clattered, lightly brushing a series of rails.

In the back seat Paul knew if he didn't get into action right pronto his soul might soon arise out of a flaming crash to greet St. Peter. He searched around the back seat for a possible weapon, found a jack and a tire rod in their cases on the floor, took out the large tire rod, and yelled, "Grab the wheel, T. I'm about to crown the crook with this rod."

Down came the rod on the drunk's head sending him into the land of shining sky blue waters followed by oblivion. Twighty guided the car to a stop.

The two stumbled out, and leaned on the guard rails to recover their equilibrium.

"Boy, that was close!" said Twighty. "Whatta we goin' to do with sleeping beauty?"

"Nothing," advised Paul. "When he comes to he can fend for himself, but will probably be taken in by the highway patrol. However, we mustn't be involved in the escapade, or our names will get into the papers, and Brother Ladislas will see it, in which case I might as well look for a frau to feed me and the kids."

The pair began the walk to the college, another two-hour expedition, picked up their gear where they stashed it, and appeared before Brother Ladislas before 7:30 a.m.

"Come along to Mass this morning, T, and thank the Lord for His mercies after you bang your chest in guilt for your life of unrighteousness."

"Well, hold on a minute there," said Twighty. "You won't be canonized after I get through testifying about you, pal."

A couple of days later, Twighty and Paul shook hands as they reluctantly parted, and although they corresponded for a few years, their paths never crossed again.

22

At the end of his second year of college Paul did not hitchhike the 160 miles to Lake Hebron, for Paul's parents had moved. The quarter section of bare land Joe Pesch had rented for twenty years was being sold, and rather than looking for some more real estate to rent, Maggie was all for moving to the city. She had been sold a bill of goods by her sister, Emma, who lived in Rochester, namely that buying a large rooming house in the mecca for the sick would bring in enough income for a family to live comfortably.

So the Pesches had had an auction sale at Lake Hebron and moved to the city of the Mayo Clinic where they took ownership of a commodious two-and-one-half story house. But they could only rent out four rooms after accommodating the Pesch family still at home.

This move turned out to be as financially feasible as investing in a factory making horse harnesses; the income was far below the family needs.

"Joe, we're going broke," Maggie announced to her spouse one day while he sat around cracking his knuckles. "Joe, you're going to have to find a job."

Joe who had never worked for another in his life except for a bit of hiring out to a farmer now and then as a young man, knew he had to take action to resolve this distressing situation. If he were to remain independent he would have to lose no time in buying a farm he could afford and resume his former life on the land.

Joe checked out the real estate ads, and found an eighty-acre farm for sale about fourteen miles from Rochester. The price was only thirty-six dollars an acre, a figure he could handle if he liquidated the rooming house.

The next day Joe drove out to look at the estate in question, and what he saw put a chill into his bones. The ad had indicated a picturesque little farm nestled in a valley. It was nestled in the valley all right, but it was not very picturesque. In fact, it was a messy looking place, which reminded him of the picture of the abode of a Tennessee hillbilly he had seen in a magazine once. The buildings were in a serious state of disrepair, with junk piled up all over, and a little mountain of manure next to the barn. "But what can you expect for thirty-six dollars an acre?" Joe reasoned. He signed on the dotted line, and would be able to take possession on March 1st.

That evening he informed Maggie that the Pesch clan was returning to the land in order to be able to keep body and soul together, and would she like to view their beautiful estate located in a quiet valley down yonder?

When Maggie saw the decrepit buildings, the mess all over, and the washed out driveway leading into it, she, who hated the idea of moving back to the farm anyway, launched into near hysterics and voluminous tears.

But Joe, who after twenty years of marriage knew she would recover from this seizure, gently patted her on the shoulder and murmured soft words of consolation.

One of the first things Maggie did was get on the phone to Paul at the college and transmit to him the tragic news and solicit his support in her grieving.

"Pa bought a small farm for thirty-six dollars an acre?" said Paul. "Sounds real good to me. He was lucky to find it."

"But it's such a mess that even a pig wouldn't live there," Maggie wailed.

"Well, what did you expect for three thousand dollars? The Empire State building?"

"Paul, it's no use talking to you. Now you get right over to the place and help us clean it up, you understand?"

"Don't forget, Ma, that I'm still committed to the books and the passing of exams in order to bring you and Pa a record of achievement that will make you proud to say you sired me. Yeah, I'll hitchike over Saturday and take a look at our new country estate."

The following Saturday Paul stood on the county road curving past the estate and surveyed the farm. Despite the messy looking sight, and nothing looked messier than a farm in early spring, Paul's poetic soul refused to be daunted. He saw what he envisioned the place would look like in the future.

A brook gurgled through the valley, ripping its way along near the farmhouse. He immediately named it "Brook Cedron." Oh, how the musical sound of that brook as it ripped over the stones would lull him to sleep at night!

He envisioned the decrepit farmhouse embellished with a fresh coat of white paint, black shutters at the windows, and new shingling on the roof—truly a worthy country home for him during the summer months. He noted the gentle slope from the house to the brook. This would be a smooth lawn, and under those oak trees Paul could lounge and read books, listening to the sounds of cattle lowing in yonder meadow.

Across the brook was a piece of fertile and fairly level land. That he would call "The Plains of Esdraelon." A wooded hill rose beyond the

Plain, and on top was another rolling field which Paul named "Golan Heights." The steeply-rising hill beyond the barn to the west he named "Mount Hermon." But what would he call the whole farm? He had run out of Biblical names for the moment.

Because a brook ran through it, he thought the place could be fittingly called, "Brookfield Farm," but that didn't sound poetic enough. With his Latin background he translated that into Latin, and it came out, "Villa Campa Rivula." Maggie said that putting all those fancy names on the miserable place was simply ridiculous.

"But, Ma," protested Paul, "this is a land flowing with milk and honey even though you fail to appreciate it."

"You mean the dump is flowing with rats and ragweeds," Maggie said.

Besides the house Paul noted what appeared to be a hiproofed barn built into the side of the hill so that on the other side of the building was a runway direct into the haymow which rested on thick limestone walls. Paul guessed the barn had not been painted since the Civil War. There was also a small granary on which barely hung a lean-to garage and a hoghouse nearly falling down.

Maggie noticed Paul standing in the yard and shouted, "Don't stand there daydreaming again, Paul. Roll up your sleeves and give us a hand cleaning up this pigpen."

She referred to the house, which had been left in a colossal mess by the previous occupants.

"We don't have electricity in the house!" wailed little Maggie, who was approaching teenage and very sad about how the place would look to her peers.

"Weep not, my darling," consoled Paul, "the REA poles go past, I noticed, and so we'll have light in no time. Look instead to a future lovely country home here where the mourning dove and meadow lark will serenade us." Having uttered that noble speech, Paul began walking back to the road to return to college.

"Hey, where ya goin'? Give us a hand and help clean up! Who do you think you are? The King of Siam?" came the chorus from the rest of the clan. Paul bowed to them and continued to walk away as Sir Edgar and little Maggie threw sticks and stones at him.

"Truly your treatment of me reflects an attitude unworthy of the children of Abraham," he called back. "I assure you that as soon as the college year ends, I shall again descend upon this charming villa to lend a hand transforming it into a place worthy of my presence during the summers when I can relax here and refresh my spirits."

Some more sticks and stones sailed in his direction. He walked a quarter of a mile down the county road from the Villa to U.S. 52 where the constant flow of traffic always provided a motorist willing to pick up a nice-looking boy with his thumb in the air.

To his credit Paul did return to the Villa after his finals and pitched in the seeming endless job of cleaning up the farmstead. He grew especially tired of throwing manure onto a wagon and hauling it to the Plains of Esdraelon where it had to be laboriously spread by hand. After a week, during which he acquired some callouses on his hands, he pleaded that he was required to spend a week at a workshop in Chicago preparatory to entering the seminary in the fall. "Now what a piece of fiction that is," he grumbled to himself, "I must needs quit telling lies like that to accommodate my love of leisure."

The next morning he took up his post on the nearby highway and headed for Chicago to be the guest of Twighty and see the sights of the city.

After a week's vacation in the city Paul discovered he still had a conscience, raised the thumb for home, donned a pair of overalls again, and climbed up on the roof of the house to assist his dad and Sir Edgar in reshingling.

Paul added a new title to Sir Edgar's name, "the Earl of Chatfield," since that village lay only five miles distant from the Villa. However the Earl of Chatfield seemed unimpressed with Paul's workmanship and threw a few shingles at him along with some uncomplimentary remarks.

"Why dost thou demean me?" Paul confronted his brother. "Have you no respect for the servant of the Lord about to enter His service as a priest? Dost thou not realize that I should be revered?"

"Aw, for crying out loud!" shot back Sir Edgar. "They'll throw you out of the seminary fast enough, an you'll be riding freight cars along with the rest of the bums."

"Shaddup, you two," commanded Pa Pesch," and get to work."

Soon the gabled two-story farmhouse was reshingled, then painted, and Maggie was encouraged to resume life on the land. She went back to her old art of raising chickens in the pitiful old shack of a chickenhouse for additional income.

"You'll have to build me a new henhouse. That's all there is to it," she told her spouse.

The rolling field up on Golan Heights was so eroded that Joe decided to sow it down permanently to timothy and clover. However, a couple of loads of oat bundles remained from the meagre harvest to be hauled down to the Villa and stacked.

With a decrepit hay rack mounted on four steel wheels and drawn by a team of old nags Joe had purchased for a few dollars at some auction, Sir Edgar and Paul went up to Golan Heights to get a load of bundles.

The two young men, having loaded a towering mound of bundles on the hay rack, began the descent from Golan Heights to the Plains of Esdraelon when Maggie's clarion call for dinner sounded from the Villa.

Paul, driving the team and being very hungry, wanted to save time by taking a shortcut down through the Cedars of Lebanon, as he called the belt of woods covering the hillside, instead of following the gentle grade down around the Cedars. The shortcut route down was known as "The Devil's Chute" because getting through it without tipping over was a devil of a job.

Sir Edgar said, "You're not figuring on going through the Devil's Chute, are you?"

"That I am," said Paul. "I figure that while the road on the curve in there slants a bit, we can negotiate it without tipping over if we shoot it fast enough."

Sir Edgar, always more conservative than Paul, shouted from his perch atop the load, "We'll never make it! We'll never make it! Swing over and take the old road."

Paul always welcomed a challenge and entered the Devil's Chute. He whipped the team to get enough speed to prevent the rack from tipping over going around the curve. But those two senior citizens of the equine kingdom were incapable of trotting on short notice. Alas, when the top-heavy wagon arrived at the slanted curve, the whole load of bundles rolled off the undercarriage.

Paul rolled free of the cascading bundles, but Sir Edgar was buried somewhere in the pile.

Paul gazed intently at the spilled bundles trying to guess where his sibling might be, when he noticed one bundle starting to wiggle a bit. Soon two bundles wiggled and moved. Shortly thereafter the face of the Earl of Chatfield emerged from the pile. From this face, now livid with rage, came forth unpleasant epithets that echoed through the Cedars, and Sir Edgar followed them up with an impassioned oration somewhat similar to that delivered in revival tents around the land. Paul got the impression that he might be worthy of hellfire.

Sir Edgar, nearly three years younger than Paul, was, as yet, a bit shorter of stature. Instead of curly hair like Paul's, his was straight but of the same light brown color. His features were somewhat plainer than Paul's more handsome face, but bore a distinct resemblance. Were he bigger physically—and he was soon to grow taller than Paul—he might have wrestled his brother to the ground.

‡ ‡ ‡

Maggie determined to have the basic amenities of life in that "dump" in the country. First, somebody had to wire the house and get the power in from the REA line on the road. After that, the male members of the household got busy and installed a septic tank, laying in pipe to the bathroom, to be installed before the crickets started singing in August. The mice population bothered Maggie no end. Mice in every building including the house.

"Hey, Ma," said Paul one day, "how would you like to get rid of all these mice?"

"The sooner the better," replied Maggie. "What have you got in mind? I won't allow no poisoning, though. Did you find a good cat?"

"Did we ever, Ma, you might not see that tomcat around, but he'll be cleaning up the mice, you can bet on that."

What Paul had in mind was not a tomcat at all. He and Sir Edgar had come up with another solution to the problem.

The day before when they had gone up to that rolling field on Golan Heights to get the second and last load of oats bundles from that sparse harvest, they spied a nice fat bullsnake snoozing on top of a shock. Bull-snakes were usually good sized reptiles, and this one looked to be at least three feet long.

Sir Edgar had been about to execute the creature with his pitchfork when Paul said, "Hold on! I read somewhere that where you find bull-snakes, you will never find rattlesnakes on the same turf, and we prefer these harmless bullsnakes. Furthermore, I'm told bullsnakes are great for eating mice. Let's take the snake along down and put him in the gra-nary and see how he does. We'll call him 'Charlie.'"

So they threw the whole shock with Charlie aboard up on the hay-rack and kept an eye on the perimeter of the wagon to see if Charlie crawled out, but Charlie stayed put. When they spotted him among the bundles they put him in a gunny sack, and let him loose in the granary after informing Pa what they had in mind.

"I dunno," said Joe. "We'll see what he does. But don't say a word about that snake to Ma. She's deathly afraid of snakes and might go nuts if she saw this one around."

Charlie stayed in the granary and got fat on mice. After he cleaned out that building, he wiggled over to the barn at night and dined very well there. Next, came the hoghouse and chickenhouse, but Charlie always returned each morning to his habitat underneath the granary.

Finally, Charlie went over to the house, crawled into the basement through a hole by the basement window and went after the mice there. He took up residence under the broad porch on the south side of the house instead of under the granary. However, nobody saw Charlie since he moved only at night, and all Maggie knew was that somehow the mice were disappearing, and she was happy about it.

Sir Edgar and Paul, noting Charlie's new residence under the porch became worried a bit. Suppose Ma should catch a glimpse of him?

Meanwhile, Maggie asked Uncle Elwin if he could wire the house for electricity. Uncle Elwin was handy but not the master of all trades like he bragged, and when he finished wiring the house, the inspector of the REA was a bit disgusted with the job. Then Charlie came into the picture.

The inspector's name was Henry, known more commonly as Hank. A short, bald man with ruffles of gray hair around his ears, he had a young-looking face and spoke with a rather high-pitched voice.

Hank went down into the basement to check the way Uncle Elwin had fastened wires to the wooden beams. The inspector was standing on the chair by the potato bin tracing the wires along the beam when he heard a "plop," and he looked down into the potato bin beneath the basement window that had a hole in the frame which Charlie used to enter the basement to dine on mice. For some unknown reason, at mid-morning Charlie became hungry, decided to go hunting mice in daylight for a change, and crawled through the hole. And instead of slithering along the partition this time and then onto the floor, he just flopped directly onto the potatoes.

Hank froze. Terribly afraid of snakes, there, right in front of him, a nice fat one uncoiled on the potatoes. The poor man's eyes bulged in fright, his lips moved, but he didn't say anything. Pa, in the basement with him, had observed Charlie's entrance and didn't know what to do, especially when he saw the terror-stricken inspector gagging in fright, his mouth open.

With a hoarse cry, Hank jumped off the chair, and clawed his way up the steps and ran out to his pickup truck, where breathing heavily, he started up the vehicle and raced down the driveway.

With a heavy heart Joe Pesch grabbed a meat cleaver off the chopping block down there and sliced poor Charlie's head off. He knew the game was up. Charlie would have to go and never come back lest Maggie find out about it, throw a fit, and faint.

Charlie had done such a good job ridding the Villa of all those mice that Joe, with sorrow in his heart, took Charlie outside on a scoop shovel and cast him into the brook where the running water would eventually float him to the Root River.

Maggie never found out that, for almost a month, she had harbored a nice fat bullsnake on the place, at times almost under her feet.

The next day Paul and Sir Edgar stood on the bank of the Brook Cedron, observed fifteen seconds of silence, and threw a few dandelions into the brook in Charlie's memory.

Back in the office in town Hank signed off the Villa wiring job as "passed" on condition that Joe keep mum about the incident in the Pesch basement. Besides, Hank wouldn't have returned to the scene again for any amount of money.

Maggie hurried Joe and the boys to the next project, the installation of a bathroom in the house. Sir Edgar and Paul went in to the county agent's office to get some literature on how to construct a septic tank. After poring over the document, they dug a trench from the house across "Solomon's Terrace," the lawn, to the site of the septic tank near the brook.

Paul took his place digging the trenches along with Pa and Sir Edgar. Blisters appeared on his lily-white hands, perspiration rolled off his brow, and the sun transformed the pigment of his fair skin into shades of tan.

As he worked, he prayed, "Lord, as I endure this crucifixion out here in the trenches, I offer my keen sufferings to Thee. And Thee, in turn, grant that I am able to stay in the seminary I am soon to enter without getting kicked out."

Paul surprised himself that he could still endure that much physical labor without trying to goldbrick on the job or finding some way to bug out.

At the end of the second day the ditch and excavation were completed, and while the trio looked at the completed job with some well-deserved satisfaction, Pa said, "We'll lay the cement block of the septic tank and the tile line leading to it first thing tomorrow."

Napoleon may have regretted making a decision or two at Waterloo, but he didn't regret it nearly as much as Joe Pesch regretted those words.

During the night a vigorous thunderstorm rolled over the Hills of Moab and the Plains of Esdraelon. Its vivid bolts of electrical energy, followed by explosions of thunder, caused little boys and girls in the county to whimper in terror as the skies opened up to deluge the earth and transformed the Brook Cedron into a roaring torrent.

The next morning brought the rising sun to reign over glistening vegetation, and a delicious odor of freshness permeated the land. But, alas, a song of sorrow rose, echoing over the Villa, a plaintive cry like Rachel mourning her children.

During the storm the earth of the sloping Solomon's Terrace shifted in the downpour and, like a sliding door, closed up the trench and septic tank excavation. The backbreaking job would have to be repeated. If only they had laid the tile and cement block the night before!

23

By the middle of August, after what seemed like a miserable summer for Paul, what with the shingling, the painting of the house, the installation of sewer facilities, Paul felt all but prostrate with sunburn and aching muscles. But he envisioned what a heaven the Villa would be in future summers after it had been restored, and he endured this temporary slavery.

To complete the restoration Paul knew that Golan Heights would have to be plowed up and sowed down permanently to preserve what little topsoil remained. Plowing up those ten acres would not require much exertion driving the tractor. So one day he suggested to his father, "Perhaps I'd better plow up Golan Heights if you want to sow it down this fall."

"Now what in the Sam Hill are you talking about? Golan Heights? Where's that?" Joe said.

"Oh, well, I was referring to that field there on top of the hill."

"Well, then, for Pete's sake, don't go calling it another one of those fancy names. People will think you're heading for the asylum."

The next afternoon Paul mounted the John Deere with the rusty two-bottom plow in tow and climbed up Golan Heights via the old trail past a gully on the neighbor's land.

Plowing that afternoon provided a few hours for Paul to daydream as he sat on the tractor. He daydreamed mostly about Lucille Nystrom, the blonde Swedish girl who lived up the road a couple of miles.

One afternoon in late August when Joe Pesch had gone up to help Einer Nystrom put up some hay, Paul went along to see what was going on up there. He was soon put to work driving a hayrack, delivering hay from the field to the Nystrom haybarn.

Then Lucille showed up. About seventeen, Paul judged, her light blonde hair was braided, and her attractive face sported a clear complexion with a healthy tint. Her body delightfully curved, she wore a faded yellow dress. A broad-brimmed straw hat clung to the back of her neck by a narrow ribbon fastened around her fair neck. Paul looked at her, and his eyebrows began quivering.

"That female beauty is capable of causing a rural revolution, of inspiring red-blooded farm lads to sing ballads as they feed their pigs, of bringing about a transformation of roosters into celestial angels," murmured Paul. "Oh, boy, oh, boy, what hath God wrought and revealed to me here!"

"Hi," she addressed Paul. "Can I ride along out to the field for the fun of it?"

"Come aboard, fair one," said Paul. As the wagon rumbled along toward the haymeadow, Paul said to his lovely passenger, "You are indeed a flower of the field in blossom, and you remind me of the first movement of Beethhoven's sixth symphony where the wind sighs through tall flowers, which, in full glory, nod in the breeze. What, pray, is your name?"

"Lucille." She giggled with pleasure at the speech Paul delivered. "You're the boy down the road who is going to college, aren't you?"

"That I am, fair daughter of Eve, and where have you been all my life?"

By the time the second load of hay had been delivered to the barn by Lucille and Paul, the girl gave every indication of being quite interested in the well-tanned collegian who looked more like a son of the soil than a college student in his bib overalls and torn straw hat, which did not entirely hide his curly hair. She edged closer and closer to Paul there in the front of the hayrack and gazed up at him with considerable ardor.

Paul became nervous. Lucille was coming on quite strong, and his libido began to gain more and more supremacy over his powers of reasoning. As they came into the farmyard with the third load of hay, the horses stopped suddenly before a closed gate. The maneuver threw both young people off balance, and they fell into the hay. Paul encircled Lucille with his arms when Einar, who had come over to open the gate, called out, "Okay, you can bring the load along now."

Paul pulled himself away from the siren's embrace, breathing heavily. In a falsetto tone because he was so unnerved, he commanded the team of horses to move forward "Jeepers!" he whispered to himself, "I was almost a goner there. Yumpin Yahosofat! I wouldn't last ten seconds in the hay with that captivating creature. Come, dear guardian angel, be my strength in these moments of trial."

Lucille struggled back out of the hay and took her position again beside him. Now she encircled Paul's waist with her arm and cuddled up to him. At this point Einar noticed his daughter's evident disposition, was not very happy about it, and yelled, "Lucille, come on down and help your mother with the lunch."

Lucille gave Paul a final squeeze, climbed down from the loaded hay wagon with the alacrity of a monkey, revealing her bare, tanned thighs in the process. Paul's eyebrows quivered some more.

The load of hay was removed from the hay rick by hay slings laid out as the wagon had been loaded. Three sets of slings took the load off and swung it into the haymow. Paul jumped off the wagon to have lunch under the cottonwood tree where Lucille and her mother served sandwiches, cool nectar, and ice cream. All the while, Lucille caressed Paul with her eyes, causing him to blush and his eyebrows to quiver again. "What if she goes along to get another load?" thought Paul. "Lead me not into temptation," he prayed.

Pa Pesch settled the issue. "I'll bring in the last load, Paul," he said. "You can go home and get the cows in for milking."

Paul waved farewell to Lucille and smiled. She threw him a kiss, and he strode down the lane of the Nystrom place to the road and on toward the Villa. As he walked along, he sighed, "Jeepers, that's some gal!"

The next day, Paul plowed up on Golan Heights, daydreaming about Lucille. He thought that farming would not be so difficult with Lucille around. The more he thought about her, the more determined he became to ask her for a date the coming Saturday night.

"Maybe I should forget about going to the seminary this fall at that," he mused. "If I married Lucille, I'd get the farm from her old man as she is the only child in the family. I could afford to buy a good tractor and modern machinery, and there wouldn't be much drudgery involved in farming then. Yep, I'm gonna have a date with that honeychile this Saturday."

At that point in the life of one daydreaming Paul J. Pesch a little disaster struck. Paul was making the last round of the plowing, at the edge of the brow of the hill. The terrain dropped off quickly, and at times the tractor tipped rather steeply.

The rear tractor tire struck a sizeable anthill, and the rubber-tired wheel bounced upward but failed to come back down. The awful truth that an upset was in the making finally dawned on Paul, and, instead of taking prompt action to steer the implement in the direction of the upset, Paul simply took measures to save his hide. He deserted the ship with the alacrity of a jackrabbit.

The tractor hung balanced for a moment with one wheel in the air, then slowly rolled over. By then the machine had reached a steeper part of the side hill, and continued to roll, picking up speed as it tumbled down to the Plains of Esdraelon. Paul, a phlegmatic character, watched the performance like an owl observing the moon coming up. However, when the spilling fuel ignited and the machine became a flaming pyre, he decided to act. He followed the burning tractor down the hill, and when it came to rest on the bottom, threw dirt at the blaze and eventually extinguished it.

Paul sighed sadly at the course of events and trudged back to the Villa thinking there must be a silver lining somewhere on this cloud hanging over his head. He dreaded the confrontation with his father for his honorable ancestor would certainly manifest considerable distress when he thought of how much it would cost him to repair his tractor.

As Paul walked into the yard Pa emerged from the barn.

"Did you finish plowing?" he asked.

"Yep," came the answer from the subdued Paul.

"Well, then, where's the tractor and the plow?"

"Got too close to the edge of the hill, and she tipped over and rolled down the hill. Paul pointed to the smoking ruins lying across the valley at the other side of the Plains of Esdraelon.

Paul thought the slow reaction was his father's counting up the cost to repair the wreckage. A look of deep disgust finally crossed Joe Pesch's face, and that soon turned to livid rage. Paul steeled himself against the vituperation soon to descend around his ears accompanied by emphatic cussing in German. But Joe Pesch suddenly dropped his arms, which had been raised on high to accentuate the outburst, and he quietly sighed, "Ach, you'd better go to the seminary. You'll never make a farmer." And he walked away.

The incident jolted Paul to the roots of his vertebrae. Suddenly gone were all thoughts of Lucille and thoughts of abandoning the seminary.

Later on Paul reflected on how the Holy Spirit operated that day in his life.

The next day a letter came from the Bishop instructing Paul to report to the St. Paul Seminary in two days. In the rush of packing, Paul did not find time to say goodbye to Lucille.

24

The St. Paul Seminary stood on a forty-acre tract of land bounded by Mississippi River Drive on the east, and Summit Avenue on the north, which meant that this place of real estate was located in the high-rent district of St. Paul. Paul gazed at the large homes of the affluent in that neighborhood for a long time.

After dumping his luggage at the door of Cretin Residence, where he would live, Paul bid farewell to his family and assured them that he would somehow get home to see them on Thanksgiving. Paul didn't know at the time that the seminary forbade hitchhiking, but it wouldn't have made any difference to him if he knew.

Paul spotted a tall, lanky lad with bushy red hair, fiery red eyebrows and thick, sensuous lips standing behind Cretin Residence, smoking a cigarette. Paul introduced himself.

"I'm Christopher P. McClanahan," the other responded. "Names are sometimes horrible things they hang on people, don't you think? I've always gone under the nickname of Punk, so you might as well start calling me that right off."

"Glad to meet ya, Punk. What diocese are you studying for?"

"Denver, for the time being."

"What do you mean 'for the time being'?"

"I'm not sure I can get along without women, for one thing. As a matter of fact, the place is already giving me the willies. It looks like a flax plant. No, on second thought, I'd say it looks more like a penitentiary. I can explain something about the history of this dreary dump if you're interested."

"Yah, go ahead."

"My pastor back home told me a little about the place before I left. He's a pious old coot who thinks I have a vocation. Wait till I go to confession to him sometime; he'll don sackcloth and ashes and pray to the Lord that Holy Mother Church be spared my presence among her holy clergy.

"Well, anyway, about this place. It was built by Jim Hill, the Great Northern railroad magnate. Jim wasn't a Catholic, but his next door neighbor on plush Summit Avenue was Archbishop John Ireland, who decided to put the touch on his millionaire neighbor to build him a seminary. The priests started to pop in on old Jim in his garden of vespertide and admired his sweet peas and petunias and buttered up Moneybags until he got a seminary out of him. You are looking at the old railroad yards the old boy built for his neighbor.

"How come you call it the railroad yards?" Paul wanted to know.

"Well, look at these residence buildings, for instance. They're built in a row, and each looks like a boxcar. Off to the side, the classroom building looks like a freight house while the administration building sure resembles a depot. Put a semaphore above that port cochere, and people will be looking for the 3:45 to come steaming in. The refectory over there could pass for the village creamery, and that power house might pass for a small canning factory. There isn't enough architecture in the whole plant to distinguish it from my grandfather's turkey farm except for the chapel, of course, built later. The chapel sitting over there in the corner overlooking the river wasn't put up by Jim Hill, who probably wasn't too comfortable building churches."

"Punk, you impress me with your keen intelligence," Paul said. "You should be able to bamboozle the profs around here. Whaddya want to quit for?"

"I'm not going to right off. Maybe I can stand it for a while. You see, my mother is bound and determined that I become a priest. I promised to give it a try to keep the old lady happy. Who's putting the screws on you to don the Roman collar?"

"Absolutely nobody," Paul answered. "Of course, I didn't like to sweat on the farm, and I figured the Lord might possibly be hanging a vocation on me. He often scrapes the bottom of the barrel."

"I'll help you get settled," said Punk. "I know my way around here a bit now. Came a day early hoping to get a hotel downtown and go out on a toot, but the old lady gave Uncle Andrew strict orders to deliver me here and no place else since she knows me pretty well. By the way, I forgot your name."

"Paul J. Pesch of the Diocese of Winona."

"Okay, Paul. Did they give you your room number yet?"

"Yeah, it's 501 Cretin."

"That's up there on top of the boxcar. I'm up there too. Makes me feel like a damned old bat. Well, I'll give you a hand with your bags as soon as I get another drag off this Chesterfield. There's no elevator in this cellblock, ya know."

Up on the fifth floor, which Paul immediately called the "Penthouse," was a chubby young man with an ingratiating smile, wearing heavy horn-rim glasses and moving an easy chair down the hall. He introduced himself as Larry Kuntzman of Kansas.

"Where did you get that easy chair?" asked Paul.

"I found it in a room left by a previous occupant. Got to grab while grabbing is good before the rest of the plebes arrive. Punk was here first so he has his pad furnished like the Waldorf."

Each student had two rooms. One small interior bedroom and the study, the outside room. Standard furniture consisted of a bed and a chest of drawers in the bedroom, and a table and chair in the study. Outside of an old easy chair with its stuffings coming out, there was no more furniture to claim from any room on fifth, Paul discovered in making a quick inspection.

"By the dry bones of Ezekiel, I gotta have more furniture!" complained Paul.

"Tell ya what you can do," advised Punk. "Go down to the lobby of the Ad building. There's an old gent in the mailroom by the name of Pat Conway. Tell him your woes and slip him a buck. The old crook has a supply of good furniture stored in the basement of the powerhouse, and he'll let you have your pick of what you need for fifty cents. The old bugger loves to nip and stuff costs money."

Having acquired a satisfactory supply of furniture from Pat, Paul plopped down in a stuffed chair, lit up a cigarette, and contemplated this new phase of his existence. "I'm not a bit favorably impressed at the moment," Paul muttered to himself. "Why would I want to be a priest if it means hanging around here for six years?"

Outside of the dormer window, he noticed a squirrel clinging to an overhanging branch of a large elm. The ends of the branch touched the dormer window, and the squirrel eyed Paul with some curiosity. Paul said to the squirrel, "Charlie, you're looking at a person, while made to the image and likeness of God, pines on occasion for the delights of the flesh as embodied in the gal I left behind me in Olmsted County. Lucille must be missing me, and I, for my part miss her. What, then, Charlie, am I doing around this dreary place? Pop in on my windowsill again, Charlie, and see how I'm doing."

Charlie seemed to nod his head, moved down the branch and disappeared.

Punk appeared in the doorway. "You sounded like you were talking to that squirrel, Paul. Not a very good sign of mental integrity. But I won't squeal on you. By the way, you can't smoke in your room. All smoking has to be confined to the rec room in Grace Residence or on the parking lot behind this building."

"The hell you say! I'll smoke anywhere I damn well please."

"Suit yourself, good looking. And, by the way, you got to get yourself a cassock and a collar to wear around here all the time, ya know."

"No, I didn't know. For the sake of Adelaide the alligator, what next! I don't have a cassock."

"Buy an altar boy cassock till you get one tailor made. Buy one at Lohmann's downtown. Meanwhile, you can get measured up for a nice-looking job tonight by Zolly when he shows up in the rec room after supper."

"Who is Zolly?"

"He's a Jew who lives in the neighborhood. Pretty good at making cassocks, and he knows it, and charges a few bucks more. The lads, I understand, give him a bad time for stealing from us poor orphans, and he in turn cries in the towel every time he comes over here because he says we Christians take the food right out of the mouth of the Hebrews and their children."

"How come you know everything around here so fast, Punk?" Paul said, very much impressed with Christopher P. McClanahan.

The bell rang for supper. "That's the bell from one of Jim Hill's locomotives," Punk explained. "That's a fact. It's mounted outside the window of one of the seminarian's rooms on the first floor. He's appointed to ring it for the various functions of the day—like mealtime and chapel time.

"Who gets that lousy job?" Paul wanted to know.

"The dean keeps an eye out for a pious-looking critter. They get all the appointments around here. The guy has to look like somebody who entertains holy thoughts all day and bumps into trees because he's afraid he'll see a girl if he looks up. Yeah, they put a premium on renouncing sex in this penitentiary."

The 185 students filed into the refectory and found places at the tables. Punk and Paul sat together. Up on a raised platform at one end of the room stood a long table draped with a white linen tablecloth. At the students' tables the china and silverware rested on bare wood.

"That's the faculty table there," explained Punk. "The bird up there now is the rector, Jeremiah K. Dobberstein. Anyhow, 'the Dobber' is angling to be a bishop and has it figured out that the more students he throws out of the seminary the better image he creates in Rome in producing a better product. And so he'll throw you out quick if you break a rule around here."

The rector tinkled his bell on the table to get the attention of his audience, for apparently he wanted to say a few words. A heavy-set man, bald on top of his head with a crown of dark hair around the rim, he reminded Paul of a fat medieval monk wearing tonsure. Mounted on his nose was a pair of black rimmed glasses. His long aquiline nose didn't seem to blend very well with his round face. He wore a black cassock and a white Roman collar around his thick neck. While Paul expected this large man to generate a powerful voice, he spoke instead in a soft tenor.

"Welcome to St. Paul Seminary," he began. "You are here to be formed into holy men of God, and we of the faculty will do our best to shape you into vessels of election, as St. Paul terms it. I will be addressing you tomorrow afternoon to explain the rules of this institution."

He sat down without looking at the students even once and began stowing salad into his mouth.

The next afternoon, Paul learned some of the rules in effect around the brickyard: No smoking except in a couple of designated spots, no secular literature to be brought onto the premises at any time, no use of any radio except the one in the rec room, no visiting in someone else's room without permission of the floor prefect, no garb worn on the grounds except the cassock and biretta, no stopping in at a bar when downtown under pain of instant expulsion.

After the session Punk cackled, "Well, that cooks your goose, Paul. Your days of being footloose and fancy free have ended. You're in the Vatican West Point now."

"Don't forget the same holds for you, Punk," said Paul. "Remember, I'm a peasant from the land quite accustomed to going without during this Depression, and of mortifying my passions as I came up the thorny road. But what about you, a semi-pagan by the looks of things, a man of the world who has had more money to enjoy the pleasures of the world than he needed? Say, you're going to feel like a wolf trapped in a cistern around here.

Punk smiled knowingly and elected not to reveal his future course of action in the "penitentiary," as he termed the place.

25

The seminary operated on a seniority system. The order of a student's registration by his bishop was his place in seniority. He could be at the top of the class or at the bottom. Since Paul's bishop never got around to things until the last moment, Paul found himself near the bottom. A student sat in class, ate, and lived in seniority order for six years. Paul ranked next to Christopher P. McClanahan, Larry Kuntsman, and Urban Neudecker, the latter a tall, dark, and handsome man who came from a solid German family, had a dry sense of humor and inclined to be prudent and conservative. In the years to follow Urban constantly despaired that Paul would ever be ordained.

Larry Kuntzman was short and plump, a lad with a ready laugh and a love for cigars or a pipe when he could not afford cigars.

All three, near the bottom in seniority, lived in the Penthouse during their first year at the railroad yards.

Paul, a night person, was at a loss when the lights went out at 10:30. He found it very difficult to get to sleep if he retired then and more difficult to rise at 6:30 a.m.

Each seminarian on the floor took his turn awakening his peers, knocking on doors and singing out, "Benedicamu Domino." (Let us bless the Lord). The drowsy mortal inside responded with "Deo Gratias" (thanks be to God) to indicate that he was awake.

If no response came, the chanticleer might find it necessary to enter the domain of the sleeping servant of the Lord and use more stimulating methods to bring the reposing servant to the land of the living. Most of the time this invasion of the slumberer's castle was not necessary, because everyone knew that should he manifest no signs of life, a thin stream of cold water descending upon him would follow.

Needless to say, the matins caller was not welcome at most doors, and, sometimes, instead of getting a "Deo Gratias" in response to his greeting, he stood a chance of being told to take a long walk off a short dock or something similar. Should the sleeper be so rash as to respond, "Go to hell," and somehow the dean got wind of it—a very unlikely scenario though that was—he might be told later in the day where he might go . . . with his suitcases.

Most mornings after Paul's feet hit the floor, he staggered down the

114

hall toward the washroom suffering no little agony. He stood half awake in front of one of the sinks and prepared to shave while whispering softly, "Lord, let his chalice pass from me for I, in truth, can scarcely drink it. But let Thy will, not mine, be done." He longed for the beautiful summer mornings on the Villa where he, upon waking, could hear the melody of the meadow lark through the open window, then roll over and sink back into blessed slumber.

At 6:55 the still sleepy crew reported to the oratory on the first floor to commune with the Lord. The communal recitation of Prime of the Latin breviary was followed by meditation. The dean attempted to teach the levites how to meditate, and they were ordered to procure meditation books. Paul had one such book on how to meditate according to the Ignation method, but, alas, this aid usually failed him. He quickly sank into the arms of Morpheus when the meditation period began.

At 7:25 the locomotive bell sounded again. Paul awoke and joined the march to the chapel for Mass at 7:30. The inmates of the red brick fortress had a chance now to breathe fresh air, and that usually woke Paul.

Often he gazed across Summit Avenue as he marched to the chapel and surveyed a few of the expensive homes there. One was a Georgian mansion, and every morning there was a light on the third floor—servants' quarters, Paul assumed.

"Bless ye, servants of the rich and mighty," he whispered, "for you share my fate on these dark mornings in winter. Trip lightly down the stairs, I bid thee, to prepare your master's corn flakes, but be sure you offer your day to the Lord."

The lads donned white surplices, and took their places in the stalls, opened the thick liturgical book, the *Liber Usualis*, and sang out the Gregorian chant, giving honor and glory to God during Mass.

After breakfast Paul dashed to his room, lit up a cigarette and lay down upon his bed to relax. John Q. Pulford, a very pious and conscientious lad living on the other end of the fifth floor, always wished to do his part in the cause of righteousness in his little corner of the world, came one morning to Paul's room, stood in the open door and said, "Paul, it is entirely possible that the dean will make a surprise appearance up here some morning, and if he catches you smoking in your room, which is against the rules, you will suffer weighty demerits."

"Yes, Pulford, you are entirely right. But, of course, I don't aim to be caught. However, I thank thee for thy great solicitude on my behalf and bid thee a good morning."

Other worthy members of the student body in Cretin Hall had already devised a system of alerting their peers upstairs if the Honorable Quentin L. O'Neill, the dean, sallied forth to make a "raid." Father O'Neill, a tall, big-boned man with a virile-looking face and a wide mouth, sported a fast-growing bald spot surrounded by thick black hair. Father

O'Neill was a very holy and conscientious man, a credit to the Holy Roman Catholic Church of America and a credit to the priest nursery where he served.

The warning system consisted of a few taps on the radiator pipe made by the first student who noted the dean on the loose when ordinarily occupied himself with his morning paper. Should the good dean ascend the stairs to the next floor, the tempo of the tapping increased, a red alert for everyone to batten down the hatches.

One September morning scarcely two weeks after gracing the seminary by his presence, Paul lay on his bed enjoying his post-breakfast cigarette and perusing the morning paper when he heard the red alert.

Paul leaped off the bed, quickly flipped the cigarette out the window, stashed the paper under the covers of the bed, and began to gather up his books for class while humming "Harbor Lights." He acted none too soon, for Quentin Louis O'Neill negotiated four flights of stairs with the speed of a squirrel, and in so doing, must have taxed his cardiac-vascular sytem to its limits. He briskly marched down the fifth floor hallway to Paul's room as if he had been tipped off he would find some mischief there.

"Good morning, Father." Paul rose to his feet and greeted the dean. "H'mm, Mr. Pesch," said the dean. "It's a good morning, I agree. But the air up here in your room is not a bit fresh and carries a peculiar odor, the fragrance of a rare perfume, I would say. Don't you agree, Mr. Pesch?"

"I hadn't really noticed, Father," replied Paul. Before he could add any more observations, the dean wheeled around and was gone.

"Sonovabitch!" Paul hissed. "He knew I had been smoking in my room. Somebody must have tipped him off, and it wasn't Charlie the squirrel."

He walked next door to Punk's room. "Punk, who do you think might be so concerned about my grevious offenses against God that he squealed?"

"What difference does it make, kraut?" Punk grunted. "In his own cute way, the dean was simply informing you that if you fail to desist from ignoring the commandments of the kingdom, you shall shortly be back feeding chickens on the farm."

Paul quit smoking in his room, and the rector, having been apprised that morning papers were being delivered to the recreation room, informed the paper boy to close that account. The world would conduct its affairs without the help of the seminarians, said the rector at his next conference, but he seemed to be more concerned with alcohol.

He informed his holy levites that if anyone should possess a bottle of the alcoholic beverage in his room, he had better unload it pronto, for a discovery of liquor in anyone's room meant instant expulsion. In addition, if one of the seminarians should be caught slipping into a bar during his weekly walk off campus, that too would also be an instant trip home to Mama. A holy fear seemed to lurk in the heart of Jeremiah Ludwig

Dobberstein that aiding and abetting demon rum to course through the veins of seminarians would lodge him into hellfire faster and more surely than anything else he could do.

"That approach to alcohol isn't going to do any good," commented Punk at the supper table afterwards. "I've been reading that alcoholism is a physical disease, an allergy, sort of, and simply forbidding anyone to drink isn't going to do any good. Well, anyway, Paul, they got you coming and going now, and I doubt if you will last beyond the first semester."

"Aw, shucks, Punk, you'll find out that booze isn't my weakness," shrugged Paul. "Breaking a few rules is more my cup of tea. By the way, I'll bet one of our hothouse plants squealed on me for smoking in my room."

"What do you mean, hothouse plants?" inquired Urban.

"They're the lads here from the prep sem on the other side of town," explained Punk. "They get hauled in there shortly after they're weaned and remain there through high school and two years of college. They never get a chance to know the ways of this cruel old world, and they could be ripe pickings for a chickenhawk after they're ordained. But it wasn't a hothouse plant who squealed on you, Paul. You know, you always have that guilty look after you pull something. All the dean has to do is take one look at you and call out the Marines."

"And you, Punk," Paul countered, "who are a ringer in the Pope's household, a communist in the convent, get by with murder because you can put on that innocent look which would deceive a Cardinal into introducing your cause for canonization."

At another conference Jeremiah Dobberstein mentioned another item forbidden to the students because it served to distract from the interior life, and that was the possession of a radio in one's room. It was legitimate, however, he said, to listen to the radio in the recreation room but only during recreation periods.

Punk poked Paul and gave him a knowing smile. He knew Paul had just inherited a little crystal set from one of the upperclassmen, who let it be known that it could be found hidden in the southwest attic of the Penthouse. These small attics were located on each corner of the penthouse where the roof sloped down beyond the dormers. Paul had lost no time making a search of said attic space, found the crystal set, and left it there. Being the owl that he was, just before the lights went out at 10:30 p.m., Paul ducked into the attic and retrieved it for a bedtime concert between lights out and when he could finally fall asleep.

The little crystal set needed an antenna, and the bedspring served well for that. Paul put on the earphones, moved the "cat whisker" over the crystal until it picked up a signal from a local radio station, and lay listening to the big bands playing from ballrooms around the nation.

But Paul's musical tastes were about to be raised. Christopher P. "Punk" McClanahan, who sat next to Paul in the refectory, announced one evening that the administration had just installed a new phonograph in one of the classrooms of the "freight house," and it could play the new 33¹/₃ records, which had improved fidelity. Punk was elated because he liked "long haired" music, and suggested to Paul that he might come to one of the music appreciation classes.

And one day Paul did stumble into the "studio" where they listened to "Clair de Lune" by Debussy. The fair-haired laddie from Lake Hebron seemed on his way to appreciating classical music. However, he still liked Sammy Kaye and Whoopee John.

However, the following summer he was dragged hollering and screaming to the level of grand opera. Paul had deplored grand opera; what little he had heard of it reminded him of a lady sounding off when she discovered a snake in her bed or a mouse in her dresser drawer.

Back in Lake Hebron, Father Joachim and his dog, Prince, were transferred to another vineyard. Appointed to succeed him was Father Herman Boecker, a thin, red-headed priest nearly six feet tall. With a ruddy countenance and a slow bass voice, Father Boecker also loved opera.

Whenever Paul hitched-hiked out to Lake Hebron, he always stopped in to visit Father Boecker because the priest always slipped him a ten spot, and ten dollars in those days was considered a fair amount of change to be lugging about.

Fr. Boecker had started an opera club in Lake Hebron for a few elite citizens, and they met every other week to listen to his opera records and lap up cake and coffee.

On a lovely day in June, Paul, upon being released from the brick yard for summer vacation, thumbed to Lake Hebron to collect another ten spot, and visit with his relatives. When he arrived at the rectory, he visited with the pastor for a while, after which Fr. B. chilled him to the bone when he said "Paul, I am inviting you to become a member of my opera club. As a matter of fact, we meet tomorrow evening. Won't you join us?"

Paul sighed as a stab of pain tore into his gizzard. "Oh, my, now I am paying dearly for my sponging off the pastor of Lake Hebron." He sighed again as the pain around his belly button intensified. "I can't refuse," he thought, "for I would displease the old gent very much, and it might dry up my source of revenue. Alas, I'm obliged to dance to his fiddle, and so have no choice but to listen to the ladies screech and thus do penance for my sins."

Paul replied, "Yes, Father, I should feel privileged to be invited to your opera club, and I thank you for the opportunity to appreciate the arts."

After extricating himself from the rectory, Paul muttered, "One thing they'll have to give me credit for is that I go down with flags flying, and I'm able to absorb the bad with the good. But, oh, my goodness, what an awful drag I face tomorrow night!"

Later on, Paul said, "Miracle of miracles! I learned to appreciate opera in one night, and for a clodhopper from the back forty like me, that's something to record in the annals of the Smithsonian Institute or somewhere."

26

The second year at the seminary resumed with Paul still aboard. Six days after the fall term began the students had a six day silent retreat. Strangely, Paul did not mind that period of silence. It gave him a chance to do some spiritual reading and think about it and gave him more opportunity to ask his spiritual mother, Mary, to lead him to her Son, Jesus, and to keep him in the seminary for another year.

For one thing, Paul was having a bit of trouble with one of the professors, Father Francis Missia, head of the music department.

The year before, a notice had appeared on the bulletin board: "All first philosophers are to report to the gym at four o'clock on Sunday afternoon to be auditioned by Father Missia."

"What's that all about?" Paul had asked Larry Kuntzman. Larry giggled, pulled the pipe from between his chubby lips and said, "It means that you're in for trouble, troubadour. You're going to have to sing the scale for the old boy, and a few other things. It's no secret around here that you drakes from Winona diocese can't sing Gregorian chant or much of anything else since you have no prep sem down there. Old Mish doesn't like you birds from Winona because of that. He's got a name for you mudhens, calls you 'lame ducks from Vinonah.'"

"Now where did you pick up all that stuff?" Paul had asked.

"It's common knowledge around here. Every year a new class of you swamp rats from Winona comes in for an audition, and you croak like frogs with tuberculosis. Old Mish gets mad and dumps you into B Chant, which is the lowest form of musical life in this institution. Hee, hee, it's going to be fun this afternoon!"

At four o'clock, Father Missia had awaited the new class for auditions and glared at them as they trooped in. About five feet six and overweight, his figure looked like a large pumpkin with a small muskmelon on top of it. He had large ears below a good crop of gray hair, a round mouth from which exploded a powerful voice on occasion, and although of Yugoslavian extraction, he spoke with a German accent.

Father Missia was a force to be reckoned with at St. Paul Seminary. The oldest man on the faculty with thirty-five years experience in dealing with young men, his opinion of individual students was highly respected by the rector and other members of the faculty. If, in a faculty meeting, Father Missia turned thumbs down on a candidate for this or that reason, the student was dropped right there. On the other hand, if he recommended a student to be given another chance, the lad was put on probation instead of getting kicked out.

At the time, Paul had not been aware of all this, nor did he know how importantly Father Missia would figure in his future. Paul thought the rotund professor was funny, and had to repress laughter, while his fellow students quaked in their boots.

When Paul's turn came up to sing the scale he couldn't make a sound because he tried so hard to keep from laughing out loud. In any event, Paul probably was not capable of singing the scale "do, ray, mi, fah, etc." in proper pitch anyway. However, Mish thought Paul was in the grip of terror, and that's why he couldn't sound a note, and the old prof hated the sight of young men exhibiting fear. Paul's name went down on the old man's hit list, which meant his days at the seminary were numbered.

"Ach, another lame duck from Vinonah," he hissed. "Sit down!"

On the way out, Larry said to Paul, "You got your ass in the sling for sure now, Paul. Old Mish is down on you. What in the devil made you giggle at the old bird?"

"Well, I think he's a funny-looking specimen, and the way he talks and acts makes me laugh. Aw, shucks, I'll win the walrus over somehow one of these days. Yeah, some day he'll discover what a diamond in the rough I am, what a good prospect I am for bringing the Church out of its doldrums, what a vessel of election I am."

"Bullshit! You'll be standing out there on Cretin Avenue thumbing a ride home before you know it, Paul."

That evening after supper Paul remained in the chapel to have a conference with his beloved Patroness in heaven. "Mother Mary," he prayed, "I'm not doing so good around here, it appears. Father Missia is on my tail and about to blow me out of the sky, I'm told. Put in a good word for me so I can win over the old hippo—I mean, the professor of music—to my cause."

Paul had Father Missia's ecclesiastical Latin class and, of course, also his B chant class, and in both classes the old professor looked at Paul like a farmer looks at a patch of sow thistles in his barley field.

Paul observed that Fr. Missia also disliked the effeminate type of student like Cecil Larkspur, who had adopted an Oxford accent and walked around the campus carrying an umbrella. Cecil was out of the seminary in six months, and Paul applauded that decision. Paul also noticed that the big mogul who scared so many lads half to death with his bombastic manner also seemed to have a secret love for young men who had a bit of nerve and took a few risks. "That sort of thing is right down my alley," thought Paul. "I'm going to pull something on the old boy one of these days."

An opportunity occurred at the end of the first semester in ecclesiastical Latin. At the end of the semester the students were required to turn in their notebooks containing all the written Latin exercises. Paul had gotten behind in this department and was scratching madly away in his notebook to bring it up to date at the last minute when his fountain pen suddenly left a blotch of nice blue ink in the middle of one page.

"By the holy pink-toed prophet!" Paul exclaimed. "Now I'll have to write the whole page all over again. This is enough to make a dog chew tobacco."

As he gazed at the ink blotch with wavy edges on the page, a light snapped on beneath his messed-up hair. He drew a couple of ribbons from the blotch and boldly printed the caption below: "FATHER MISSIA'S SEAL OF APPROVAL FOR EXCELLENT WORK."

While the class labored over semester exams, Fr. Missia inspected the notebooks. When he came to Paul's and noted the seal of approval, he hissed; "Vell, derefore, vat's diss?" Paul held his breath. His fate rested on the reaction of the professor.

Father Missia proceeded to scratch the end of his nose with his thumb, a sign he had gotten a kick out of Paul's seal of approval gimmick. Paul could now hang around the seminary for a while longer, that is, until the next episode.

In the meantime, Father Missia said not a word, but Paul noticed that the old professor's demeanor toward him changed. He no longer growled and called him a "lame duck" when Paul rendered a piece of Gregorian chant rather badly. The worst he ever said after Paul goofed up an "Ite Missa Est" for instance was, "Vell, derefore, Mr. Pesch, dot hass been composed before."

One day Fr. Missia noticed Paul reading the *Commonweal* magazine in class. (Paul would have preferred *Time* or *Life*, but no secular literature was allowed on the grounds.) Without a word Fr. Missia simply took the magazine away from him, and at the end of class, gave it back saying, "Go up to A Chant."

‡   ‡   ‡

The conscientious and holy Fr. Quentin O'Neill, professor of history of philosophy lectured one morning on the Chinese philosopher, Confucius. Paul was at the edge of falling into the arms of Morpheus when the good professor, to rescue him, called on him for a comment. Paul stood up and said, "It sounds rather Confucius to me." Father Quentin's countenance looked a bit pained for a moment, told Paul to resume his seat, and went on with his lecture.

"Ah, the man is such a gentleman," Paul said after class, "I'm sorry I let that one slip out."

"You, my friend," said Punk, "have just driven a nail into your coffin."

"Ah, well," sighed Paul, "a man has to keep life interesting around here, you know. But at the same time you should pray that I squeeze by to the priesthood. The Church is in great need of me to survive in this difficult era."

"I'm too cultured to use the apt response to your egotistical assertion," replied Punk. "But the word is bullshit!"

The next professor to suffer under Paul was Father Thomas Houlihan, homiletics. Fr. Houlihan, a serious man of short stature who usually manned the library, spoke very little, and neither he nor anyone else on the campus knew much about homiletics, but he was deputized to conduct a class in it.

One day Fr. Houlihan announced that everyone in the class had to give a practice sermon on the life of a saint, and please, not everyone select the same saint.

Paul scoured through the *Butler's Lives of the Saints*, and picked the last entry, St. Zozon, about which Butler had written but three lines. Paul used his fertile imagination to come up with a ten-minute homily on this obscure Greek martyr, a ridiculous account of this man's tribulations that earned him the crown of martyrdom.

"Zozon was diligently tending his sheep that afternoon on the hillside of a lovely Greek isle," Paul said, "and praising God all day when a trio of soldiers came along.

"'We heard that you are a Christian,' they said to Zozon.

"'I am a Christian,' professed Zozon.

"'You will then comply with the edict of the Emperor and denounce Christianity and give fealty to our great god, Zeus, they commanded.

"'That I shall never do,' responded Zozon.

"Whereupon these cruel soldiers threw Zozon to the ground and chopped off both of his feet above the ankle leaving him to contemplate the loss of his feet. This made him feel a bit depressed.

"'Ah,' he said, 'I must go into the village and warn the good Christians there about the Emperor's soldiers who go around chopping of people's feet.'

"So Zozon got up and walked to the village on his stumps, but, lo and behold, the wicked soldiers were there ahead of him, and they were extremely annoyed to see Zozon hopping along on his stumps. So they lopped off his head sending his soul straight to heaven.

"And, so, my dear brethren, we must learn from the example of St. Zozon not to be afraid to profess our faith boldly at all times even though our feet are killing us."

Paul delivered his tragic tale of Zozon very solemnly, but his peers who comprised the audience roared with laughter all the way through it.

Father Houlihan, though puzzled for a while, finally caught on and, besides flunking Paul, resolved to lodge a complaint against him at the next faculty meeting.

The next time Paul gave a practice sermon in Father Houlihan's class it came out even worse. Supposedly preaching on Christ walking on the water, Paul cleverly pictured Peter as the rector of the seminary, and the other apostles as the professors, but on the surface it all sounded very orthodox, Fr. Houlihan again puzzled over why the class rolled in the aisles. He smelled a rat in the freight house, however, and the more he thought about it, the angrier he became. He made a big production of it all at the faculty meeting even to the point of reading part of Paul's sermon on St. Zozon, during which Father Missia tried to repress laughing and got himself a stomach ache.

At the next Chant class, Father Missia called Paul to his desk after class and told him to lay low as a word to the wise. Paul read between the lines and realized "Mish" had persuaded the faculty to put him on probation instead of expelling him, but the old professor also let Paul read between the lines that there would be no help for him next time he pulled something.

27

A "word to the wise" dished out by Father Missia proved not sufficient; Paul soon gained another enemy on the faculty, Father Herbert "Squeaky" Nolan.

Father Nolan, professor of moral theology, also prefected Loras Hall where Paul moved after his sojourn in Cretin Hall. "Squeaky" Nolan's nickname came from his habit of throwing his voice into falsetto whenever he became excited or befuddled, and that was frequently.

One spring day the workers of the railroad yards were granted a free day to leave the premises after breakfast, but they had to report back in by 5:30 p.m. On this particular free day Paul and three other inmates of the yards went out to Lake Minnetonka, west of Minneapolis, where one of the boys had a friend who let them use his cabin cruiser on the lake for the day. They ran out of gas in the middle of the lake, and, by the time they procured a tow and got back to the seminary, they were three hours late. Paul undertook to be spokesman for the lost sheep when they reported to Squeaky's office.

"And what is your excuse for coming back so late?" asked Squeaky.

"Father," said Paul, "we were out on the lake in a motorboat, and we ran out of gas in the middle."

"What did you do?" Squeaky squeaked.

"Well," replied Paul, "we got out and walked."

Squeaky had made up his mind then and there that Paul J. Pesch had just hung himself and would soon be departing from the holy halls of St. Paul Seminary.

Poor Paul, in enough trouble, had to make it worse only a short time later. One Wednesday afternoon the whole student body was given a "4:30," that is, instead of having to report back at the usual time of 3:15 p.m. following a two-hour walk off campus, they were given an extra hour and fifteen minutes, which meant they could go to downtown St. Paul to shop or go somewhere else.

Squeaky felt almost certain that someone in the student body would sneak into a bar downtown and lift a few, and that Paul would be the one to watch. However, the zealous faculty member decided he would have to devise some strategy to procure the evidence, in other words, find some way to detect the smell of liquor on the breath of a guilty one. The students, however, were not much interested in consuming alcoholic beverages anytime and anywhere. Squeaky really wasted his time sniffing at this tree trunk.

Squeaky arranged that when the residents of his building reported in, he would have them check off their names from a list on his desk in his office. He would sit at this desk and thus be in sufficient proximity to the student checking in to be able to detect one who might have acquired a "snootfull," as the expression went. Very probably Squeaky was out to get Paul by this strategy.

Paul swung into Squeaky's office and smiled broadly as he bent down and drew a broad check mark behind his name.

"Felix the cat won't trap his mouse this time," he chuckled. "I haven't had a drink for over a year."

"Did you have a pleasant time this afternoon, Mr. Pesch?" Squeaky said as Paul bent down close to this proboscis.

"Yes, Father," answered Paul. "I most certainly did. I got drunk."

A scarlet tinge diffused over Squeaky's fat countenance, his anger near explosion.

When the word spread through the brickyard about what Paul had told Squeaky at check-in, a certain sadness settled on the air, for the student body had grown fond of Paul. Now he undoubtedly would be expelled.

Then the Vinegar Shampoo Caper. Squeaky, making himself obnoxious popping into seminarians' rooms, hoped to catch them redhanded with some liquor on the premises. The conscientious dean intended to collect a decoration from the rector, Jeremiah K. Dobberstein. Jeremiah had two great worries: one, that a potential alcoholic lurked among the saints in his kingdom, and two, a ringer hid among the holy candidates, only hoping to avoid the draft. Jeremiah felt that the Lord would favor him with the title, "good and faithful servant," if he could detect and escort to the gate any such unworthy candidate infesting his bailiwick. Knowing that, Squeaky determined to be a good and faithful servant himself in assisting Jeremiah in his zealous quest.

At his weekly conference with the students, Jeremiah let it be known how zealous he was to spot any such unworthy servants in the ecclesiastical enclosure.

"About the only ringer I can think of here in the brickyard is you, Punk," Paul commented at supper to his comrade. "But you're so clever you can fool them all."

Punk smiled and added his bit of wisdom. "An alcoholic priest didn't drink while he was in the seminary, the old bugger ought to know that. He catches that disease out in the front lines. I doubt if you, Paul, will ever go down hugging the jug some day—hugging a woman, perhaps, but not a bottle. But I think they're after you, nevertheless."

"You're right, Punk," said Paul. "You seem to be in tune with the

Holy Spirit at the moment, despite being the prime weasel in the chicken-house around here. As far as liquor is concerned I was cured of that one day when I was eleven. Uncle Thorval, a bootlegger during Prohibition, used to cache some of the stuff in our granary when the law was hot on his heels. Pa would leave a jug of the stuff in the cellar for guests. It was 180 proof stuff, and people liked to spike their pop and stuff with it.

"One day when I brought the eggs into the cellar, I decided to take a swig of Uncle Thorval's nectar to see how it tasted. It took only one swallow to put me into agony and firmly convince I had burned out my gizzard. Well, I lost my taste for demon rum for evermore."

Squeaky, not aware of all that, of course, felt that with the way Paul carried on with his brand of mischief he must be importing alcoholic contraband into this room too. And he longed to get the goods on this rascal who always made life miserable for him.

Paul knew sooner or later Squeaky would make a surprise raid on his room, so he procured a bottle of vinegar, tore off the label, put it on top of his wardrobe in plain sight, and awaited the arrival of the Secret Service.

One evening, as the boys were all quietly studying, Squeaky stole up the stairs and on tiptoe made for Paul's door.

Paul worked on an assignment and listened to the contraband radio when the dean rapped on his door and almost immediately stepped inside to better his chances of spotting contraband before Paul could hide it.

"H'mm, Mr. Pesch," he beamed, "how are your studies coming along these days?" All the while his eyes shifted about the room to detect what he was looking for. "A'ha! What's that on top of your wardrobe?" he asked with some glee.

"It's a bottle of vinegar, Father," said Paul.

"A bottle of vinegar, eh?" Squeaky sneered and fairly leapt at the "contraband," brought it down from the top of the wardrobe, screwed off the cap and smelled its contents.

"Vinegar!" he said dejectly, "What on earth do you want with vinegar?"

"I use it to rinse out the soap from my hair when I wash it." replied Paul. Not true.

The dean quickly slid out the door. Paul looked down and giggled. Squeaky had failed to notice the only contraband in the room, the radio on the floor next to Paul's chair. But Paul knew Squeaky had only one goal in mind—to nail Paul at the next faculty meeting and get him thrown out.

The next faculty meeting took place soon after, and Father Missia must have had a difficult time saving Paul's hide that time, for the morning after that, Fr. Missia beckoned Paul to his desk after A Chant class. "Ach, Pesch," he said, "I varned you about laying low before. Dis time you eider do vat I say or out you go. Verstehe nicht?"

"Ya wohl," Paul replied.

Paul immediately went over to the chapel and thanked Mary, the mother of priests, for looking after him when he wasn't using his noodle and begged her help in the future to be able to hang around until ordination.

A couple of months later Paul found himself summoned before the Prussian rector, Jeremiah K. Dobberstein. Jeremiah handed Paul a letter and growled, "I would appreciate it if you would let me know when you have been elevated to the hierarchy."

The letter, from Twighty O'Toole who kept up a correspondence with Paul, had been addressed, "His Excellency, the Most Reverend Paul J. Pesch."

"Inform your correspondent that, fortunately for the Church, you have not yet been made a Bishop, and that he should cease to assume a prerogative of the Holy Father by trying to name you one."

Father "Wooley" Becker, dogma professor, had developed a fear that the female of the species would pose quite a danger to priests after ordination and warned the class to stay away from them. One day in class he raised his long lanky finger and groaned, "Gentlemen, I beg you, never, never, touch a woman as long as you live. If you wish to remain celibate, again I say, never touch a woman."

During the few minutes of relaxation between classes, Paul said, "I think Wooley put it on pretty thick, don't you?"

"Yeah," said Larry. "How am I supposed to say goodbye to my ma. Hee, hee! Okay, Paul, you heard him. Keep your paws off the girls."

"No problem," said Paul. "I'll be content to offer up the adorable creatures of God, who made them, and faithfully hoe my way down the row of celibacy. I wonder what Wooley would do if a woman ran her fingers through his curls."

Wooley got his nickname from the heavy stand of hair he had, a light brown mass of naturally curly hair, which would have elicited admiration from any woman. Otherwise he was not particularly handsome.

In James J. Hill's railroad yards, however, a half dozen or so girls worked. Fresh out of high school in some small town, their strict Catholic fathers had moved them into the domestic department of the seminary, thinking they would be safe there from the incursions of the wicked world.

Usually one or two of these girls were real beauties, and the seminarians had a natural interest in inspecting what feminine pulchritude labored faithfully back in the kitchen. However, the view was much restricted. Between the refectory and the kitchen two small windows opened only wide enough to slide trays through, set low so that to get a peek into the kitchen to survey the field of females back there, one had to stoop down. That was a big "no, no" around the institution, since it indicated a predilection to taste forbidden fruit. Members of the faculty at their table on the raised dais could observe any of the boys doing some "peeking" and mentally chalked up a demerit. If someone made a habit of peeking, the faculty voted to dismiss him to pursue his love for women with much greater freedom in the outside world.

Punk expressed his unorthodox opinion on the situation one evening at supper. "It does not pay to be human around here," he said. "What we ought to have is a couple of dances a year in the gym inviting the k.m.s. (kitchen maids)."

The seminarians at the table laughed but knew that would never happen in a hundred years. (Actually, with the temporary collapse of discipline in some seminaries after Vatican II, the equivalent happened in less than fifty years.)

"What the Church ought to do, and be done with it, is to abolish celibacy entirely," Punk said.

In those days, to say that in Catholic circles was tantamount to advocating that a few subpoenas be served on the Pope, but the boys paid little attention to Punk's unorthodox views.

Urban Neudecker, usually quiet, spoke up at this point. "We can criticize and make fun of the faculty for entertainment, and characters like Paul bait them until he gets booted out, but the fact remains that despite their human quirks they are doing a rather good job of training us wild stallions to serve the Church and stay under the saddle when things get rough out there on the range."

‡ ‡ ‡

A few days later Wooley Becker got off the subject in his dogma class and made a few prophecies. "Gentlemen," he began, "the day is coming soon enough in this country when great affluence will replace much of the poverty present now in this country. Luxuries as we know them now will become necessities. A people taken up by comfort and convenience will be tempted to shortcut the moral law. They will not want to carry crosses anymore and will be deaf to sermons on penance and mortification. They will demand instant gratification, which they will obtain on the installment plan. And thus they will also vote themselves largesse from the public treasury and spend their grandchildren's and great grandchildren's money as they plunge the nation into a horrendous debt to finance their desires.

"In the days to come, gentlemen, celibacy, among other things, will be attacked since it calls for sacrifice and self-restraint. The attack will come mostly from clergy inside the Church swallowed up by the world and its ways because they stopped praying and cultivating the interior life. Gentlemen, this is no vocation for a man who does not value holiness."

The years at St. Paul Seminary passed rapidly. The fierce Armistice

Day blizzard came and went, affecting the seminarians very little. The Japanese attacked Pearl Harbor, and that didn't affect Paul much either, but it did his brother, Sir Edgar, who volunteered for the Navy and was sent to Washington, D.C. to work on a classified project at the Bureau of Standards. Toots, Paul's sister got married and settled down to raise children as Paul had told her to do only to be told to jump into the lake. Margie and Little Maggie, Paul's other sisters, after graduating from high school worked in Rochester and whooped it up on dates. Paul solemnly warned them that the wages of sin was death. "Who's sinning? Ya dumb duck," they replied.

28

A student from the Winona diocese traditionally held the job of representing the downtown McCluskey clothing store at the seminary. When the agent became a deacon he passed the job down to one of his diocesan cohorts. And so in his fifth year in the railroad yard when Ed Klein offered to hand down the job to him, Paul said, "Sure thing. Anything to drop a few shekels into my ragged pockets."

The McCluskey job consisted of advertising the line of seminarian clothing offered by the firm. To effectively accomplish that, Paul wrote up a sheet he called "The Fortnightly Review," which contained a lot of bull but always featured an item of clothing. He tacked a copy of it up on the Bulletin boards of all three residences about the time all came down for night prayer. After prayers, the lads crowded around the bulletin boards to read the infamous sheet. But the paper proved excellent for business, and while Paul received credit of only one percent on all purchases by the holy joes at the brickyard, he soon accumulated sufficient credit to outfit himself with a few new wardrobes and even stocked up a few for after ordination.

Of course, Squeaky also read the "Fortnightly Review" when it appeared on the bulletin board in his kingdom, but, to his credit, while he must have had fierce urges to take it down, he refrained, and Paul said that this good deed would probably get him a thousand years off his purgatory sentence.

During most of the academic year the theology students (the first two years were philosophy, the last four, theology) took their turns delivering practice sermons during the supper hour in the refectory. But with all the dish noises, the bulk of the sermons could not be heard except by most of those up there at the faculty table.

"Preaching is the weak link in the chain of salvation in the Catholic Church," observed Paul after one of the sermons. "There isn't enough emphasis put on it here in the seminary. Guys go up there and spell off dry prose and expect the laity to get something out of it. There has to be attention-getting introductions, stories illustrating points, more Scripture used, and a greater prayer life on the part of the preacher."

"Okay, Laacordaire," Larry said, "we'll see what you can do when you get up there. Say, why don't you give that one on St. Zozon again?"

When Paul's turn came, he mounted the dias next to the faculty table where the preachers and readers during dinner stood and began: "A p-41 fighter plane screamed over the Panama Canal in a high-speed dive, its machine guns spitting hot lead. . . ." And Paul never heard the end of that p-41 from his peers.

"Didn't I tell ya, ya gotta get their attention?" Paul insisted.

"What was our fighter plane doing over the Panama Canal in the first place?" asked one. "You know we own that bit of real estate."

"Well, ya blasted dumpkopf," Paul said, "If ya would have listened to the rest, ya would have known there were a bunch of Japs fishing for bullheads in it."

One day came the electrifying news that three of the candidates for the Winona diocese had been dropped by their bishop for low grades.

"How come he didn't drop you too?" Punk asked. "You certainly don't look like you are going to become a 'luminary of the Northwest,' to use the terminology of Father Missia."

"My friend," replied Paul, "You may be right that I don't seem to possess exceptional talent, and I'm certainly not an intellectual genius like the bishop seems to favor, but thou knowest, dear Christopher, that the Lord doth not require excellence in human talents and qualities to do His work. All he needs is a humble man who faithfully plods along doing the will of the Lord."

"Aw, go piss against the wall," snorted Punk.

"I'm glad, Punk, that you know a little Scripture. That phrase of pissing against the wall occurs in Josue 25:16."

Paul walked over to the chapel to thank his spiritual mother in heaven for putting a good word for him with the Commissar of the Diocese enabling him to escape the purge.

"The trouble with me is that about the only time I really pray around here is when I suspect that axe is being laid at the foot of my tree, and I beseech Heaven to allow me further residence in the railroad yards," Paul mused as he left the chapel.

At his next conference with the students, Jeremiah Ludwig Dobberstein talked about the weasel in the woodpile. He said he feared some student in the institution was there only to hide from the draft. At which Punk poked Paul in the ribs.

"Were you indicating that I am the Judas the old boy is worrying about?" Paul confronted Punk while they walked over to supper. Even if I were, honorable hypocrite, it would be justified for me to escape the draft lest the great tragedy of having my handsome face shot off should occur for the human race. On the other hand, it would be a great boon for the human race if your ugly mug were removed from the gaze of holy men who may becoming accustomed to gazing upon the face of the Lord. And, furthermore, Heaven forbid that you should father a clone to perpetuate ugliness among humankind, but that would still be preferable to placing you, another Judas, into the ranks of the priesthood."

Punk didn't laugh very often, but he did that time.

During the mellow Sunday afternoons of late spring and early fall when not engaged in his favorite sport, handball, Paul joined the promenade around the perimeter of the seminary grounds not only for exercise but also to get a glimpse of pretty young girls cruising up and down the Mississippi River Boulevard. Some years later a song got on the hit parade entitled, "Standing on the Corner Watching All the Girls Go By," and Paul remembered how he had engaged in the vulgar occupation himself once and at, of all places, the holy seminary!

The girls in their turn seemed to look with some longing at the handsome young men strolling along in long black cassocks.

"You know, Ed," Paul said to Ed Petka one afternoon during one of these strolls, "I can almost hear these gals saying as they observe us seminarians, 'Isn't it a shame that such good-looking boys should be cooped up like that? And what's worse, they are going to have to live all their lives without a wife. It's just too bad.'"

"Me, I'm just too busy envying their dates to be wondering what they think," said Ed.

"Now what you should do in a situation like this," said Paul, "is to offer up to the Lord all these lovely creatures He created and give glory to Him for creating them."

"Aw, pipe down, Paul," growled Ed. "You sound like an old monk with T.B."

But Paul decided to launch into a sermon for the fun of it.

"Remember, brethren, we are witnessing the secular world going by, the world which is not much interested in eternal things as in immediate gratification of the senses. But soon the gleam in the eye will pass, the flesh will expand into ugly folds and eventually wrinkle and shrivel. So, what charm doth you see in this passing world? Work rather for the things which do not pass away, aye, work not for the gold that rusts, the flesh that corrupts. Seek ye first the kingdom of heaven and these things will be added for you besides."

"Aw, what a hell of a sermon," moaned Ed. "You can't even keep your Scripture straight. Hey, look at that convertible. It's stopping. Maybe they want to talk to us."

And indeed that is why they stopped. In a shiny black Chevrolet convertible sat three nubile girls but only one male, the driver, and all seemed of college age.

Paul put his foot on the running board of the Chevy and his elbow on the top of the door. He gazed into the eyes of the girl in the front seat who had long blonde curls resting on her shoulders. She wore a freshly ironed cotton blouse of pale blue color. Her shapely knees emerged from her pleated white skirt. Paul decided to give her a speech he hoped she would still remember when baking cookies for her grandchildren.

"My dear young thing," he began, "you are indeed a ravishing sight for eyes usually glued to prayer books, and I confess, you distract me no end from the holy thoughts I gleaned this morning as I meditated on Holy Writ. What can I do for you this lovely afternoon? You servant awaits your command."

Ed stood a few feet away from the convertible and had not quite made up his mind yet whether to smile as tempted or retain a severe countenance befitting one called to eschew such worldly and vain speech. The blonde girl giggled with pleasure while the male driver, her escort apparently, listened and grew troubled of face. The two co-eds in the rear seat seemed entranced.

"It is indeed fortunate that you came along," Paul continued, "for I was saying to myself that while I can gaze upon those flowers up yonder in the yard and admire their beauty, their loveliness fades to nothing compared to the fresh beauty of the roses of Sharon I see before me now."

The girls now began to cast admiring glances at Ed, who was very handsome, at six feet tall and with black hair—"Tall, dark, and handsome" would describe him well. Although he possessed a pleasing voice he remained silent as Paul poured out the poetry.

"I am almost intoxicated with the sight of God's glorious creation in the form of you beautiful creatures," Paul continued. "I am almost tempted to sing the Canticle of Solomon. And before this inspiration leaves me, I must retreat from this vision of paradise and withdraw into prayer, asking the Lord to hasten the day when I can enter the gates of paradise. Adios, ye delightful creatures of Beauty itself."

Paul backed away from the Chevy and bowed gallantly to the girls, who remained transfixed, gazing at Paul and Ed. The male driver, meanwhile, had heard enough, shifted the car into gear and drove off with the girls looking back.

"Boy, you sure unloaded the biggest cargo of horse manure I've ever heard," Ed growled. "'The Canticle of Solomon!' Bet you can't quote a line from it."

"My friend," Paul answered, "what harm is there whispering sweet nothings into the willing ears of pretty young things? They hunger for poetry like that while their boyfriends can't get an inch above the mundane. 'Tis a sad situation."

"You keep on dishing out lines like that to females, bub, and you'll end up soon enough with one wearing your dime-store wedding ring," Ed said. "Hey! they're coming back. Hope they don't stop again. Neither that driver nor I could stand hearing any more of your bullshit."

Paul bowed to the girls in the passing Chevy, which did not stop this time.

"Brother," said Ed, "You'd better not be walking this trail again for a long time because I suspect those gals will be cruising by here pretty regularly from now on hoping to hear you pitching the woo again, and if

Dobberstein happens to find out you're a car stopper as you tramp on his turf, you'll be the one he'll be escorting to the gate. You heard him gloating how he'd like to kick the weasel in the woodpile out of here, and, weasel, you're the one he dreams of catching."

"It's indeed most fortunate that one aspiring to the priesthood these days should be prevented from acting like a human being in the presence of the female of the species, but I'll keep clear of Dobberstein's traps, I promise you," concluded Paul.

The walks Paul took from then on were twenty-minute journeys to the cancer hospital to visit the patients. Paul began to be quite fond of visiting the sick in his latter years in the seminary.

The Hawthorne Dominican Sisters operated Our Lady of Good Counsel Cancer Home, the cancer hospital in question. In order to be admitted a patient had to have terminal cancer and be unable to pay his way. The Sisters ministered lovingly to these unfortunate people.

When he entered the men's ward, Paul would sing out, "Hey, you fellas, time to get up, pack your lunch pails and head out for the factory before you lose your jobs!" The men in their beds or sitting in chairs would smile.

"Hubert," Paul directing his attention to the man in the corner bed who had been a farmer, "have you got your cows milked already? And it's time to get the oats seeded."

Hubert loved to talk about his days on the land, and since Paul shared his background, he loved to talk with him and looked forward to his visits.

One afternoon when Paul dragged along a couple of his friends with city backgrounds, he edged them over to Hubert's bed and said, "Hubert, these two fellers are city slickers. They have never milked a cow, never harnessed a horse, fed chickens or gathered eggs. They have never pitched hay into a haymow when the temperature was one hundred in the shade or plowed corn under a June sky. One wonders, Hubert, how they managed to keep from landing in reform school. Why, I doubt if the lazy bums ever even weeded a garden as they grew up. Now, Hubert, you and I have had it over them and became the salt of the earth, haven't we, Hubert?"

Sister Precopius, the Superior at the hospital, was always on hand to chat with the seminarians, and one afternoon Paul asked her what happened to little Stevie, a little three-year-old who had cancer of the larynx. Stevie used to run around the wards, and he especially delighted the women patients.

"Oh, Father, don't you know what happened to Stevie? That's right, you haven't been back since Christmas. Well, you will hardly believe what happened to little Stevie."

"I can hardly wait to hear this, Sister," said Paul, cheered by their joy. "Hey, you fellas," he called to his companions who were visiting on the other side of the ward, "Come over and hear what happened to little

Stevie."

"Well, you remember that Stevie had cancer of the throat," said Sister Precopius. "Christmas was coming, and Stevie was failing with each passing day. So we Sisters gathered around him on Christmas Eve, and we decided to try to get him to say the holy name of Jesus once more before he completely lost his voice. It took a long time, but finally Stevie did utter the Holy Name once more. That's when it happened. Stevie was instantly cured of his cancer."

"Marvelous!" Ed murmured. "How wonderful! Jesus heals today as He did in the New Testament times. What a story to remember for future sermons!"

29

That spring the call came out of the Chancery Office of the Diocese of Winona for seminarians to volunteer teaching summer vacation schools in small rural parishes where the number of children was so small it hardly warranted sending out the well-seasoned troops from convents. Paul volunteered and was assigned to Stockholm, a small village on the prairie. At Stockholm the small parish consisted only of a tiny frame church. Here Paul was to teach some twenty children, grades one through six, for two weeks. Classes began at eight thirty in the morning and ended at noon. Most of the sixth graders didn't show up because they lived on farms, and their parents deemed them old enough to help with the farm work.

"It's the old story," Paul observed to a knot of seminarians down in the rec room as they discussed vacation schools. "Farmers put the kingdom of corn and hay ahead of the kingdom of heaven in their lives. Someday when I'm a priest I'll remind them who sends the rain for their crops."

"Yeah," commented Ed Petka, "and they'll go to sleep on ya."

On a sunny June day, Paul thumbed his way out to Stockholm. As he stood on the side of the road he thanked the Lord for making that meadow lark which sang so beautifully from the top of a fence post nearby, and in the next breath he mumbled, "C'mon, somebody, give me a ride."

Stockholm had a population of 345, half of which were retired farmers and their wives, and the other half ministered to the needs of the farmers who tilled the fertile soil around the village.

Paul arrived at Stockholm just as the setting sun silhouetted the grain elevator against the pink western sky. The first person Paul called on upon arrival that evening was Mrs. Angus Duncan, the president of the Altar Society and also the reigning ecclesiastical power in St. Jerome's parish. Father Malachy, the pastor, lived in Winner, some twenty miles away and came to Stockholm usually only on Sundays for Mass. Georgia Duncan reigned as queen of St. Jerome's in his absence.

Georgia chuckled when she met Paul and, after sizing him up a bit, said, "All the girls around here will soon be after you because you are so good-looking. By the way, we have arranged for you to stay with the Olsons. They live only a block from here."

Honus Olson, head of the household, a big, brawny man with well-developed muscles that threatened to pop the buttons off his faded blue cotton shirt, had a thick crop of light brown hair and a plain face that mirrored his honest but forthright character. When he laughed he displayed an even row of yellow teeth, but he did most of his laughing down at the local bar, rarely at home.

Howdie (nobody called him Honus except Maria, his wife) ran a blacksmith shop where he welded things for farmers instead of shoeing horses, which his father had done in the days before the mechanization of farms.

Maria Olson, a small wispy sort of woman with a gentle disposition, said a lot of novena prayers and preached incessantly to her children, but always in a soft voice.

"They ain't gonna listen to you unless you holler good and loud at them like I do," Howdie informed her many times.

Howdie usually bellowed instead of speaking in a normal tone of voice. "Maybe you think I holler too much," he explained to Paul, "but I found out a man can't be heard down at the shop unless he yells, and it's got to be a habit."

So the Olson household was no place for a guest like Paul to sleep on Saturday mornings because the Olson chidren, three boys and a girl, took after their father and screamed most of the time instead of talking normally. The neighbors often commented on what a noisy household the Olsons were.

In addition to the four young Olson children—Eric eight, Josephine seven, Harold five, and Wayne four—was the Olson dog, "Horseshoe," a mixed-breed animal that resembled a bulldog.

"This is Horseshoe, our dog," explained Howdie when Paul first appeared at the Olson domicile. "His father was a purebred bulldog, but he wasn't particular who he jumped on around town, and so the pups were mixed breed. Horseshoe is one of the pups, growned up."

"Please, Honus, be more delicate in your language," pleaded Maria, pushing back a lock of her dark brown hair, "especially in the presence of the children." Maria was very sensitive about anything having to do with sex. At the end of each novena she always added, "St. Joseph, pure as a lily, pray for us."

"Well, for Pete's sake, Maria!" bellowed Howdie, "what are you aimin' to do if a bitch shows up on the street and Horseshoe takes after it—blindfold the kids?"

"Honus, it's just that you should try to be more delicate about these things," Maria replied softly. "While I teach the boys to imitate the purity of St. Joseph, you talk about dogs carrying on."

Howdie tolerated Maria's long prayers before meals and the many invocations that followed it like "Eternal rest grant unto grandfather Olson, and may he rest in peace." But when it came time for the family rosary after supper, Howdie skipped out, pleading he had to sharpen some plow lays for a farmer who needed them "first thing in the morning." Maria knew he never went to his blacksmith shop but rather to Mecklinberg's Bar for an evening of beer and sociability.

"Maria wanted to name our first son Aloysius after St. Aloysius," Howdie complained one day, "but I put my foot down on that. I figured that at least one of my boys would be named after one of my Viking ancestors and not always after some of those holy joes she thinks about all the time."

"Howdie, did you actually join the Church?" Paul asked him once.

"Yep, I had to do it, or Maria wouldn't marry me, and I had quite a hankering for that gal. But I'm not much for religion of any kind. Say, come to think of it, I can't figure out a good-looking guy like you wanting to leave the women alone the rest of your life."

Paul set up class in the church every morning at half past eight. Queen Georgia had made arrangements to start digging for a basement below the church as soon as vacation school finished that June. She said she didn't want little kids falling into the excavation during vacation school and get all full of mud.

"Say, Georgia," Paul inquired one day when he entered the implement shop on Main Street where the Queen sat behind a counter all day, keeping books, and waiting on farmers coming in for parts when the men were out delivering a new tractor or something. "Say, Georgia, I don't know how you can get away administering a parish like you do. That's the priest's job. Most of them would raise hell with you for trying to do what you are doing. Where did you get the money to put in the new basement under the church?"

"It's all in the treasury of the Altar Society. All the church money goes there, and I take care of it, pay bills, and so forth."

"Holy Toledo!" Paul exclaimed. "Canon law forbids that kind of arrangement. What's the matter with Father Malachy?"

"Well, he doesn't know what's going on and doesn't bother his head about it. There's nothing he can do about it anyway. I rule the roost around here."

And so Queen Georgia continued her reign at St. Jerome's during the tenure of Paul Pesch, who was supposed to be in charge of the department of Christian education.

At half past eight on the first morning of vacation school some seventeen future members of the holy Roman Catholic Church in southern Minnesota trooped in and put themselves under the tutelage of Paul J. Pesch, seminarian, whose knowledge of pedagogy never did amount to much.

Paul divided the children into two groups: the older group and the First Communion class, which included the first and second graders even though the first graders would not make their Communion until the following year. Paul spent most of his time with the younger group because first Communion was the number one priority at a summer vacation school. To teach doctrine and illustrate the life of Jesus, Paul used the colorful "Jesus and I" charts much in vogue then.

At the beginning of the week, Paul started working with the younger group. First, he wanted to find out how much they knew about religion.

He asked a little second grader, Patrick Nolan, to come up to the front and began interrogating the little buy.

"Patrick," he asked, "who is Jesus?"

Patrick stood there and fidgeted, ran one hand through his thick, tangled red hair and said nothing.

"Patrick," repeated Paul, "I asked you who Jesus is."

Patrick fidgeted some more but said nothing.

"Patrick, don't you know who Jesus is? You never heard of him?"

Patrick jabbed one hand deep into his pocket and the suspender snapped. He looked at Paul and said, "Nope."

That a child could reach the age of seven and not know about Jesus was beyond Paul's wildest imaginings. Paul was shocked clear down to his big toe, and, before he could catch himself, he blurted out, "Well, I'll be damned!"

Paul quickly recovered and fervently hoped the children didn't hear what he said or, if they heard it, would forget about it during recess.

However, Eric, one of Howdie's boys, had been up in the front of the class erasing the portable blackboard at Paul's request, and he had distinctly heard what Paul had said, and Eric knew what the phrase meant having heard his dad say it often enough.

Fortunately for Paul, Eric did not tell his mother, but that evening when he helped Howdie fool around with a lawn mower out in the garage, he told his dad. Howdie burst into such a fit of uproarious laughter that Maria, hearing it, sighed and murmured to herself, "I wonder who is out there telling Honus a dirty story tonight." The good woman never did find out about the unjudicious remark Paul, "a boy studying to be a priest," had made in front of the tots at Bible school. The next time Howdie got Paul alone he slapped the seminarian on the back and laughed uproariously again, "Eric told me what you said in class when one of the kids didn't know who Jesus was. Hee, hee, you're a man after my own heart."

In the afternoons and evenings Paul got on a borrowed bicycle and rode out into the country to call on delinquent parents who didn't send their children to the academy of Christian education. They, in their turn, got him off the subject and talked about farming and livestock, both subjects the salesman for the faith enjoyed more than the purpose of his visit. He usually ended up drinking a cup of coffee and consuming a piece of strawberry shortcake before sallying forth again. Even then he made little impact. "Man," he said to himself, "I just got to lean on these people more. I guess I'm not much good talking religion. And I want to be a priest?"

One afternoon while Paul walked past the Olson blacksmith shop, Howdie hailed him. "Hey, Paul," the burly blacksmith said, "there's a barn dance tonight out at Fleckheim's place. Wanna go along? I gotta pump beer out there?"

"Well now, Howdie," Paul replied with some hesitation, "I don't know how the good people of the parish would take to seeing their Sunday school teacher out at a barn dance."

"Aw, shoot," Howdie spat into the forge, "they ain't gonna make no fuss. Fact is, I think they might like to see you at one of their community social affairs. And you'll get a chance to get acquainted."

"Okay, if you say so, Howdie."

Maria Olson elected to stay home from the barn dance and cautioned Honus about drinking too much beer. She also looked reproachfully at Paul for electing to attend the affair instead of staying home and telling her children some more about Jesus. After Howdie and Paul left, Paul imagined she'd be paging through her prayerbooks, looking for a new novena to protect seminarians from the wicked ways of the world.

The community barn dance out at Fleckheim's intended to raise money for a new fire truck and seemed a suitable enough social at which Paul could be seen. The orchestra consisted of two fiddlers, an accordian player, and a drummer. A caller stood ready for square dances and circle two-steps. In one corner Howdie manned a couple of kegs of beer and ministered to a thirsty clientele.

In another corner, the Queen and a few of her cohorts from the Altar Society manned a lunch stand. "Have to make some money for our new church basement," the Queen said.

After all his dancing experience at the Chicken Coop, Paul experienced little hesitation in joining in and discovered he could dance better than any male up there in the barn haymow. His handsome, youthful appearance, his light curly hair, and his expertise in the terpsichorean art drew the attention of every girl in the hayloft. He tried to give them all a chance to dance with him instead of giving attention to just one lest the word got out he was "sweet" on somebody special.

The seminary faculty would be horrified at the thought of any student dancing during vacation times. "Wooley" especially warned his students "to stay away from contact with members of the opposite sex except when absolutely necessary, and then to conduct oneself with very appropriate decorum. I want you to know," he continued, "that temptations are rampant in some social gatherings where girls and women are present."

"Father Becker," asked one student, "you mean dances?"

"Oh, by all means stay away from dances," Wooley had answered. "If you take a girl in your arms at a dance you are inviting the sins of the flesh to take over and lead you down the path of perdition."

"Well, I wonder what Wooley would do if he saw me now," thought

Paul, as he swung Dorothy Anderson around. Dorothy, one of the girls he ran into when visiting farmhomes in search of his lost lambs, was a dark-haired, about sixteen years old and had about as perfectly formed a female body as he had ever seen. The sight of her made Paul's eyes dance the polka. Here she was in his arms and seemed to be as attracted to him as he was to her. Paul considered giving her another dance and whispered to her that he would be around again.

When he went over to the ladies' lunch counter for a glass of cool lemonade, the Queen leaned over and said softly to him, "Better not give much attention to Dorothy Anderson. Her dad watches her like a hawk and has no time for Catholics of any description. He's liable to get rough if you aren't careful. A word to the wise."

Paul decided to forget about Dorothy for the good of his health and next asked a girl he noticed giving him the eye. Wilma, unbeknownst to Paul, was the wildest girl in town and the most dangerous for a boy like him. About sixteen years old, with a volupuous looking body, Wilma's face however, was dotted with pimples. Still, her long blonde hair, shining after a thorough combing, framed her face rather attractively.

Out on the dance floor Wilma cuddled up to Paul as closely as she could, placed her cheek against his while her arm around his neck pressed his head closer. The presence of her soft body against his excited Paul so much he became uncomfortable after being so well trained in chastity. He also knew all the eyes in the haymow were on him and that made him more uncomfortable. "I'm putting on a show here," he thought, "which is going to cause a lot of talk here on the prairie."

The orchestra wailed out a slow waltz popular then, "Goodnight Irene," and Wilma looked up at Paul with adoring eyes, while he feared looking into her eyes lest she might impulsively unloose a kiss upon his lips. Paul began to perspire more freely than when pitching bundles of grain on a hot day.

When the music faded away, Wilma whispered huskily, her voice full of passion, "Paul, let's go outside and sit in my car for a while."

Paul, his libido burning white hot, was quite receptive to Wilma's suggestion, but then Queen Jacoba the Fierce popped into his mind, saying, "The only way to deal with a temptation against purity is to flee from it fast! Then your Guardian Angel can help whisk you safely away."

Paul excused himself, telling Wilma he had promised the next dance to Lulu Herrick, the niece of Queen Georgia, and he needed to find her but that he would be back for another dance. He bolted from Wilma before he could change his mind.

"Hey, Paul, come over and have a beer," Howdie hailed him from his bar. Paul actually had no commitment for the next dance despite what he had told Wilma, and, since she had disappeared, he stopped and took a paper cup of beer from Howdie. As he drank it, he muttered to himself, "Boy, I'd be as safe with Wilma in a car right now as I'd be with a trapped rattlesnake."

"Paul, how do you like Wilma?" asked Howdie.

"Well, Howdie, she sure comes on strong as you probably noticed when she had me in a half nelson there on the dance floor."

"You can say that again, Paul!" Howdie roared. The word is that if Wilma takes a real liking to a boy she usually has him rolling in the hay by midnight."

"Well, she's not going to have me rolling anywhere tonight," replied Paul. "Wow! I didn't think there were girls like that out here in the country."

"Aw, hell, I don't care where you are, Paul. There'll always be one or two gals circulating around whose mothers didn't bring 'em up properly. You know, Paul, Wilma is pretty choosy, though. The word is that she lays only one or two boys a year at the most, and they have to be topnotch. But, Paul, laddie, you're already nominated. No doubt about that. So stay out of the bushes with that gal. She's dynamite!"

"Thanks for the tip, Howdie," Paul said. "I'd better get the devil out of here before she traps me into another dance. See you back in town. Don't worry about getting me a ride. I need the two-mile hike back to town to cool off."

Paul quickly vanished down the ladder and out of the barn into the soft June moonlight. "Maybe the moon tonight made that gal daffy," Paul muttered. "They tell me she lives in town, and I suppose I'll be running into her again before this vacation school is over. I gotta stay away from her. I won't be able to hold out very long with that Delilah."

The next afternoon Paul stopped in to chat a minute with the Queen who said, "Say, the town's buzzing about you and Wilma. The odds are going up that she'll have you in her web within a week. Think you can hold out?"

"Aw, come on, Queenie, she isn't the first one to try tying me down," Paul said. "As long as Maria is praying for me, I'll escape."

Paul headed for the post office to mail some letters. Cutting across the street toward him come Wilma dressed in brief shorts, her bare midriff exposed below her tank-top blouse. Paul reflected, "She may have a few pimples on her face but she's pretty well stacked otherwise. Whew!"

"Hello, Paul," she greeted him with a about as sweet a smile as she could conjure up. "Where did you disappear to last night? You promised me another dance, you know."

"Well, I had to get out of there right away. My mother-in-law blew in and threatened to squeal about my bigamy if I didn't come up with some money."

"Oh, aren't you a joker!" laughed Wilma. "Listen, I have a little party tomorrow night out at the gravel pit. Just a few of us. We'd love to have you come. Swim, roast weenies, and mess around—you know. What do you say?"

"Thanks, Wilma, but I'm scheduled to go down to Winner and take a half dozen of my kids on a picnic along with my second wife whom I've been thinking about shooting."

"C'mon, honey," Wilma gushed, "stop giving me the runaround. Your second wife, my eye! I'd settle for being your first one. You know, Paul, I could just hug you to death!"

With that she waved her finger tips at him and slowly backed away. Paul quickly strode the other direction because he didn't want her to see how much he blushed.

"Wow! Imagine being down at the gravel pit with her!" Paul said to himself. "I'd be worse off than David closeted with Bathsheba."

Meanwhile, Maria had been informed about the brewing Wilma-Paul alliance and began saying two novenas a day instead of one.

30

On Friday evenings Father Sylvester Malachy, pastor of St. Ignatius parish of Winner and pastor of the mission parish of St. Jerome's, drove up to Stockholm to pick up Paul and take him along back to Winner for the weekend. There Paul helped get out the parish bulletin and stood up in the pulpit on Sunday to explain what was going on as Father Muldoon offered the Latin Mass. Paul liked the job and thought he did very well at it. Nobody told him that, because he mumbled a lot when engaged in public speaking, the people could hear only half of what he said.

Living with Father Malachy was very pleasant although he was a bit deaf in one ear, and when he didn't understand somebody, he always smiled and said, "God bless you."

Father Malachy, medium of height and slender of build, had a mouth and teeth a bit large for this thin face. When he smiled or laughed, one saw mostly teeth. The older priest possessed a keen sense of humor and was quick to laugh and tell jokes but also was a bit absent-minded and forgot to pray his breviary much of the time. His main virtue was his great kindness to everyone.

One of the neighboring priests, an old man wise in his years, told Paul that Fr. Malachy's kindliness still counted as a very important virtue in a priest, and Paul could do well some day to be half as kindly as the pastor of Winner.

When Fr. Malachy took Paul back to Stockholm Sunday evening to commence the second week of vacation school, they were surprised to see a large circus tent erected on the vacant lots between St. Jerome's Church and the corner oil station. Howdie explained the phenomenon right away.

"There's a medicine show moved into town," he said. "The village council—I'm a member of it, you know—decided to let them come in if they coughed up a hundred dollars for a license, and they did. They's gonna have a show every night all week long clear through Saturday night, and it's gonna be free. You're welcome to come, Father, and, of course, you too, Paul."

"Thank you very much, and God bless you," said Father Malachy with his toothy grin. Paul guessed that he had failed to hear Howdie's invitation.

Paul turned to Maria, whom he had started to kid a little now and then, especially about her novenas. "Maria," he said, "I'm sure you'll be down there at the medicine show every night buying booze under the name of some medicine, won't you?"

Marie smiled a bit wanly at Paul and said nothing. She had become very fond of the seminarian and made allowances for him.

"No, I don't think Maria will be at any of the shows," said Howdie. "She'll stay home and pray that the women in the show will always dress modestly and not give the men and the boys any bad thoughts."

The Hillburton Medicine Show opened on schedule Monday evening at 8:00 p.m. and the farmers did their chores a bit earlier than usual in order to come and see the free show. Even on the first night the company played to a full house.

When Paul escorted the Olson children to the show Monday evening, he ran into Wilma, who also waited in line to get in. She came over to Paul the second she spied him and squeezed his hand.

"Hello, Paul," she murmured. "I missed you a lot this weekend. How did you like it in Winner?"

"Oh, just great, Wilma," answered Paul, I helped make some mash for the still Father's got in the church basement."

Wilma squealed with laughter. "That's what I like about you, Paul," she said. "You're not stuffy like I'd expect a student preacher to be. Say, why don't you join us kids down at the City Cafe after the show. You know, lots of other kids are dying to meet you."

"Okay, Wilma, but you inform them that I'm going to try to make them all Catholics by midnight."

"I'm sure you'll convert them," said Wilma laughing again. "All except me. I'm going to give you a lot of trouble before I kiss the Pope's toe." She moved in close to Paul and whispered, "I'd rather kiss you instead," and kissed him on the cheek.

The show was entertaining enough for the country folk, consisting of vaudeville, melodrama, and, of course, regular interruptions to sell medicine. Max Hillburton, the boss, conducted a hard sell of his product, "Dr. Quadro's Elixir," which relieved most of the ailments of the human race. Taken by mouth or rubbed on painful areas of the body, the price was one dollar a bottle.

"That stuff really would be a bargain if it cured everything they claim it does," said Howdie the next day in the blacksmith shop, "but, of course, all the stuff is, is just moonshine with some sassafrass juice mixed in to make it taste a little like medicine. I bought a bottle last night for nipping off and on today, and it ain't bad hootch for a dollar a bottle. In fact, it's a bargain. You can't buy any booze like it in a liquor store for twice the money."

Howdie didn't confess that he had drunk a whole bottle of it with his friend, Hank Thulford, behind the train depot after the show, and they had had a little trouble walking home. Howdie had slept it off in the garage and was only back in circulation at ten o'clock in the morning.

After the show, Paul sauntered over to the City Cafe where Wilma and her friends sat crowded in a booth enjoying ice cream sundaes.

"Come over here, Paul," Wilma shouted when he came in the door. Paul sat on the chair placed at the end of the booth even though Wilma wanted him to sit beside her on the bench.

Paul looked over the collection of Stockholm's bubbling girls before him and said, "Hail, you beauties of this fair village! Your presence at the show tonight indicated your noble desire to heal the sick and bury the dead. But if you drink that medicine he sells this week, somebody will be burying you. But leave these mundane matters of medicine shows and follow me as I lead thee over uncharted seas to a paradise you have always dreamed about. You will, dear flowers of the youth of Stockholm, achieve this paradise if you but let me instruct you in the truths of the Catholic religion."

The kids responded with a lot of laughter. In those days Catholics feared asking any Protestant to join the Catholic Church and offending him, so the invitation Paul gave to the kids was quite refreshing. The young people enjoyed him. But all the time Wilma gazed at him as if in a trance. Paul felt uncomfortable with her eyes constantly on him, and left the company after telling them he had to go back to the tent and help Max make some more medicine for the following night's show.

The next day at vacation school all that the children talked about was the show the night before, and at recess they stormed over to the tent to look around. Here they caught Max Hillburton lying in a hammock smoking a cigar and taking regular swigs from a bottle of his second product, "Miss Cora's Remedy for Aches and Cramps," which he sold only to women.

"Get those damned kids out of my tent!" he roared at Paul, who had arrived to do just that. "For Chrissakes, a man can't have any privacy right in his own castle anymore!"

Paul didn't blame him for objecting to being caught boozing with his own product. He decided to tip Howdie off on the "Miss Cora" line since the proprietor seemed to favor it over the "Dr. Quadro" line at least for a morning picker-upper.

Paul give a severe lecture to the children after he shepherded them back to the confines of St. Jerome's and threatened them that if they set foot in the tent again during recess the devil would catch them and burn a hole in their big toe.

Howdie switched to the "Miss Cora" label for his drinking at Paul's bidding and delighted in the product. "The stuff doesn't have that bitter sassafrass flavor the old crook put in the men's bottles, and it's dang cheap whiskey. I'm going to stock up on some for the winter."

Maria was not happy to hear that. She had been praying for twelve years that he would stop drinking.

Max Hillburton was a good showman in building up an audience as the week progressed.

He sent out an agent to snoop around the village to get wind of some shady goings-on during the last fifty years, and he ran into the "The Stockholm Murder Case" which had never been solved. It had happened about fifty years before, but it was still talked about. The case involved a local farmer who heard a disturbance in his grove one dark night, went out to investigate, and ended up very much dead with his skull split by an ax. In that Max smelled possibilities for packing the tent the rest of the week.

Just before the finale Wednesday night, the house lights dimmed and the head honcho, Max, appeared on the stage dressed in a black tuxedo. The spotlight focused on him. He waited for dead silence before he began his speech in a somber tone.

"My dear ladies and gentlemen. It has been called to my attention the other day that many years ago a man in this community was savagely murdered. When one of the oldtimers related the details of this heinous crime to me, I shuddered with horror to the depths of my toes that a hundred years ago a heinous murder was committed in this community, and that to this day the crime has not been solved nor the murderer apprehended.

"By now, of course, you have become acquainted with our great Dillo the Magnificent, magician unparalleled. Dillo has graciously undertaken to solve the murder. But this difficult job can be done only by degrees, and each night on this stage you will witness Dillo the Magnificent as he breaks open the barriers to communicate with the murderer of this poor farmer. And on Saturday at our final show, Dillo will bring the ghost of this murderer onto this stage. Yes, you shall behold the ghost of the man who perpetrated one of the vilest crimes committed in this country, and he might confess to all of us who he is. Don't miss the shows on Thursday and Friday as Dillo prepares to bring the ghost of the murderer before you on Saturday night."

A murmur swept through the crowd at this announcement, which also drew a collective astonished breath. There was no doubt about the size of the crowd each night for the rest of the week.

"Now what do you think of that bird?" Howdie asked Paul after the show. "Can he conjure up a ghost, do you think?"

"Heavens no," Paul said. "That's just a good gimmick to get the crowd to show up every night."

"Well, he sure has the whole town eating out of his hand," said Howdie, and I gotta admit his medicine is good tax free whiskey. What do you think they got cooked up?"

"I don't know," said Paul, "but in any event you and I are going to have some fun Saturday night.

"Doin' what?"

"Messing around with Max's show Saturday night."

"Doin' what?" asked Howdie again. . . .

"Let's go over here out of the way, and I'll explain the deal."

Howdie listened and began to laugh deep in his throat. He agreed to go along with the plan.

During supper at Olson's, Maria mentioned she was adding Wilma's name to her novena intentions because Wilma had been running around town that afternoon clad in short shorts and causing the boys and men to have bad thoughts—a veiled hint to Paul to take pains to avoid her more than ever.

"Hell's bells, she shore had nice looking legs," Howdie remarked out in the garage where he and Paul went after supper. "Here, Paul, have a short swig of 'Miss Cora's Remedy.'"

Paul took only a mouthful, and it made him shiver like a dog emerging from the creek and shaking off water.

"Man!" Paul gasped, "that stuff's got a kick to it. Must be dang near pure alcohol. I don't want any more of that stuff, Howdie. It'll burn out the insides of my gizzard."

"Ya know, Paul," Howdie said, changing the subject, "I think Wilma was on the prowl after you this afternoon. Good thing you wuz out in the country on that bike. But if she gets wind of your biking she'll get on her bike, catch up to you out in the country somewhere, and then you will be in a pickle."

On Saturday night the tent jammed full for the final performance. The show followed its usual format of song, dance, and melodrama, with plenty of time given to marketing the miracle medicine. However, tension filled in the air as everyone awaited the climax of the Adams murder case at the end of the show.

Came the moment. The house lights dimmed except for the one spotlight directing its beam to a spot on the stage. Max Hillburton, dressed in a black tuxedo, white shirt, and black tie appeared on the stage. A murmur of anticipation arose from the audience.

With a flair for the dramatic, Max Hillburton waited for perfect silence and began in his sonorous bass voice.

"One hundred years ago in this quiet little community of hard working, God-fearing citizens, there occured a murder that was to shake the very foundations of this town. It was a brutal, bloody murder perpetrated in the darkness of the Adams grove that summer night.

"Many years passed, and still there was no progress in solving this heinous crime. The sands of time flowed ever onward, and the memory of this despicable crime gradually dimmed leaving only a tale told to children around the fireside on stormy nights.

"And so the murder remained an unsolved crime on the books of the Sheriff of Cottontail County until the day scarcely a week ago when this majestic production, 'The Hillburton Galaxy of Stars,' moved into town. Dillo the Magnificent felt some bad vibrations the minute we entered this community, and he immediately made inquiries among the older citizens if there had been an unsolved crime committed around here at one time.

"Upon learning of the horrible murder, I asked Dillo to gather all the powers of concentration he could muster and bring into focus the ghost of the murderer if he could. Obviously, the guilty man has been dead for many years, and all we can do is to bring the ghost of the murderer up from the infernal regions to stand before you and beg pardon of all for his crime."

Hillburton stood aside leaving the center of the empty stage in the spotlight.

"Ladies and gentlemen," Mr. Hillburton addressed the audience in hushed tones, "in a moment I will give you the ghost of the man who killed Orrin Adams a hundred years ago. Let all be silent now. . . ."

From the back of the stage the figure of a man with a large black cape around his shoulders, a three cornered hat on his head and his face covered with a veil shuffled to the center of the stage.

From the lips of Max Hillburton came a husky growl, "What the hell. . . .!"

The figure stopped in the center of the stage and yelled "I am George Washington, the founder of the country, and I committed the murder!" then back through the curtain.

"Goddammit, get that sonuvabitch," yelled Max and headed for the spot where the figure had disappeared.

The audience sat frozen at first, then burst into a laughter that went on and on, completely forgetting that they had come to se a serious climax of the drama, and not some comedy.

Hillburton, a veteran showman, had the presence of mind to capitalize on the unfortunate turn of events. He got the lights back up, signaled to the orchestra to strike up a crescendo, and came out to the center of the stage. "I must say you were surprised tonight, weren't you? The Hillburton Galaxy of Stars can always be counted upon to provide a maximum of entertainment, even providing endings with strange twists. And now I wish to bid you all goodnight, Ladies and Gentlemen. We have enjoyed playing in your beautiful little town, and we hope you enjoyed our performances. Come up and get your supply of our remarkable remedies for your ills before you leave tonight. Good night to you all."

Hillburton came out of the thing smelling like a rose. The incident could have gotten him ridden out of town on a rail.

In the nearby church basement Paul helped get the cape off of Howdie's back and divest him of the rest of his colonial costume. "You did fine, Howdie. Perfect, in fact. I doubt if anybody in the audience recognized your voice when you made that dramatic announcement. Hail to the Ghost of Stockholm! This should go down in the annals of the village for a hundred years."

"Yeah," replied Howdie, "little do the trusting souls around here know that you pulled this off and teach Sunday school besides. You're a man after my own heart, you young scoundrel. Let's go downtown and wet our whistles."

Paul decided not to accompany Howdie into the Municipal bar, and as he went into the City Cafe he spotted Wilma coming out toward him. She had seen him on the street from her booth by the window, left her friends, and dashed out to meet him.

"Hi, handsome!" she said as she snuggled up to him. "I hear you're leaving tomorrow. Am I ever going to miss you!"

Wilma wore short shorts again and a man's blue shirt. She had tied the shirttails together leaving a patch of midriff bare. In the early Forties such a style of dress was extremely daring.

Mrs. Lena Galveston sat in her car parked on the street where Wilma and Paul stood. She weighed over two hundred pounds, and Paul noticed her double chin quivering with horror as she gazed at Wilma. He steered Wilma back into the cafe saying, "C'mon, I'm dying of thirst. Let's get a coke."

Paul knew he'd better keep out of dark alleys with Wilma in tow or he might be the father of a child before the moon set that night. In the cafe he brought Wilma to a booth full of kids and announced that it was time for all of them to accompany him to the park and get a revival meeting going with Wilma testifying on how she got saved. After a chorus of laughter, "Pokey," one of the girls sang out, "Oh boy, what I'd like to hear is Wilma confessing her sins." That produced hooting and shouting of approval. Wilma shot Pokey a dirty look and urged Paul to go for a walk with her.

Paul knew going for a walk with Wilma would be like walking into a cage with a hungry tiger. He motioned for silence and announced to the celebrating bunch of kids, "I must needs repair to my room and take a few swigs of 'Miss Cora's Remedy for Aches and Cramps,' lay my head on the pillow and dream about all the charms of you lovely creatures. In the morning I must take leave of this bit of paradise and head back for the farm where my cruel father awaits to enslave me for the rest of the summer. Good night, dear girls, and may you all be swept to Camelot before midnight by a handsome knight charging in on a white horse."

Paul dashed out of the cafe and went straight to the Olson home where, surprisingly, he found Howdie home already. Paul was greeted by a guffaw from Howdie.

"Hee, hee, Maria, your prayers have been answered. Paul's guardian angel saved him from sin tonight. Wilma almost had him, but the forces of good prevailed. Man, was that gal decked out tonight! She could have seduced a wooden Indian the way she looked. But our Paul survived. Maria, you have indeed saved the day."

Maria smiled. "I wonder if you two didn't have something to do with the way that show ended tonight. Georgia thinks it was Honus who came on the stage and busted up the show. And I wouldn't put it past him. And Paul, I'm wondering if you didn't put him up to it. With all my praying, the devil still gets you both into mischief now and then. I just feel it in my bones."

And Maria sighed some more, and clasped her prayerbook tighter.

"Ah, shucks, Maria," Howdie said, "don't worry so much. Paul keeps me on the straight and narrow 'cause you pray for him all the time."

The next morning Paul guided his little lambs through their beautiful First Holy Communion, and Sunday afternoon Father Malachy came back to Stockholm to pick up Paul to take him to Wilder where he could start hitchhiking home on the highway going through Wilder the next morning.

Maria and Howdie and the children followed Paul to the car to say goodbye. Howdie bragged Paul up a lot to Father Muldoon and said Paul was the best thing that happened to the parish in the last fifty years. Father Malachy, as always, murmured, "God bless you."

"You must have had a swig of Miss Cora's Remedy this morning, Howdie to be putting out that line," commented Paul.

Maria who had become attached to Paul during the previous two weeks gave him a little hug and whispered she would always pray for him.

"I might be back next summer if Father Malachy invites me to teach vacation school again," Paul announced.

Howdie sidled up to Paul and said softly, "I know somebody in this town who'd love to kiss you goodbye."

"Howdie, you kiss her goodbye for me."

"She'd sock me one on the kisser. She don't take any guff from us old bucks. I'll tell her you'll be back next summer to keep her from committing suicide."

As the hot late June sun bore down on the sleepy village of Stockholm, Paul gazed upon the field of his first missionary activity with a little tug in his heart and hoped he would be back again the following summer.

31

The next day, at Wilder, Father Malachy handed Paul a generous check for teaching vacation school for him and said, "You got enough for the bus to get you home and some spending money for the rest of the summer besides. I'll take you to the bus station. God bless you."

"Don't wait for the bus to come, Father," said Paul. "You have things to do. Goodbye Father, and keep your liver in good condition. Maybe I'll see you next summer."

Paul wanted to get rid of the gentle Father Malachy so he would not see him starting up the road on the thumb instead of getting on a bus. Seminary rules forbade students to hitchhike, but Paul ignored that rule as long as he could keep this thumbing under cover. "Hells Bells," he grunted, "I'm not going to waste what little coin of the realm I can garner to buy bus or train tickets."

A dirty old Buick that smelled of cow manure and cigar smoke inside and driven by a livestock buyer took him the first twenty miles; a milk machine salesman, who gave Paul a lecture on mastitis, took him another twenty miles or so. Without very many delays, waving his thumb in the breeze from the side of the road got Paul to Mankato by noon. A little old man who took a liking to Paul went out of his way to take Paul to the east end of Mankato where it would be easier to pick up a ride going east on Highway 14.

Here a lady who was quite obese picked Paul up. She said she was heading for the Mayo Clinic in Rochester, and Paul clicked his tongue with joy, for that would take him almost all the way to the Villa.

The lady was probably not more than forty-five, Paul thought, even though her overweight condition made her look older. He thought her double chin made her face resemble that of an iguana. She wore a pink dress made of gauzy material with many frills. Her hat was a small bellboy type which seemed too small for her head, and she wore pince nez glasses which always fell off her nose and caused her to say "goddamit."

Every twenty miles or less, she reached into her purse on the seat beside her and pulled out a small bottle of whiskey and took a drink. Each time Paul declined her invitation to have a "swig."

"Madam, are you afraid of the Clinic doctors or something?" Paul asked.

"Why do you ask?" she snapped.

"Because you are always fortifying yourself out of that bottle."

"That's none of your damn business. It so happens that I need a dose of schnapps regularly to properly maintain the sugar level in my blood. That's why I'm going to the Clinic—to get that fixed up. Bill, my husband, couldn't stand to see me suffer anymore and sent me to Rochester."

"You mean he couldn't put up with your alcoholism any more and hoped the doctors at Rochester would somehow steer you into proper treatment," said Paul who had learned about the technique of confrontation when dealing with alcoholism the year before in the seminary and decided to try it out.

"You sonuvabitch!" she yelled. "I should stop right now and throw you out of my car!"

"Sorry, lady," Paul said, "I was just trying to be helpful. Alcoholics need to face up to their sickness and stop trying to kid themselves and others."

"You little bastard!" The woman shot an angry look at Paul with her bloodshot eyes. "For a nickel I'd dump you into a manhole."

"Now, Madam, please stop the car right now and let me drive before we both land in the ditch deader than a couple of mackeral in Boston on Good Friday."

"The hell I will," she screamed.

Paul leaned over and turned off the ignition and guided the car over to the shoulder of the road. Paul took command of the car.

As they cruised into the next town, the woman, who at one time said her name was Lydia, waved a twenty dollar bill at Paul and lisped, "Here, stop and buy me a bottle of Scotch."

"Okay, lady, but when we get to Rochester I'm going to take you to a house where you can get some help."

Lydia said nothing and sucked on the new bottle of Scotch until she fell into a comatose state. Paul drove her to the St. Mary's Guild house, a home for working girls presided over by Aggie Houlihan.

"Aggie," Paul pleaded, "give the old girl a bed, and when she wakes up, get Teresa Conway to take her over to AA if she'll go. But you'll have to go through her purse to find where she lives and so forth and call her people to find out what they want. If you have any difficulty, call me up at the Villa."

Paul thumbed on to the Villa and arrived late in the afternoon. The house was empty, and he opened the refrigerator door to find a bottle of pop to slake his thirst when he remembered the Pesch clan didn't buy luxuries like pop but drank plain cold water from the well.

Maggie Pesch came into the house from feeding and watering her chickens and saw Paul standing in the kitchen.

"Glory be!" she exclaimed and gave him a hug. "When did you get home? I supposed you hitchhiked again like you always do and one of these days somebody is going to shoot you."

"Naw, Ma, don't worry about that. When are we gonna have supper?"

"While I get supper you tell me all about what you've been doing the last two weeks out there in the sticks."

During supper Paul recounted his vacation school experience emphasizing what a great missionary endeavor it was and leaving out his part in goofing up the medicine show finale and, of course, not a word about Wilma.

Paul's siblings who lived at home at that time were Sir Edgar, Paul's younger brother; Margery, who was at home visiting from her job in Rochester; Maggie, a senior in high school, who was not home at the time; and Darlene, the latecomer in the family who was still in grade school. Sir Edgar was impressed by Paul's recital of his missionary journey "comparable to St. Paul's first missionary journey in the Acts of the Apostles" as Paul put it. Marge was not impressed and expressed her guess that Paul probably spent the entire two weeks bumming around on the thumb.

A leisurely summer for Paul there on the Villa, all he did was mow the lawn and sit under the oak trees out on the terrace between the house and the creek and read books, the novels of Thomas Hardy that particular summer.

One day Sir Edgar suggested that they overhaul the tractor which was about seven years old by then. The idea appealed to Paul although his expertise in tractor engineering was nil.

The next morning the two busily disassembled the engine of the John Deere Model B.

Joe Pesch came along and said, "What do you two think you're doing?"

"Well we was gonna overhaul the engine," said Paul. "She seems to be losing compression. You even said yourself once that it might need to be overhauled."

"All I can say is that you two better have it running in the morning to start plowing or you're going to have to plow by hand behind a team of horses." Then, shaking his head, he added, "Ach, you two dumkopfs, you can't overhaul no tractor!"

And mumbling to himself, Joe went on toward the barn lugging parts of the milking machine which Maggie had washed.

"Jeepers," said Sir Edgar, we sure better get this job done right. Think we really can do it?"

"Well, shucks," said Paul, "there really isn't much to it." But he thought that maybe when they took the block into town to have the valve seats ground, he would ask around in the shop about some of the details of reassembling the engine. It was easy enough to take it apart, of course.

The kind mechanic at the John Deere implement shop in Chatfield took some time to instruct the two budding engineers on the procedure of reassembly and timing, warning that they might have to remove a shim or two from the bearings in the connecting rods to make up for the past wear.

The two amateur mechanics resumed their operation at the Villa after lunch, and fortunately everything seemed to fall into place without difficulty. However, they made one mistake, namely, they removed two shims from the connecting rod bearings instead of one.

Reassembly of the engine ended by three-thirty. An inkling that there was trouble ahead manifested itself when it came time to start the engine. Paul grabbed the flywheel to turn over the engine but it wouldn't budge.

"Well, of course, an engine is stiff after an overhaul job, you know" Paul said to Sir Edgar. "Let's get some more leverage on that flywheel to loosen up the bearings."

They found a crowbar and by inserting bolts into the holes of the flywheel they were able to clamp the crowbar between the bolts and put their weight on the crowbar. That turned the engine over but only inches at a time.

"I don't think we can get it started by the ordinary cranking method," Paul observed. "Yet we have to get it started somehow in order to loosen the bearings a bit. All newly overhauled engines are tight, you know. They have to be broken in."

"I got an idea," Paul continued. Let's go over and borrow the neighbor's tractor and pull the John Deere of ours to the top of the hill above the barn, and then we'll run our tractor down the hill to get some speed, and then we'll throw the clutch in. That'll spin the engine and she'll start."

It was a hare-brained scheme.

They pulled the John Deere up the steep slope of the hill above the barn (which Paul had named "Mt. Hermon") with Paul Wright's tractor, turned the John Deere around so it headed downhill.

"I'll mount our beast and after I get it rolling down the hill, I'll throw in the clutch," Paul said.

Sir Edgar leaned against the borrowed tractor to watch the performance.

Paul, released the brakes, and the John Deere began to roll. The tractor, still equipped with steel rear wheels with long spade lugs, took a few seconds to build up some speed even on this steep grade. At the proper moment when the rig rolled along at a fairly good clip, Paul threw in the clutch. Since the engine was too tight to turn over, the spade lugs dug into the ground and the tractor literally stopped on the proverbial dime. Paul plunged forward, his body grazing the steering wheel, and he went headlong into one of the small piles of hay drying in the sun. His guardian angel put it at the right spot to break his fall.

Paul got up, brushed the hay from his clothes, retrieved his straw hat and, with his dirty handkerchief, tenderly daubed the scratches on his face acquired by his abrupt descent back to the bosom of Mother Earth. Sir Edgar came over to check the condition of his brother who had outdone the performance of any human cannonball in Barnum and Baily's Circus.

At this point some semblance of wisdom returned to Paul's cerebellum, and he said to Sir Edgar, "I think maybe we took out too many shims from those bearings. Let's put one back in each one."

They got the machinery back down the hill and proceeded to repair their oversight on the bearings. After replacing the shims, they were able to turn over the engine by hand and get it started.

"Oh boy, am I glad Pa wasn't around to see what happened," said Sir Edgar.

"Oh, yah, that's for sure," said Paul, thinking about the time only a couple years before when he had rolled the John Deere all the way down Golan Heights to the Plain of Esdraelon, denting it up considerably. On that occasion his honorable ancestor had impressed upon him his obvious unfitness to be a farmer, concluding that he was, in fact, a menace to agriculture.

Joe Pesch would probably have been confirmed in this judgement had he witnessed another performance of said offspring the following afternoon.

Joe told his sons to hitch up a team to the hayrack and bring in the haycocks on the slope of Mt. Hermon and stow them in the haymow of the barn.

Paul decided to load them all on one load, but that was too much. The horses couldn't hold back that much weight going down the hill, resulting in the loaded hayrack careening out of control. Paul, with the reins in his hand, standing on top of the load, knew it was folly to head the runway into the haymow, for then both horses and load of hay would plunge through the opposite wall of the haymow and crash to the ground one story below.

The only alternative would be to take the driveway from the slope down into the farmyard below and head out toward county road. Paul managed to guide the team into the driveway and prayed the galloping horses and the hurtling load of hay wouldn't clip off the yard light post and possibly crash into the granary after arriving in the farmyard. Paul's guardian angel went to work, and the mess finally came to a halt at the entrance to the county road.

Paul let out a sigh of relief, and just then Lucille Nystrom came along in her dad's car, slammed on the brakes, sang out, "Paul, c'mon over and see me sometime."

Paul said to himself, "Golly, I got enough trouble without a roll in the hay with that curvy creature."

32

A few years passed, and there were only two years before ordination of one Paul J. Pesch, if he could continue to survive the temptations of the world, the flesh and the devil.

The nation had been in war for two years, and the bishops had decided to accelerate the seminary course for two reasons: A shortage of priests had developed with so many in the chaplain's corps of the armed forces, and the sooner the seminarians were ordained the sooner they could be put to work in parishes. Secondly, the bishops decided that healthy-looking young males from the seminary should be kept out of the public eye when their age counterparts had been drafted. Summer vacations, therefore, was shortened from three months to one.

Paul returned to the Brickyard that fall of 1943, and the thought struck him that during the previous year he had been on fairly good behavior. In the meantime, his bishop had died and had been replaced by Bishop Louis Betka. This new ordinary of the diocese was trying very hard to alleviate the shortage of priests in his bailiwick, making it unlikely that he would clip Paul from receiving Holy Orders on schedule unless he publicly denied the doctrine of the Blessed Trinity or called the Pope the anti-Christ. Paul breathed a bit easier and decided to let up the restraints a bit and have a little fun again.

Mid-year vacation began as usual on January 25, and Paul boarded a bus to Rochester for two weeks of relaxation at the Villa.

It was night, and he was garbed in a new black suit, white shirt, and black tie, all courtesy of his commissions as the stellar sales representative at the seminary for McCluskey's. He had stored his new black hat and woolen topcoat on the rack above the seat.

A woman he judged to be perhaps thirty-five, sat beside him. She peered at Paul in the semi-darkness and opened the conversation. "H'mm, I see you're a Naval Officer," she said, With the black tie, white shirt, and black suit Paul might pass for a Navy man. At the time there were many such personnel to be seen.

Paul was about to deny her mistaken identity of him, but decided that they would be on that bus for almost three hours and he might as well make the ride interesting.

"Yes, as a matter of fact I am serving in the Navy," he replied gravely.

"In what branch of the Navy are you?"

"I'm in Naval Intelligence, Ma'am."

"Oh, my goodness, how interesting!" she gushed. "Have you had many unusual experiences in that type of service?"

"Yes, ma'am."

"Call me, Lillian, won't you? Could you perhaps tell me about one or two of them without violating classified material?"

"Well, Lillian . . . I might be able to relate a few of them without violating Naval secrecy. However, I'd rather you did not repeat them."

"Oh, I'd never breathe a word to a single soul," Lillian pledged.

Paul used his fertile imagination and related a few capers, during which she gave him her full attention.

"Perhaps," Paul continued, "You might find our Operation Bedpost recently completed in Germany quite interesting."

"Oh, my, I can hardly wait to hear about it!" she said with bated breath.

"I was working in conjunction with British Intelligence at the time," Paul said in a very serious tone of voice. "The British were getting desperate with the German U boats ravaging their merchant marine and seriously threatening the war effort. It was imperative, therefore, that information be obtained concerning the location of as many U boats as possible and their projected movements. But in particular we needed information on the sailing orders of the new German super battleship, the *Bismarck*, due to sail from Bremerhaven on her initial voyage."

"Yes, yes, do go on!"

"Information had leaked out that Adolf Hitler had been talking in his sleep. Since the details of the German war effort were constantly on his mind, our high command felt that he might also talk in his sleep about these matters. I had been briefed on the arrangements of Hitler's Eagle Nest retreat, the Kehlsteinhaus, where Hitler was spending a few days. I managed to sneak into the house one night and, very fortunately, attained my post under Hitler's bed where I could listen to him talk in his sleep."

Paul looked over at the woman, an attractive fur-lined cowl resting on her shoulders, and it seemed to him she not only listened with rapt attention to his every word as he spun his fantastic fabrications but apparently believed every word!

"What kind of creature is this anyway?" Paul asked himself. He looked closely at her and noted that she was quite attractive. Maybe she just wanted to believe the nonsense he told her. Maybe it was a simply temporary fascination on her part. In any event, Paul knew he would have to puncture the balloon soon, as the lights of Rochester came up in the distance.

"My dear Lillian," Paul said, "I can see you are a very charming person, and I have been enjoying talking to you lo these many miles. But now I have to make a confession. All I have been telling you has been pure fabrication to pass the time. I'm no naval officer but a seminarian expecting to be ordained a priest within a year or two, a person who shouldn't be telling you tall tales. Can you forgive me?"

Lillian shook her head slightly as if coming out of a trance. Her face, seemingly frozen, broke into a smile.

"Of course, I forgive you," she murmured. "You've made this a most enjoyable trip, and I must say you possess a great imagination. Your sermons should be masterpieces."

"Not necessarily, my charming lady. To be a good preacher one has to be a man of prayer, not a dang liar like me."

The bus pulled into the depot. They exchanged names and addresses, and Lillian invited Paul to visit her at her home where she would be delighted to listen to some more of his "war stories."

Paul decided that gracing her home with his august presence wouldn't contribute anything to making him a better priest. Rather, it might be a rose garden of temptation. "I most certainly must decline your gracious invitation, sweetheart," Paul whispered under his breath.

The following summer Paul returned to the Villa for the month of vacation the seminarians were allowed. In the meantime, Sir Edgar had enlisted in the Navy after the draft board started breathing down his neck. He figured the Navy offered more training in electronics than any other branch of service, and at the moment he was stationed at Oklahoma A & M College down in Stillwater, Oklahoma, learning Naval radar.

"Ma, I'm gonna hitchhike down to Stillwater to see Edgar," Paul announced after lying around the Villa for a few days instead of helping with the work.

"Paul, are you going bumming again?" Maggie said, a bit aghast at the idea. "That's a long ways down there, and nobody will pick you up, and when somebody does pick you up he might shoot you."

"Ma, I'm such a charming person that people thank the Lord just for the privilege of giving me a ride. Besides that, as an official mouthpiece of the Lord soon I'll get some practice at preaching to the kind souls who pick me up especially if they need someone to lay out the road to Heaven for them."

"You'll more likely start flirting with the women who pick you up, Paul. Sometimes I don't know why you want to become a priest. You're not very pious and you sure don't act like a priest."

"Ma, you always say you can't judge the book by the cover. You don't know what's going on inside me. I could be a holy joe for all you know."

A holy joe, Paul knew he was not. But a priest, he knew he wanted to be, and he decided to leave it at that for the moment.

On a warm August morning, Paul walked the half mile down the country road to US 52, dressed in his black suit, white shirt, and black tie. "Only a wretch blinded by the devil would refuse to pick me up today considering how neatly I'm dressed," mused Paul.

Because of gasoline and tire rationing during the war, traffic was light and rides short. However, by evening Paul had traveled through Iowa and found himself at Muscatine as the sun set.

Paul sat down on his suitcase along a curb at the edge of town, noted a hamburger stand nearby, walked over and bought one for supper. As he ate his hamburger, Paul listened to the chorus of locusts filling the evening air with their unmusical serenades and started thinking about plans for the night.

He didn't want to hitchike all night because that didn't work. People seemed to hesitate picking up anyone at night for the same reason they didn't picnic in cemeteries. It made them nervous. On the other hand, getting a room at a hotel would be too expensive for Paul's limited financial resources. Another option entered Paul's mind—get on a bus and you automatically have a place to doze off while moving closer to your destination.

Paul went over to the hamburger stand again, and asked the proprietor, a middle-aged balding man, "Say, is there a bus heading toward St. Louis from here this evening?"

"Yep. Leaves in about an hour and gets into St. Louis in the morning sometime. Kind of a rattletrap, though, but I guess they have to make do with it with this war going on."

"Will he stop for me if I flag him as he goes by? Or does he go out of town by another road?"

"Oh, he'll come by here all right. This leads to the river road going to St. Louis. Yah, he'll stop if you flag him."

While waiting for the bus, Paul studied the huge elm tree that shaded the hamburger stand, trying to guess its age and wondering how many people had died in that town since that tree had been planted and how many went to heaven and how many went to hell.

A pretty, teenage girl came walking down the sidewalk. Instead of wearing shorts on such a warm evening, she wore a plain blue dress with a high collar and sleeves which came to her elbows. "I must get to know this unusual girl better. She looks like a diamond in a coal bin," thought Paul.

"Good evening, Miss. You are indeed a lovely looking girl. Do you live here?"

The girl smiled faintly at Paul, but soon her face took on a fearful look. She edged over to the other side of the walk, giving Paul as wide a berth as possible. After a few more steps she started running. Paul addressed the man at the hamburger stand.

"Do I look like a lizard from Livermore or a scorpion from Salt Lake? She took off like a scared rabbit. What's the problem?"

"Oh, she's Dan Pentard's daughter. He's awfully strict with her and won't allow her to say a word to a stranger. Say, what are you doin' all dressed up in black like that? Look like an undertaker."

Paul took up the rest of the time while waiting for the bus enlightening the man about himself and that being dressed up helped like the deuce getting rides.

"Well, blow me down!" the stout hamburger maker said. "A preacher bumming rides. Do you preach to everybody who stops to pick you up?"

"No not unless they seem interested in religion. Then I do. I always try to convince them that Jesus Christ founded only one church nineteen hundred years ago, and that one happens to be the Catholic Church."

That statement riled up the hamburger chap. He shouted, "You're dead wrong there, brother! I'm a good southern Baptist, and I know the Roman Church is the whore of Babylon as the Bible says."

The bus came along at this juncture. Paul picked up his suitcase, flagged the bus and gave a parting wish to his Baptist friend, "My good man, may the Holy Spirit guide you into the harbor of truth, the Holy Roman Catholic Church. Adios!" Then Paul climbed onto the bus.

"I don't have a ticket," Paul said to the unshaven driver. "How much to St. Louis?"

The driver, with a cigarette hanging from the side of his mouth, waved him to the back of the bus. "Buy a ticket at the next town we stop at."

Paul spied an empty seat in the back of the bus, the window seat next to it occupied by a young black. Paul sat down beside him, and that seemed to make the black very nervous, and he started to fidget.

"What's the matter with these people around here?" Paul mused to himself. "This black, for instance, seems to be scared of me."

Giving the driver the ticket he bought at the next stop, Paul remarked, "How come that black man I sat with back there was so scared of me?"

"Them niggers," the driver said, "they's scared of whites when whites sit with them 'cause they think the white man is going to get after them for being 'uppity' for having the nerve to sit with a white man. Course, you ain't supposed to be sitting with a nigger either. You either stand up until a nigger offers you a seat or better still, you order the nigger to get the hell out of that seat he's got so you can sit down. Jes' don't go sittin' alongside of no nigger no more."

Paul returned to his seat in the back, but now the black stood in the aisle in the back. "My goodness," Paul whispered to himself, "if this isn't the dangedest situation I ever ran into!"

That was Paul's first encounter with racism. Up until then he hardly knew the meaning of the word, since he grew up without seeing a black anywhere.

The bus, hardly more than a rusty old school bus, was noisy, the windows rattled, and the skimpy upholstery was torn in about every seat.

About one o'clock in the morning the bus rattled into a deserted village to leave off a passenger. On the sidewalk in front of the bus stop stood an intoxicated man, in his fifties perhaps, and a woman, apparently his wife. She shouted at him at the top of her voice, obviously showing keen displeasure because he was drunk. In order to escape her stinging tongue, the poor man ducked into the bus, which left with him aboard.

"Where do you wanna go?" asked the driver.

"I wanna go to shee my horsh," the drunk managed to spit out while swaying back and forth as he stood in the front of the bus.

"Where is your horse?"

"Shomwhere in a barn dere." He pointed down the road.

When the bus came to the next barn situated fairly close to the road, the driver asked him:

"Izzat where your horse it?"

The drunk swayed back and forth some more and finally said, "Nope."

The bus passed two more barns near the road, but the drunk denied his horse was in any of them. At the next barn the driver stopped, persuaded the fellow that his horse was indeed in that one and half pushed the man off the bus. By that time, the poor man had traveled fifty miles from home.

About eight in the morning when the bus arrived in St. Louis, the heat became oppressive. Paul had had little to no sleep in the poor excuse of a bus. His black suit crushed, his white shirt soiled, and feeling clammy, he wished he was back at the Villa bathing in the cool waters of the Brook Cedron.

Paul ate breakfast in a cheap restaurant near the bus depot, found a bus heading out on US 66 toward Springfield, rode it to the first stop outside of St. Louis, and resumed thumbing. The sun made Paul feel like a lizard in a blazing woodshed.

A rattletrap of a pickup truck hove into view, and, although Paul didn't want to ride in it, anything seemed better than standing on the side of the road suffering in the heat of a Missouri midsummer day.

The wreck stopped, and Paul climbed into a very messy cab, with an array of rusty wrenches, a half ball of twine, discarded paper bags, and quite an accumulation of peanut shells scattered on the floor. The driver wore a tattered black felt hat with many holes in it and a greasy denim shirt tucked inside bib overalls, which looked like they had never seen a laundry tub. He sported a black beard, and Paul decided he must be a hillbilly from the Ozarks.

"Good morning, sir!" Paul sang out in a cheery greeting as he usually did when about to embark upon a journey fueled with somebody else's gas.

No response. The driver popped a peanut, shell and all, into his mouth, ground it with his teeth, and blew out the remnants of the shell. Then he chewed the peanut. "That's a slick trick," thought Paul, "but I wonder why the old bugger doesn't say something."

"Where are you heading for?" Paul tried again.

"Up the road a piece," he grunted, and said nothing more for the next hour, but continued shelling and chewing peanuts. When his right hand was empty of peanuts, he extended it in the direction of Paul and motioned toward the glove compartment. Stuffed in the glove compartment was a paper sack still half full of peanuts. Paul grabbed it and poured some into the man's hand. When the driver consumed this ration, they repeated the procedure. However, when the man blew the shells out of the window, the wind blew half of them back inside, and two or three inches of them accumulated on the ledge above the seat in back, a couple of inches on the seat, and maybe six inches on the floor because the driver occasionally swept them off the ledge and the seat.

About fifty miles up the road the man drove up to a beer joint and motioned to Paul to accompany him inside. There he ordered two bottles of cold beer and pushed one toward Paul. Paul welcomed the libation on that hot afternoon. The hillbilly uttered not a word while he drank his beer, motioned to Paul toward the truck, and they resumed their journey.

After another fifty miles the bearded driver got thirsty again after eating all those salted peanuts, and drove up to another beer dispensary. The third time Paul politely declined another bottle of beer.

"No thank you, I've had enough," he said.

Then the hillbilly spoke the second time. "Drink it, damn ya."

Paul, who didn't know much about the code of hospitality practiced in the Ozarks, had read somewhere that they started feuds at the drop of a hat and decided to play it safe and drink as much beer as he could. Meanwhile, he tried to think up an excuse which might allow him to part company with Peanut Sheller without offending same.

While engaged in thinking up this excuse, Mr. Peanut Sheller slowed to make a turn off US 66. "Going south to my cabin in the hills," drawled the bearded one. "If youse is aimin' to stay on 66, youse gets off here."

Another ride, this time with a cream separator salesman, brought Paul into a small hamlet in the heart of the Ozarks as dusk settled over the hills. Paul strode around the bedraggled village looking for a hotel where he might get cleaned up and make up some of the sleep lost the night before.

Paul hiccupped some from the oversupply of beer in his gizzard and spied a dilapidated hotel, which he decided at least to look over. Any port in the storm.

Two cats, contentedly perched on top of what could pass as a registration desk, didn't move as Paul approached.

"Anybody here?" Paul whooped. From the back room came a heavy-set woman in a soiled gingham dress.

"You wanna room? Is that it?"

"I thought I'd at least look over one of your luxurious suites," said Paul.

"What are ya? One of them smart aleck coons from Springfield? Whaddya doin' here. You look like maybe you're a revenue'er."

"Naw, I'm just a salesman. How much for a room?"

"Maybe you won't want one. Rooms ain't so fancy. Never had time to get at 'em lately."

"How much ya want for one night?"

"Fifty cents. In advance."

She pushed one of the cats off the top of the desks but couldn't find the register, took the coin Paul offered, and motioned him to go upstairs to room three which she said wasn't locked.

The room looked like it hadn't been cleaned for a month. The bed, however, was made, but the sheets were "tattletale gray" and worse and smelled musty. There was a hole knocked in the plaster of one wall—perhaps the result of a recent fight in the room.

Paul leaned down to peer through the hole and looked into the eye of someone gazing at him from the other side. The hole was large enough to give Paul a view of the adjoining room. A naked little girl about four and with a dirty face peered at him. Her mother lay on the unmade bed, her head propped up by pillows against the bed head. Clad in a kimono, she read a copy of "True Confessions," and smoked a cigarette.

Suddenly the woman yelled, "Lucy, get in the tub as I told ya, and I'll wash ya up."

Paul noticed a galvanized tub near a small stove at one end of the room.

"Mama, there's a man in the next room," piped up Lucy.

"What does he look like?"

"He's got on black clothes."

"Jeez, that's all we need—a damn preacher next door," moaned the figure on the bed. "I wonder what he's doing in this flea trap. She rose from the bed and lumbered over to the hole in the wall to take a look at her neighbor.

"How do you do?" greeted Paul. "Let me introduce myself. I'm Ambrose Heckler, the coroner from Springfield. We came to check on the body reported to be under the bed in this room."

"Christ! A stiff next door!" the woman moaned.

"She appears to be a woman about your age," Paul continued. "Been stabbed to death. Now we know you didn't do it because the killer has been apprehended. Nevertheless, I would advise you to clear out of that room for this night anyway, otherwise you'll be questioned. Just make yourself scarce until tomorrow afternoon, and don't say anything to anybody, and you'll be all right. Sound okay?"

"Yes, Lucy and I will get out of here and spend the night with a friend, but dammit, I'll lose some bus—" And she clammed up. Paul already guessed she was a hooker.

Paul was so tired he didn't care if the room wasn't so clean. Having gotten rid of the distractions in the next room, he crawled into the musty sheets and slept for nine hours straight.

Before dropping off, he had just time to utter this brief night prayer: "Dear Lord, forgive me for pulling that deal on the lady of the night next door to get rid of her, but . . ."

33

The next morning dawned overcast. Hitchhiking proved to be slow, the worst that Paul had experienced. He got to Joplin by afternoon when the rain began. Paul got on a bus for the rest of the way to Stillwater, but it traveled so slowly that it arrived in Tulsa after midnight. During the long layover there Paul took a hike around town. On a dark street a couple of young men saw him, and Paul ducked into an all-night diner when they pursued him. Paul hid out in the supply room off the kitchen for ten minutes, and then high-tailed it back to the bus station.

"This is not very hospitable country," Paul grumbled, and continued to read the book he brought along until his bus was called.

At three o'clock in the morning that bus broke down, and Paul, accompanied by an army serviceman on leave, started hoofing it down the road until the relief bus was due to come along. On this walk, with lightning flickered around in the southern skies, the army man spun tall tales about his exploits in the army.

"This chap is as bad as I am at putting out bullshit," Paul thought, only he hasn't as good an imagination as I have, and he's about as entertaining as looking into the eyes of a cow."

Paul arrived on the campus about eleven Saturday morning just in time for convocation. WAVES of all descriptions converged on the auditorium. Paul thought that the place would be a great institution for him at which to pursue studies only he would probably get no studying done.

He wondered where his brother, the Earl of Chatfield, could be located and finally found him, giving them a short weekend together until Monday morning when Paul took the highway again back to the land of ten thousand lakes.

Paul's brother, Sir Edgar, was then a petty officer third class studying how to make radar effective on planes and ships and had little time to entertain a guest.

Back on the highway waving his thumb in the breeze, Paul saw a farmer driving a pickup pull up. The driver, a "local yokel" in hitchhikers' parlance, was about fifty, hadn't shaved for a week, and was clad in denim bib overalls, the usual attire of rural workers in America. He had a straw hat on his head shaped like a cowboy hat.

"Where ya goin,' friend?" asked the driver.

"Back to Minnesota after visiting my brother, a navy man here at A and M."

"How come you ain't been drafted?"

"I'm in the seminary, and they don't draft seminarians."

"You gonna be a preacher?"

"Naw. I'm going to be a priest."

"A priest? You mean one of those goddam Roman Catholic priests?"

Paul knew then that he was in the "Bible Belt," a term they used in the seminary. In the Bible Belt most of the people practiced fundamentalism of one kind or another and were sorely ignorant of Catholicism.

"Yessir, I'm going to be a Catholic priest, but I'm not aware that priests have been damned by the Almighty."

The Oklahoman rolled down his window and directed a stream of tobacco juice into the wind.

"Tell me somethin' . . . and you ought to know the answer to the question being one of them hypocrites yoreself . . . they say in these parts that Roman priests got the right to spend the first night with all brides they marry up. That right?"

That was the first time Paul had heard that one. He burst out laughing. "That's a new one," Paul said trying to control his laughter. "but it's another one of those canards somebody invented and bigots like to believe and hope it will make more people mad at the Catholic Church."

"Waal, goddamit, don't go using all those big words. Jes tell me if it's true or not."

"Of course it's not true. Can you imagine any man allowing something like that on his wedding night? Use common sense, man."

"Waal, them Catholics is a strange breed from what I hear."

"The trouble is that you don't know any Catholics," Paul said, "and, therefore, don't know much about them. Catholics are scarcer than purple camels in these parts."

"Waal, yah, I guess I don't know no Catholics. One of my damfool cousins got married up with one in Milwaukee, I hear, but I never got a look at the varmint. Another question: Why in the hell don't priests get married if they ain't allowed to screw all those brides?"

"Simply because the Church made a law about that," Paul replied. "The Church figures that priests can do a better job tending to the flock without a wife and family taking a lot of their time. A priest offers the Holy Sacrifice of the Mass every day. That's a mighty holy act, much more so than the sacrifices of the Old Law. But even then the priests had to refrain from intercourse for a while before offering those sacrifices. So, now it's fitting that the modern priest refrain all the time since he performs such a holy act at the altar every morning."

"Bullshit! It don't make a damn bit of sense to me. I don't know what in the hell yer talking about. All I know is that cellarbussy or what you call it—it jes' ain't natural."

"No, it isn't natural. It's supernatural, and the priest needs and receives supernatural graces to live that kind of life. These graces or helps come through the Sacrament of Holy Orders at ordination."

"Who gives them orders? The Pope, I s'pose. Nothin' in the Bible about it."

"On the contrary, there's something in the Bible about it although it's not called 'Holy Orders.' For that matter you can't find the words 'Baptist Church' in the Bible either, but that doesn't mean the Baptist Church doesn't exist, isn't that right?"

"Talking about the Bible," the Oklahoman, introduced as Jason T. Edder, continued, "why can't you Catholics read the Bible?"

"Can't read the Bible?" Paul whinnied. "Let me show you something, my good man." Paul reached into his suitcase and brought out his breviary. It looked like a Bible, with most of its contents Scripture. "Take a look at this? It's my Bible. I carry it with me all the time, and read out of it every day." Paul, to be ordained a subdeacon when he got back to the seminary in a couple weeks and was getting some practice reading the Divine Office. As a subdeacon he would be obliged to recite every day and that would continue after being ordained a priest.

"Holy cow!" exclaimed Jason. "By Gawd, you do have the holy book at that! I wouldn't have believed it iff'n you hadn't shoved it to me.

"I'm turnin' off here. I reckon you wants to stay on the highway, so we'll let ya off. Glad to meetcha, young preacher. Hope you don't let a woman getcha and get kicked out of the church."

"Thanks for the ride, pardner, and keep the commandments," said Paul as he stepped back on the parched earth.

Paul looked around the barren landscape of Oklahoma in August and soon felt the sun boring through his black suitcoat.

"I'm a deuce of a ways from anywhere out here," he murmured. "Can't see a ranch or farmhouse anywhere. Brother, I hope a car comes along pretty soon."

He had hardly enunciated his wish when, as if a genie had granted his request, a black Chrysler braked to a stop. The only person in the car was the driver, a lady about forty dressed in a black suit and a black net around her hat.

"Get in, my dear Horace," she chirped.

Paul, sorely puzzled, thought, "What's the matter with this gal anyway? My name isn't Horace."

"Pardon me, young man, for calling you Horace. Horace, you see was my son who was killed in the war last year, and you remind me so much of him. You look just like him."

Paul let her talk and talk. He always figured that was the least he could pay for a ride. When they arrived at Ponca City, the good lady, whose name was Lily, took Paul into a first-class restaurant located in a hotel and bought him lunch, insisting he select the most expensive items from the menu. And the lady kept talking while Paul said nothing. After lunch she invited him to stay at her home for a few days, but Paul declined. Lily took him to the north edge of town and left him off. As he shook her hand he found she left a piece of paper in his palm.

While waiting for the next ride, Paul examined that slip of paper. It was a fifty dollar bill.

"Yumpin' Yahosaphat!" Paul exclaimed. "First time I have ever seen a fifty-dollar bill. Man, this bumming on the turnpikes can be lucrative once in a while. Well, anyway, I'm glad I looked like Horace. The old gal must be rolling in cash, and if I were a crook I'd go back into town and get some more of it."

A middle-aged man, who looked to Paul like a bank president and driving a 1941 Chevrolet sedan, picked Paul up and took him to Wichita. He said he had some business with aircraft manufacturers there and preached for an hour, berating President Roosevelt's idea of sending "lendlease" planes and equipment to Russia. He felt that Stalin and his communist gangsters were as bad as the Nazis. "And after we win the war for them," he said, "they'll gobble up eastern Europe and plan on taking over the world."

The next ride took Paul to Newton, Kansas, where he arrived at dusk. He went to a cheap diner by the railroad station for some supper. While chewing on some overfried potatoes, he looked out the window and saw a sign that the Santa Fe railroad operated through the town.

"Does the Santa Fe Chief run through this burg?" he asked the waitress, a pretty teenage brunette.

"Yessir, she sure does, and she's a classy streamliner."

"Does it stop here?"

"Oh, yes. Every day." She looked at her wristwatch. "She's due in here in another fifteen minutes at 8:50. But you probably can't get on if that's what you got in your mind."

"Why not?"

"Well, she's always full up, and you have to have a reservation. You got a reservation?"

"Sure thing. I'm with the government and defense contracts and so forth."

"Aw, don't give me that stuff! A minute ago you didn't even know the train came through here. You don't look like a crook, but still I wonder about you."

Paul gave her one of his captivating smiles and said, "You're a pretty smart little cookie, do you know that? And if your boyfriend ever tries to give you that old line about 'proving your love,' hit him over the head with a tire wrench."

She gave him a sweet smile and then another one when she noticed he had left her a quarter tip. Ordinarily Paul inclined to be a bit stingy with his money, but, after all, he had just collected a fifty-dollar bill that afternoon.

Paul ambled over to the railroad station, which looked like a thousand other train stations except larger than those in small towns. While waiting for the train and trying to figure out a strategy to ride the Chief without a reservation or ticket, he noticed a girl standing on the platform also waiting for the train. She appeared to be about eighteen with light brown hair and dressed in dark blue cotton skirt and a light blue blouse. Paul thought she looked quite attractive. He walked up to her and noticed a spray of freckles on her beautiful face.

"Are you going to get on the train?" Paul asked.

"Yes, I am." she replied. "Are you?"

"Well, to be frank with you, fair daughter of the Kansas prairies, I've been thinking about it. However, lacking a ticket and a reservation, I suspect I'll encounter some difficulties." Paul looked at her and flashed a smile.

"I'll give you a tip." She showed more than a passing interest in Paul now. "All you have to do is get aboard, head for the nearest john in front of the car, stay there exactly two minutes which is the time it takes for the conductor to check for new passengers in the car, then move back one car and repeat the action and continue the process until fifteen minutes have passed when the conductors will hole up somewhere to have a smoke or something."

"Is that how you work it?" asked Paul.

"Sure, I go down to my uncle's farm by Topeka, and most of the time I ride the Chief free that way. Pop raises hell about it and says I'm stealing from the Santa Fe. Say, what are you dressed up like an undertaker for? I mean all those black clothes and stuff. Who are you?"

"Ah, permit me to introduce myself," Paul said. "I am the Reverend Josiah Hezekiah, secretary of the National Council of Churches, and I must be in Topeka for an important conference in the morning. Unfortunately, I seem to have lost my ticket and reservation on the Chief."

"Aw, c'mon, you're no secretary of any church organization. You look too young for that. But you do belong to some outfit supposed to wear black. What's the deal?"

"Well, my dear little barn swallow," answered Paul, "the truth will out. I'm an official escort of dead bodies from the Mormons who insist on being buried in Missouri."

She gave out with a tinkling laugh. "You certainly have a great imagination. Well, we both told lies to each other. I have my ticket and reservation, see? What I told you about riding the train free is not true. Here comes the Chief! Good luck. I hope they don't tear your nice black suit when they throw you off the train."

"My dear little chicadee," said Paul, "it behooveth me now to evade members of the railroad brotherhood after I get aboard in order to remain a passenger in good standing on this trip."

Paul smiled at her and gave her a wave as she boarded the train, and she smiled back. And then he followed a couple of smartly dressed businessmen aboard.

Paul threw his bag into an empty slot he spied above the seat in the car he entered, hurried down the aisle and out of that car into another, and upon leaving that car, squatted down in the connecting area between the cars so the conductor could not see him if he looked out of the door of the car. After about ten minutes, Paul's leg muscles ached, and he stood up. By now, they should be through checking tickets, he thought and moved from car to car to find an empty seat but to no avail. Finally, he arrived at a darkened car. He opened the door anyway and took a step inside. An anguished yelp rose above the noise of the clicking rails. Paul lit a match and discovered that he had entered the dining car where the black employees slept on the floor. He had accidently stepped on someone's hand.

Paul quickly backed out of that car, reversed his course and headed for the rear of the train. He arrived at the last car, a parlor car for first-class passengers who relaxed there before retiring into their small bedrooms in the last two cars.

In the parlor car he spied his chicadee. She sprawled on one of the sofa seats smoking a cigar, although not very gracefully and exhibited a pale color in her face.

"Hi," she greeted Paul rather weakly. "They bet me a dollar I couldn't smoke this cigar without getting sick, and I'm afraid I lost the bet."

"Here, I'll help you get some fresh air," said Paul and reached down, took her hand, and, half supporting her with his arm around her waist, assisted her out to the noisy passageway between cars, and held her while she breathed in fresh air.

"Feeling better now, my prairie miss?"

"Yes, I'm coming around. How did you make out with the conductors?"

"No problem. I sidestepped them all. Say, you're a delectable bundle to hold, I must say, and I'm gravely tempted to smother you with kisses, but, alas, I'm bound to the law of Kashmir not to touch the lips of a girl until I'm thirty. Therefore, I must deposit thee back upon your feet and disengage my arms from thee for, verily, thou dost charge my battery."

"What do you mean, the law of Kashmir? You're no foreigner. And you haven't told me yet why you wear those black clothes in summer. Now I'm beginning to suspect you are a crook of some kind."

"Ah, wouldn't you like to meet more crooks like me, honeychile from the land of timothy and wild roses? My little indiscretion of failing to pay for my passage on this denizen of the rails is indeed regrettable for a person of my great rank, but I did have to catch this train."

"Why did you have to catch this train?" She turned her freckled nose up at him, and Paul had to stifle an immense urge to kiss her.

"Because, my dear Kansas blossom, I have been telling you too many prevarications, and now I must needs spake the truth least my honorable ancestors disown me before the Grand Vizier of Abadan."

"There you go again! Can't you be serious for a minute?"

Paul looked thoughtful for a moment and then said, "Okay, let's be serious for a moment. What is your name, prairie rose?"

"Amelia. What's yours?"

"Paul. But, ah, I see the dawn about to come up like thunder there in the east, and we must be nearing Topeka where I disembark with thee, and our paths will separate. Come, leave us move up to the car where I stowed my bags."

When the train slid to a stop in the pale light of dawn, Amelia and Paul, hand in hand, moved off the train to the platform where Paul faced her and delivered the following valedictory: "My heart indeed, Amelia, has been ignited with love for thee, but cruel fate tears us apart now, and I still cannot divulge my identity and mission. And so, dear one, as the sky in the Orient takes on a pinkish hue announcing the arrival of Mazda, I bid thee fond adieu, my darling of the prairie."

Paul brushed her lips with a kiss, turned and quickly walked away leaving her with eyes swelling with tears as her Uncle Henry, or somebody waiting to pick her up, took her by the hand and led her to his car. He seemed very much concerned about her tears and swung his arm around her shoulders to console her.

Paul walked swiftly away, not daring more than a peek backwards. Just then a quote from the Gospel popped into his mind, "He who puts his hands to the plow and looks backward is not worthy of me."

"But, hell, I'm not worthy even though I don't look backward," Paul thought.

34

After fortifying himself with some breakfast, Paul walked up Highway 75 to the edge of Topeka, sat down on the curb to rest while keeping his thumb raised. A sleek Lafayette came to a stop.

"This is certainly an interesting trip," Paul muttered to himself. "Now look at the chariot that just stopped to offer a ride to this vagabond of the plains. You just don't see Lafayettes around much, but what a car! I'm surprised that Wooley Becker, our conservative dogma prof back in the seminary would drive one. He must have mistaken it for a Buick."

The driver, a very attractive young lady about twenty-five, had on pale blue slacks and a white blouse and had her dark brown hair gathered up in a pug on the top of her head. Her dark eyes seemed to regard Paul with some interest as he threw his bag into the rear seat and sat down beside her in the front.

"Hi," the lady said, "I picked you up because you seemed like you might be someone with a bit of education considering the way you're dressed. I'm looking for somebody who can carry on an intelligent conversation. I left my husband off at Fort Riley to serve Uncle Sam, and I'm driving to Sioux City."

As she talked she deftly moved the gearshift through it's four speeds. The engine growled through the special muffler, a modification, among many Paul detected about the unusual vehicle.

"It's a long ways from here to Sioux City," she continued, "and a bit boring without someone to talk to. By the way, if you happen to be one of those bums who dress up only to lure women into his net and has nothing but sex on his mind, declare yourself right now, and I'll stop and leave you off to walk off your libido."

Paul smiled at her and said, "My dear young lady, I am indeed what the doctor ordered for you as a conversationalist. I have just completed college majoring in philosophy, and I'm now in graduate school of theology. I have been traveling all night and apologize for my unkempt look at the moment rather than appearing fresh as I usually do at this hour of the day.

"I do indeed consider it a privilege," he continued, "to be able to accompany you on this journey today. I'm on my way back to Minnesota. Finally, sex is not my usual bill of fare, nor a subject that concerns me

174

terribly as I'm studying to become a priest and, as you know, am vowed to celibacy."

"You're a very refreshing person," the lady smiled, "and I'm delighted that our paths crossed. Do me the honor of accepting my invitation to accompany me the rest of this day in our mutual journey toward the land of the sky blue waters."

She pressed on the accelerator as the environs of Topeka gave way to open country, and the speedometer smoothly moved up to eighty miles per hour.

"My husband modified this car in his spare time," she said, "and it's capable of doing 120 very easily. By the way, my name is Leora Burns. And yours is . . . ?"

"Paul Joseph Pesch, your devoted servant." Paul bowed low.

"Oh, aren't you the gallant one!" Her laugh was a pleasant tinkle. "I daresay you won't find much opportunity to use your charming manner with women once you're ordained. You'll have to be quite reserved then. You know, I'm wondering if you'll really become a priest at all. You don't seem to be the type."

"Well, as a matter of fact, my religious superiors in the seminary would be aghast at my manner of speaking to you and would likely cut me off from Holy Orders were they ever to see me in action when I'm on the loose like now. They consider a candidate for the priesthood one who conducts himself like one of the saints they read about. But the accounts of the saints are spurious and doctored up a bit to edify the reader according to the standards of heretics like the Jansenists and so forth. I'm afraid that to be human in the Church today, alas, is not considered a virtue."

As the August heat shimmered over the dormant wheat fields of Kansas, the Lafeyette speeded on while its two occupants talked philosophy by the hour since Leora has also majored in the subject at college.

When lunchtime arrived, Leora insisted on entertaining her passenger in a small town restaurant on the main street.

During lunch Paul said, "Your generous offer of treating me to this repast comes at a time when I'm dreadfully poor in the way of liquid assets so I am particularly grateful for your generosity. However, I'm inclined to be tight-fisted with money since I have so little of it now during my student days. However, I'm afraid the parsimonious fashion of laying out the coin of the realm might become a habit and one of the reasons why marriage would be difficult for me, I suspect. I might find myself denying my wife funds she would need to run the household, for one thing."

"Maybe that is the underlying reason you want to become a priest," Leora asked over dessert. "You don't want to face up to the responsibilities of being a husband."

"No," Paul answered, "I suspect the Lord might be calling me to the exalted state of the priesthood because He sees that in any other vocation I might easily land in hell."

"You're funny," Leora laughed. "By the way, how do you know the Lord really called you? Did He tap you on the shoulder one day and or speak to you in a dream?"

"No, He just arranged the circumstances of my life in such a way as to get the message through my thick skull. But I'll never know for certain if I have a vocation to the priesthood until the bishop calls me to Holy Orders. That's the clincher."

"You Catholics, it seems to me, depend too much on the hierarchy, as you call those in the upper echelon of your church," Leora observed. "It's better that an individual depend more on what the Bible tells him. It's a sort of slavery to have other men tell one what he must believe and do to be saved."

"It depends on who the other men are," answered Paul. "It's okay if they are the authentic spokesmen of the Church Christ established and participate in the power Christ gave to the leaders of his Church."

"You don't need all that organization," Leora argued. "All you need is God's word in the Bible."

"Here we go again," Paul sighed. "I'm surprised to hear an intelligent woman like you, Princess, putting out that theory that can't hold water."

"What do you mean?"

"Well, what is the Bible? A collection of books written under God's inspiration. Right? But the Bible can't interpret itself and needs a divinely established agency to do that and do it without falling into error in the process. That's the function of the Church, which was established before the New Testament was written. She was in business for a hundred years before the first book of the New Testament came on the scene, and eventually some of her members also wrote the rest of the books of the New Testament."

"Oh, come on now! Don't hand me that stuff! Are you trying to tell me that the Pope has some magic which enables him to interpret the Bible without error?"

"No, he doesn't have any magic. He, along with the council of bishops, has the guidance of the Holy Spirit on these matters. It sure works a lot better than each man interpreting the Scriptures according to his own lights and ending up with hundreds of different churches all based on the same Bible, like we have now."

She elected to change the subject, apparently finding it more pleasant to admire Paul's curly locks. "You know, Paul," she said dreamily, "You're too good-looking to be a priest."

"Pardon me if I blush and stammer 'shucks' a few times," Paul murmured and did blush. "But you embarrass me. Even if it's true what you say, the Lord has a right to pick out whomever He chooses to be His priests. And the arrangement of my features is God's work and no credit to me personally."

Leora smiled and said, "Yes, that's true, but it won't prevent some babe coming along someday and laying a trap for you, and that'll be the end of Paul, the priest, while your bishop will cuss under his breath like a trooper."

Paul laughed. "I simply can't feature a bishop cussing like a trooper under his breath," he said. "But what you say is certainly possible. Like all men I'm weak and need the assistance of Christ to do his work. But there's another factor you don't take into consideration. I could fall in love with Christ and not with a girl."

"Yes, but you might tire of Christ after a while and welcome the arms of a blonde instead."

"Yes, it's possible. As a matter of fact, I'm being captivated by your pale blue eyes right now, and may not be able to hold out much longer against your charms. Maybe we'd better start sailing down the highway again."

"You damfool!" Paul thought to himself "always giving out a line like that to women. Like the rest, Leora eats it up, but you don't have to pay for your ride doing that. If you ever do get ordained, you'll have to quit that or you'll end up having the shoes of one of them under your bed, and you'll be trying to make a living supporting a wife and family probably by embezzling the company you're working for."

They arrived at Sioux City at dusk, and Paul boarded a train for Worthington where he planned to stay the night at his aunt Veronica's house. But this time he bought a ticket for the ride.

"Adios, Princess," he bid goodbye to Leora. "Thank you so much for the ride and the meals. When I get back to the seminary in a couple weeks I remember you at morning prayer just before I drop off to sleep in the pew."

‡   ‡   ‡

At the Villa Maggie pumped all the information about Edgar she could extract from Paul who, of course, did not divulge any details of the journey there or back.

Joe, who by then was beginning to feel his age a bit, sat there in the kitchen and listened, saying nothing. He no longer cracked his knuckles because they were no longer supple enough to be clicked anymore.

Young Maggie, now a senior in high school, called Paul "a bum," as usual and went to the neighbor's house up the road to talk about boys with Kay, her classmate.

Paul returned to the Brickyard a few days later to begin his third-year theology course at the end of which would come ordination to sub-diaconate. In the preconciliar Church there were three major orders: Subdiaconate, Diaconate, and Priesthood. If he qualified, the candidate was ordained a subdeacon at the end of his third year in theology, and was ordained a deacon at the beginning of the fourth and last year theology. And finally, if he had not been "clipped" in the meantime, he was ordained a priest at the end of the fourth year.

Paul had no doubts about wanting to be ordained, but he feared getting "clipped." His seminary record might warrant this exclusion from Holy Orders. He felt he might have been clipped already by his bishop, but Bishop Kelly was too ill to take care of that matter, and Paul's fate hung in the balance.

In the meantime, a new bishop was assigned to the Diocese of Winona to assist the ailing Kelly. Leo Binz breezed into the diocese as co-adjutor bishop as they called him.

"What's this co-adjutor business, Punk?" Paul asked one evening at dinner. Punk seemed to know everything ecclesiastical.

"It means that the new man will take over being a full-fledged bishop as soon as his predecessor dies. In the meantime, however, he will be in command and, among other things, might dump you even though you're close to ordination. You won't go down in history as a model seminarian, you know."

In those days the ordination to subdeacon posed the decisive step because it involved taking the vow of chastity for life and with it the obligation to pray the entire Divine Office every day for life. As Wooley Becker said one day in class: "When Mother Church imposes perpetual chastity on her clergy, she at the same time gives him a prayerbook, the Divine Office or breviary, which will give him sufficient strength to keep his vow of chastity."

Because it was the decisive step, some of the boys tended to "sweat it out" for the last few days before taking it. Paul, however, went over to the chapel and told his Boss: "Lord, unless you bar me from Orders, I'm going to go ahead and clutter up Your Priesthood. But if You want to get rid of me, then, You'll have get the Smiling Buddha to clip me pretty soon."

Paul called his new bishop, the "Smiling Buddha" because the man somehow reminded him of the statue of the sitting Buddha, only Bishop Binz smiled a lot, and Buddha didn't.

"When he clips you, he'll do it with a smile on his face," commented Urban Neudecker, Paul's classmate also awaiting ordination for the Diocese of Winona.

On the morning of ordination to the Subdianconate, Paul was a calm as an owl on a tree branch and bravely took the step that would bind him for the rest of his life "For richer, for poorer, in sickness and in health until death do I serve the Lord as a priest, and may God have mercy on my soul."

"I hear Bishop Binz is quite short of priests," said Paul the evening before at dinner, "so short, in fact, that he is taking a chance on me, and so I have not been clipped from ordination tomorrow. By the way, where is Punk?"

Punk who had threatened for five years to quit the seminary finally did so before he took the final step.

35

aul became a deacon in the early summer of 1944. He went to the Villa in July when the troops were released for six weeks. But after a few days lying around on Solomon's Porch, as he called the terrace or lawn between the modest farmhouse and the Brook Cedron, the wanderlust set in. One August day, Deacon Paul packed his worn and ragged suitcase. When he dragged it downstairs, Maggie confronted him. "Now where do you think you're going? My goodness, boy, can't you stay put for a week anywhere?"

"My dear honorable ancestor . . ."

"Now don't call me an 'ancestor.' I'm not that old."

"My dear honorable progenitor . . ."

"What does 'progenitor' mean?"

"It's a fancy word for mother. Now what I was about to communicate to you was a message of great tidings of joy for all men, namely, that I'm off to procure the salvation of more souls."

"Now don't give me more of that fancy talk, young man. Just where are you going bumming to this time?"

"I must needs travel to Chicago, mother dear, to attend an event of great import, namely, the SSCA."

"Now what's that supposed to stand for?"

"Summer School of Catholic Action, to prepare me for greater effectiveness in the vineyard come six months or so when the Bishop ordains me and sends me out to preach the Gospel to all creatures, baptizing them in the name of the Father, and of the . . ."

"Ah, stop your foaming at the mouth again. Okay, go to Chicago but be careful in your hitchhiking so you don't get picked up by a gangster and get shot."

"Far be it from me, mother mine, to expose my precious body to the ravages of men bent on destruction. I shall return in four or five days to grace the Villa again with my august presence. Adios, and keep the hens laying."

Paul walked down County 7 a few rods to where it joined concrete US 52, and parked his suitcase on the side of the road. The suitcase, made out of wood and not much bigger than an attaché case, and was covered with a cheap imitation leather. Because of the sturdiness of the suitcase,

Paul could sit on it and pray the Divine Office as he waited for a ride. While praying he raised his thumb to alert passing motorists that this praying monk dressed in black sought transportation.

Paul, getting drowsy reading the Latin text of the psalms as frequently happened, heard the squeaking of worn brake linings and saw an old four-door Plymouth move onto the shoulder after the driver finally slowed the chariot.

"Methinks riding in a conveyance with such bad brakes," sighed Paul, "might give my Guardian Angel extra work."

He walked to the car and saw an elderly couple in the front seat.

"H'mm, usually old people don't stop to pick up hitchhikers," mused Paul. "Where are you going?" he asked them.

"We're goin' home to Burr Oak, Ioway," said the man, "That's just across the border on this here Highway 52."

"Fine. I'll be happy to accept your kind invitation to ride with you that far," said Paul and he crawled into the back seat.

The old man didn't know much about coordinating the clutch with the gears and ground them quite badly. When he finally reached high gear he kept his speed down to thirty five miles per hour. To save gasoline and tires patriotic Americans were asked not to exceed thirty-five on the highway, and this man must have been quite patriotic, Paul thought. Most motorists exceeded the recommended limit.

Paul opened his breviary and continued reciting his prayers.

"Me and the wife been down at the Mayo Clinic," the old gent sang out. "Alma here's been ailing a bit."

He eyed Paul in the rearview mirror and noticed that he was reading. "Are you a preacher?" the old man asked. "Seems like you a preacher. Seems like you're reading the Bible."

"No, I'm no preacher," said Paul. "However, I'll be ordained a Catholic priest in six months or so."

"Izzat so?" cackled the gent, his face singularly free of wrinkles compared to his prune-faced spouse. Both had silvery hair, hers gathered up in a pug in the back of her head and his cut short and very thick. He didn't wear a hat as if to show off how much hair he had for his age.

"A priest, huh?" said the old man. "Me and the missus ain't Catholics ourselves, but we have good friends who are, and I always figured we all worship the same God and are going to the same place. Doesn't make much difference what church ya go to." He turned around to look at Paul as he talked.

"That's a lot of baloney," Paul said. "Christ established only one true Church and not a whole slew of them." But his remark was drowned out by Alma shrieking, "Ludie! For heaven's sake, keep your eyes on the road."

"Never mind, Alma," Ludie growled, "I ain't gonna run into no ditch jest 'cause I look around at our young preacher boy. Didn't know you Catholics wuz allowed to read the Bible, been told you ain't allowed to touch it."

"That's nothing but a damn lie," Paul blurted. "Oh, I'm sorry. I shouldn't have used that bad word."

Alma turned around and gave Paul a steely look. "Seems to me," she said with compressed lips, "that your church could find a better candidate for the priesthood than somebody who swears."

"Aw, shaddap, Alma." said Ludie, "I cuss plenty when yer not around."

There was silence. Paul tried to resume reciting the breviary but soon fell asleep.

A warm sunny day graced downtown Dubuque where Paul found himself at the end of the next ride. His cheap watch said 1:10 p.m. as he started walking across the bridge over the Mississippi. On the other side of the river he hoped to snag a driver heading down route 20 toward Chicago.

Paul had walked about halfway across the bridge, when to his surprise, a semi-trailor truck stopped. Truck drivers usually were forbidden by their employers to pick up hitchhikers, and, at any rate, they wouldn't stop on the bridge holding up traffic to pick one up.

Paul hoisted himself into the cab. The driver, a middle-aged man of large build, with sandy hair and wearing no cap, looked at Paul's neatly pressed black suit and spotted the Knights of Columbus pin on the lapel. He extended his large rough hand and bellowed, "Welcome aboard, fellow K.C. I'm heading for Chicago. Where you going?"

"Chicago also. Glad you stopped. May St. Christopher keep you in the middle of the road." Little did Paul know then how fitting it was that he uttered this short prayer in view of the journey he commenced.

"How come you're dressed up like an undertaker on a hot day like this?"

"For some reason, my good man," said Paul, "when I present myself along the turnpike desirous of free transportation, my appearance is the deciding factor motivating the driver to stop. Dressed like I'm going to the Opera I get rides real quick although they don't know that I'm really the Earl of Chatfield. May I introduce myself? Your servant, Paul J. Pesch, the Earl of Chatfield by order of Mary, Queen of Scots."

"I'm Gordie C. Burke. Glad to have you aboard. But, hell, you ain't no Earl anymore than I'm the Duke of Diesel. If ya were you'd be tooling along in a Rolls Royce instead of standing along the road waving your thumb. Now what about all that wool on your back?"

"I'm a seminarian. Be ordained in a few months, and really we're supposed to be wearing black anyway. True, we're not supposed to be hitchhiking, but while I'm usually an obedient cuss, I do take a few liberties now and then."

"You're a man after my own heart," said the driver. "I like a guy with a little nerve. Yessir. Son of a bitch! Look at that guy. He's going to have to get off on the shoulder. I can't stop."

By now they were among the steep hills around Galena. Gordie drove wide open. He pushed up his speed to almost eighty miles per hour going down one hill and then shoot up the next hill. A car chugged up the steep hill. Gordie passed him like a meteor. But on top of the hill appeared another car in the passing lane. This poor driver had no choice but swing off on the shoulder or go head-on into the truck. He pulled off on the shoulder.

Meanwhile, Paul went rigid and called on St. Christopher. The crisis over, Paul knew at once he rode with a mad driver who could easily put them both before the tribunal of the living God. He said, "My good man, as a Catholic, you should know the Act of Contrition. I would suggest that we both recite it while we have time. The way you drive we'll both soon find ourselves catapulting into eternity, and I'm not so sure you're in the state of grace."

"Aw, hell, don't worry so much. I been driving like this for years."

Up ahead lay a railroad crossing. The truck swept across the tracks full speed.

"Look back and see if there was a train coming," instructed Gordie.

"What's the use?" said Paul. "We're across the tracks."

"Well, I sort of like to know if there was a train coming just for the heck of it."

"Gordie, I would advise you to abandon truck driving for your health," suggested Paul.

"You're right. I don't like this job anyway. You know what I'd like to be? A funeral director."

"The closest he will come to getting his wish," Paul thought, "will consist in being the guest of a funeral director in his embalming room after he runs his truck into kingdom come one of these days. Just as long as it won't be this day.

"Angel of God, my Guardian Dear," Paul whispered, "to Whom God's love commits me here. Ever this day be at my side, to light and guard, to rule and guide. Amen."

In the late afternoon they arrived in the outskirts of Chicago. Gordie stopped the truck and said, "Look, I ain't s'posed to pick up hitchhikers. I can't take you all the way to where I'm going. If they see you in my cab I'll get my ass in the sling. I'll leave you off here. You catch that street car there and stay on it, 'cause she'll take you all the way to the Morrison Hotel. That's where you said you was going, didn't ya?"

Paul thanked Gordie and promised to pray for him so he don't meet up with a train at a crossing one day, shook his large, rough hand, and high-tailed it for the street car.

When the street car reached Clark and Madison in the loop, it was dark, and Paul walked the few yards to the Morrison, which, at the time, advertized itself as the tallest hotel in the world and rose like a wall in the Grand Canyon.

"I'm sorry, sir, but we're full up and will be for the rest of the week," said the clerk at the desk.

During the war hotels and trains were always crowded. In addition the SSCA was going on at the Morrison, which meant a thousand or so Catholic young people on the premises for a week of speeches, workshops, seminars, and good times. Paul came primarily for the latter. He hoped to flirt with teenage girls who fell for his line. "Jeepers! In only a few more months, I'll have to quit that stuff," he mourned.

Paul made the rounds of all the hotels within a couple blocks of the Morrison, but no rooms were available in any of them. Paul wasn't the type to be daunted by the vicissitudes of life. He always kept a smile on his face and made the best of things.

What to do next? During a previous SSCA trip to Chicago he recalled scouting around the neighborhood of the Morrison to see the sights one afternoon, and recalled observing some flophouses a couple blocks away on North Clark Street. He decided that, with his limited options, if he was to find a bed that night, maybe it would be a good education to experience how some of the less fortunate brethren live. The next day at the SSCA sessions, he'd find somebody he knew who would slip him into his room.

Paul must have looked like a well-dressed banker carrying his attaché case full of important documents, or, more likely, in this neighborhood, a government bureaucrat bent on no good. The winos leaning in the doorways of cheap liquor stores eyed him with suspicion and hostility.

Paul noted a sign in the transom of a door, "Rooms 50 cents."

"H'mm," he mused, "this must be the Waldorf Astoria in this district. Most of the gorgeous hostelries in this neighborhood advertise their suites for 25 or 35 cents. I'll register at this one and wait for a smartly dressed bellhop to come, pick up my luggage, and lead me into my damask-curtained sitting room."

Paul mounted the steps. At the head, a fat lady confronted him. Well past her prime, dressed in a gray kimono, her thin, gray-flicked black hair frizzled into a mess. Around her waist she wore a leather belt from which hung a holster containing some sort of handgun.

Paul thought that the better part of valor would be not to cross this gal. "Jeepers, what kind of a place is this where the landlady packs a hunk of artillery on her person?"

"Good evening, my good hostess," began Paul, bowing to her as he arrived at the top of the stairs. "As the shades of vespertide clothe the city within her shadows, I must needs find shelter for the night soon. May I ask if you have a room available?"

"For Chrissake, look at the bastard!" the woman shouted in hoarse tone of voice. "Just what in the hell do you mean coming up here and trying sweet talk on me? Now you know damned well you have no intention of sleeping in this dive. Are you an FBI man coming after one of the men around here?"

"Truly, madam, I do not have ulterior motives in coming here. You must believe me, I'm looking for a bed for the night. All the hotels are filled, and it would seem that I am forced to seek accommodations in less luxurious hostels."

"Well, I'll be . . .!" She looked at Paul as if wondering if she should believe him. "Yeah, I got a room, but you ain't gonna like it, that I'm damn sure of. You look like one of those who faints at the sight of a bedbug, and I wouldn't be surprised if the bed in that room had a few."

"I'm sure I can adjust to that for one night," Paul sighed. "Leave us gaze upon the royal suite."

The room appeared to Paul to be in a sorry state, with the paint on the door badly chipped and the lock hanging loosely in its slot obviously having been forced several times; it would not be much of an obstacle to any intruder. The sheets on the brass-posted bed were gray, not white. A sorry-looking chest of drawers and a chair which smelled like a cat's litter box, furnished the room.

"The biffy's down the hall," the "Duchess of Bedbug," as Paul named his landlady, said and waved to Paul to follow her toward the quite dirty and thoroughly uninviting "bathroom."

They walked back to the "registration desk," a hacked up table at the head of the stairs at which the Duchess usually sat. Paul reached for his wallet and extracted a dollar bill from it. "I shall dwell in your hostel for the night," he said.

"Better not flash that billfold around here, Mister," cautioned the Duchess. "Plenty of people around here would conk you over the head for just a glimpse of it."

Paul accepted a fifty-cent piece in change. "I'll run over to the Morrison for some supper," he said, "and be back in time to retire. And what did you say your name was?"

"Millie, and what's yours, banker boy?"

"Paul, at your service. I'm a seminarian about to be ordained a priest, and, frankly, I choose to stay here for the night for the experience of it and observe Christ in some of His more unfortunate brethren in the Mystical Body."

"Holy buckets of blood!" Millie shouted. "A holy joe, and the bastard can't seem to talk plain English. So yer gonna be a preacher, huh? Well, tonight you'll get your bellyful of stuff to preach about, I'll tell ya that."

At the Morrison coffee shop, Paul lapped up a cup of soup when he spied Carl Ludington. He waved, and Carl hurried over and stuck out his hand, "A fellow convict from the Brickyard! What brings you to the wicked city, Paul?"

"They got this SSCA going, you know, and I suppose that's what brings you around too. Me? I'm going to flirt with some pretty young chicks for a few days, and maybe learn something from Daniel J. Lord. The old pamphleteer is on the roster, isn't he?"

"Yep, the Jebbie sure is, and he'll have the kids eating out of hand at his workshops as usual. Where are you staying?"

"That's the problem, Carl, old saint. You have a room in this palatial palace?"

"Yeah, but I can't sneak you in tonight. Basset's already occupying the other half of the sack, but he's scurrying back to Iowa tomorrow. Still, you could bed down on the maple in my room, if you want."

Thanks, I'll be around tomorrow. I've contracted a flophouse for tonight on North Clark to see how the other half lives. You're going to have to pick bedbugs off my hide tomorrow like the monkeys do at the zoo."

"By golly, Paul, you'll try anything! I'll give you a good sendoff at your funeral. You know those birds up there don't play around. They'll put a blade in your liver for a fiver at the drop of pigeon shit."

"The Lord will look after his faithful son whom He wants to Proclaim His Name over hill and dale during the years ahead," Paul answered. "See you tomorrow."

Back at the walled off Astoria on North Clark Street, Paul found another chair and sat with Millie to learn more about life on skid row. Paul told her everything about himself she wanted to know, and the woman softened, her voice talking on a shade of tenderness, and she apparently began to entertain a bit of affection for Paul. "I must be appealing to her maternal instinct," Paul thought. "I always do that to women."

Millie divulged a resume of her life story, starting by confessing that she thoroughly hated the place, but it was the only living she had. Her husband, Albert, had left her the building when he died from a "pickled liver" after suffering alcoholism for thirty years. He had been a bootlegger during Prohibition, but Al Capone's men threatened to break his legs if he sold another pint in their territory. He took on a mistress, which enraged Millie, and she put him into the hospital several times because she underestimated her strength in wielding a shovel handle on him in her rages.

At that point a bedraggled wino appeared struggling up the stairs.

"Alfie, you owe me ten dollars back rent," Millie yelled at him, the tenderness in her voice entirely gone.

"Yeah, I know," mumbled Alfie. "I'll be getting my pension day after tomorrow. Right now I'm broke."

"Of course you're broke!" shrieked Millie. "Spending it on that stinking wine."

As Alfie stumbled down the hall, a figure emerged from one of the rooms and tried to drag Alfie into his room. Alfie let out a howl of distress, and Millie stomped down the hall, removed her gun from its holster. She proceeded to pistol whip Alfie's attacker, screaming: "You goddam son of a bitch! Always trying to rob Alfie of his pension, but you never seem to remember the day he gets it. Next time you lay for Alfie again, Boxer, I'm going to drill a hole in your gizzard, unnerstand?"

When Millie returned from putting out the brush fire, Paul said, "Man, when they spot me in these glad rags they'll think I'm loaded and move in to relieve me of my sparse resources."

"Ah, don't worry about it," Millie said. "I'll be hanging around here all night, guarding your door. If anyone come prowling into your room, I'll plug him with my .38. They don't mess around with me because they know I can handle this rod pretty good."

"Did you ever have to use it?"

"Lord, yes. Scarcely a year passes that I don't send one or two customers down to Cook County Hospital with a slug in 'em. Only way I can run a place like this."

"What do the cops think of you shooting up the place?"

"They wish there were more landlords up here on North Clark as handy with the artillery as I am to keep peace in the district. Saves them a lot of trips up here."

"Well, Millie, not to try to change the subject, but your turn to appear before the High Court up yonder will be coming up too, and I want you to be on good terms with the Judge on that occasion. Better think about getting your sins forgiven and getting your ticket for the Kingdom. I'm just the one who can help fix you up."

"Yeah, I know. But don't give me any of that mission ear-banging, sonny. Down the street they got one of them missions goin' all the time, and they bribe the guys to come in by giving them some free soup. In return the guys have to listen to a scrawny preacher threaten them with hellfire all the time. That ain't no way to sell religion."

"I know that, Millie, but maybe the only language the customers can understand is the prospect of getting their livers cooked. Of course, I'll admit the boys really go down there to get something in the belly, and naturally would prefer to slurp the soup in peace. Now, what I am trying to sell you, Millie, is an entirely different product, namely, the love of God, not His vengeance."

At this point, "Hobo" Jones struggled up the stairs and complained to Millie of a "helluva bellyache" and gasped out that he thought he was going to die.

"Hobo," Millie stormed, "I'll bet you bought some of that cheap rotgut from Bernie's, and now you are going to have to pay for it. Get to your room and let it burn a hole in your gut. Maybe that'll teach you to leave the stuff alone next time. But don't you croak, Hobo. You still owe me some rent."

Millie and Paul resumed talking at the table at the head of the stairs, and Paul hung onto the topic of religion. Millie had little background on the subject but seemed game to learn more about why she was on earth. She had been thinking about having to die some day and wondered about the future life "if there was any." Paul suggested some easy ways to begin praying. As they talked, Millie's hard exterior seemed to change, and her voice softened.

"Her maternal instinct is reviving," Paul thought. "She's starting to become a bit fond of me. I can tell it in her eyes. I guess I won't have to worry about being assaulted during the night. She'll see to that."

"Paul, a nice-looking young man like you should get married," Millie, said resuming the conversation. "I can't see why that church of yours would wanna keep you boys away from women, for Chrissake. After all, you're human, and I'm sure you have the urge to go to bed with a woman a couple times a week."

"Sure," Paul replied, "I also have the urge to swipe somebody's Cadillac once in a while, but I don't do that either, because I know what's going to make me happy and what's not. Now, Millie, we're talking about the holy priesthood of Jesus Christ here and not a vocation to be a plumber. When we, unworthy as we are, are ordained and given the power of changing bread and wine into the Body and Blood of Christ at Mass, the Church expects a bit more of us as befitting that high calling."

"Aw, don't give me that pious crap the Pope brainwashes you with. There's nothing wrong with getting married. Good people do it all the time."

"Certainly," Paul replied. "But here we're talking about giving up a good thing for something better, and that we do freely. I can go out and get married tonight if I want, and the Pope isn't going to summon the Swiss Guards and put out a contract on me. As far as keeping the vow of celibacy is concerned, you have to remember we receive extra helps to live that kind of life. We call them the graces of our state in life. We're not just carrying a heavy burden, growling every foot of the way and wishing we had enough guts to tell the Church off. No, it's a joyful life and allows us to love everyone better than if we were married."

"Aw, hell, I give up!" Millie sighed. "It still don't make much sense to me."

"I'll pray for you, Millie," Paul smiled. "And now I'd better get some sleep. It's a big day tomorrow down at the Morrison. Goodnight, Millie."

"Goodnight and sleep tight, you cute kid, and don't let the bedbugs bite. I'm afraid they'll be all over you before morning. This whole dump is full of them. I'd suggest you sleep on top of the bed with your clothes on."

He took off his suit coat as the stale air was very warm, and the window had been nailed shut. Paul had hardly touched his head to the dirty pillow after throwing himself on top of the dirty bedspread, when he heard somebody arrive in the adjacent room, the soundproofing between the rooms being almost nonexistent. A woman said in a loud tone of voice, "Now look here, Mister. If you want me to do that you cough up some more money, or I don't do it, see!"

"Oh, is that so, you bitch! I don't have no more money, and you'll do as I say or I'll beat the shit out of you."

"Get your stinking paws off me," she screamed, and then screamed louder and louder as if he tortured her.

"Oh, goodness gracious!" sighed Paul. "It doesn't look like I'm going to get any sleep at all tonight."

Just then he heard a "thump, thump, thump," as Millie advanced toward the scene of battle, and even before she arrived at the door she started bellowing "Leave her alone, you bastard or I'll put a .38 slug into your gizzard. And, Lana, you get outta here before you get strangled. You ought to know by now that some of these johns are weirdos. And you, mister, get the hell outta here right now."

Paul got up on his feet, padded to the door, and poked his head out. "What's going on, Millie?" he croaked.

"This ain't the kind of thing for holy joes like you to be involved in. Try to get some sleep, Paul, and I'll see that no more of these creeps disturbs you."

In the meantime, Lana got a good look at Paul, and Paul got a good glimpse of her. She was a slim woman, in her thirties perhaps, and wore too much makeup on her small face framed by frazzled brown hair. She wore a sort of housecoat, and Paul feared she wore nothing else underneath. Her body, which at one time might have been quite attractive, had a dissipated look reflecting the kind of life she lead. Paul guessed she was a prostitute. He was a bit scandalized by finding himself so close to one. He decided to say a few prayers for her while waiting for sleep to come.

Again Paul was about to drop off to sleep when he heard the loose knob of the door rattle. He opened his eyes and saw Lana quietly slip into his room. She whispered, "Just five dollars, man of my dreams, and we can both sail into dreamland. What d'ya say?"

"No sale, fallen daughter of Eve," Paul growled and quickly sat up in bed. "Better move out of here before I call Millie."

Lana loosened the sash about her waist in preparation for divesting herself of her housecoat. Paul thought he faced the most difficult moment in his young life, when "thump, thump, thump" came the sound of Millie approaching. Even before she arrived at the door she bellowed, "Get out of his room, you bitch!" And there followed a string of epithets not sung in the sanctuary of a church. Lana quickly made herself scarce.

"Thanks, Millie," Paul sighed. "I'll see to it that you get good treatment at the pearly gates some day."

"Sorry we bothered you." said Millie. "Ordinarily she's is not around here, but she wanted a one-night stand. I get fifty percent. Well, you won't have to worry about any more disturbances tonight, Paul. I think I have things under control now."

Paul woke at 6:30 a.m. anxious to clear out of the unusual hostel. "I wanted to get an education on how the dregs of society live, and I certainly did," he sighed.

Millie still at her post at the head of the stairs, dozed her head dropping off toward her right shoulder. When Paul approached, she gave a stir, straightened up, moved her tongue about in her mouth, and tried to focus her bleary eyes on him.

"You pulling out already, Paul? How'd you sleep?"

"Oh, so-so. But I want to thank you for your kindness to me last night, and may God bless you. Adios, Millie, I'll pray for you."

"Goodbye, Paul . . ." She smiled, and that was the first time Paul had seen a genuine smile on her face. She stood up and seemed to want to hug him, but Paul raised his hand in farewell to her, blew a kiss in her direction, and quickly descended the stairs.

While Paul busily spooned oatmeal into his mouth in the hotel coffee shop, Carl reappeared.

Carl sat down on the opposite side of the table. "Well, old boy, do tell me about your adventures last night among the down and out in skid row. I wasn't sure you'll be back alive this morning."

"Carl, my friend, what I have to reveal to you will only provide distractions for you all day at the workshops. Leave us defer the telling of the tale tonight in your room. You do have a corner of your palatial suite for me, don't you?"

After three happy days among the young people at the SSCA and much flirting with the teenage girls who lapped up his line, Paul, found the contents of his purse rapidly dwindling. He boarded a Greyhound bus at nearby State and Madison, and slept through the rest of the night to Dubuque. There in warm sunlight he resumed his journey on the thumb back to the Villa.

While waiting for rides, Paul reflected on the fact that in only a matter of months he would be ordained a priest unless he was clipped at the last minute when the authorities found out about his bumming around the country. After ordination his whole life would have to change. No more hitchhiking, no more levity, and the assuming of a solemn mode of conduct.

"Will I really change much? What will happen if I don't? Should I drop out now at the last minute? No, by golly, I won't drop out, but I might get kicked out. We'll see."

Paul walked into the driveway of the humble rural abode of his honorable ancestors at about four o'clock that afternoon. He noted that

Pa had already had the four stacks of grain threshed in the cattle yard, and he was sorry he had missed that since he always loved threshing time on the farm.

"Well, look at our prize loafer!" Maggie exclaimed as Paul entered the house. "Where have you been this time?"

"I told you I was going to Chicago, didn't I? To preach the Gospel to the down and outers in skid row down there." Paul reflected that what he said was at least partly true.

"Now stop that foolish talk, and tell me what you really did in Chicago," Maggie said adamantly.

Paul did what she asked leaving out the interlude on North Clark Street, or she would have been shocked. He also left out the fact that at the SSCA he "horsed around" instead of studying. But there was enough left to hold her interest.

At the end of his narrative, Maggie looked very serious and said, "Paul, are you going to be ordained or not? There isn't much time left for you to decide."

"I've already decided, Ma. Long ago. Sure, I'm going to be ordained if they'll have me."

Six months later, Paul's great advocate in heaven, Mary, the Mother of Jesus, decided she could still handle that happy little levite of hers even after he became another one of her Son's stand-ins in the priesthood, and Paul was ordained.